PAINT THE WHITE HOUSE BLACK

PAINT THE
WHITE HOUSE BLACK

Barack Obama and the Meaning of Race in America

Michael P. Jeffries

STANFORD UNIVERSITY PRESS
STANFORD, CALIFORNIA

Stanford University Press
Stanford, California

©2013 by the Board of Trustees of the Leland Stanford Junior University.
All rights reserved.

Printed in the United States of America on acid-free, archival-quality paper

Library of Congress Cataloging-in-Publication Data
Jeffries, Michael P., author.
Paint the White House black : Barack Obama and the meaning of race in America / Michael P. Jeffries.
pages cm
Includes bibliographical references and index.
ISBN 978-0-8047-8095-7 (cloth : alk. paper) —
ISBN 978-0-8047-8096-4 (pbk. : alk. paper)
1. Obama, Barack. 2. Post-racialism—United States. 3. United States—Race relations—Political aspects. 4. United States—Social conditions—21st century. I. Title.
E907.J44 2013
973.932092—dc23

2012035312

Typeset by Bruce Lundquist in 10.5/15 Adobe Garamond

To those who died, and survived, and toiled, and spoke,
and sat, and sang, and marched, and bled, so someone
like Barack Obama could have the slightest chance
at the presidency and I could teach and write

Contents

Acknowledgments

Thank you, Kate Wahl, for your patience and dedication to this book and my ideas from start to finish. I appreciate the efforts of the reviewers and all those at Stanford University Press who had a hand in this project.

Ira Katznelson and Eric Foner have been friends to my family for quite some time. I will not speak on behalf of my father and grandfather here, but I cannot let this moment pass without acknowledging what their work has meant to scholars in the fields I draw from, and to me personally. Their books were among the first I read in college, and the first that showed me what this enterprise can be. I am incredibly lucky to have benefited from Ira and Eric's careful consideration of my writing, and from their honesty.

Jennifer Nash took the time to read multiple drafts, and her feedback was at once incisive and encouraging. I am immensely grateful for her work and for the intellectual fellowship we share.

William Julius Wilson's comments and guidance were impeccable, and full of the passion that defines his career and continues to inspire me.

Simone Browne and Ben Carrington were so thorough and influential in responding to the chapter they read, and I am thankful for the interest they expressed in my work before things had fully taken shape.

Sarah Willie-LeBreton and Robin Wagner-Pacifici were my mentors when I was an undergraduate, and each read very early versions of half-baked ideas that proved to be the foundation for this book. I have never taken their support and friendship for granted, and they continue to serve as my models for teaching.

Kimberly DaCosta is another friend and mentor who has believed in me for over a decade. Thank you, Kim, for your input at the very beginning of the publishing process.

My colleagues at Wellesley College have helped me claim the space they prepared, and thanks to Jonathan Imber, Elena Creef, Yoon Lee, Susan Reverby, Paul Fisher, Selwyn Cudjoe, Beth DeSombre, and many others, my life on campus has been exquisitely rich and fulfilling.

Thank you to all the young men and women who gave up their time and spoke openly with me about their lives for the interview-based chapter of this book. I am proud to include your thoughts and voices. Additional thanks to all the scholars and other writers cited in the book, and to my students at Wellesley, who fuel so much of what I do. Shout-outs to B-A and Eric, who accompanied me to the inauguration in 2009, and to Frank, who missed that trip, but has joined the three of us on many more.

Love at the beginning, middle, end, and beyond to my family. To my wife, Sarah, who patiently endures my silence and narcissism while I stare at the screen and bang my keyboard, and saves me every single day. To my parents, Emily and John, who continue to teach me the vast majority of what I know, including how to think and how to care. To my siblings, David and Julia, who do so many difficult and courageous things I cannot, and who laugh with me, even when we're apart. And to Emily, Dawn, Fred, Ruth, and Carole, whose love and support never cease.

Last but not least—thanks to everyone who worked to elect Barack Obama president of the United States. It would be tough to write a book about Obama and race without this minor detail. Impossible until it wasn't.

PAINT THE WHITE HOUSE BLACK

CHAPTER I

THROUGH THE FOG

There would be no great problem if, when the things changed, the
vocabulary died away as well. But far the more common situation in
the history of ideologies is that instead of dying, the same vocabulary
attaches itself, unnoticed, to new things. . . . In this they resemble
those creatures of horror fiction who, having neither body nor life
of their own, take over the bodies and lives of human beings.
—*Barbara J. Fields*[1]

On December 18, 2006, months before Senator Barack Obama formally announced his intention to seek the presidency, Pulitzer Prize-
winning journalist Diane McWhorter discussed the obstacles to
electing a black president in the United States. The primary barrier,
according to McWhorter, was whites' reluctance to give up white privilege. She explained, "[during the civil rights movement] one of the
reasons that the whites were so obstinate about giving into any quote,
'demands'—as they called them, quote, 'Negro demands'—was that,
you know, the expression was if you give them an inch, they'll take a
mile. To me, the primitive fear of white people is that, if you have an
African-American as the leader of the free world, that they're going to
give away white privilege—you know, that we are going to have to give
up something that we have taken for granted."[2]

"White privilege" is a slippery phrase. McWhorter's understanding
is rooted in measurable economic and political advantages. As a group,
white people sit atop the unjust racial and economic hierarchy, and they
collectively benefit when people of color are mistreated or denied opportunity. But white privilege is not just about quantifiable economic ad-

vantage and clearly identifiable acts of injustice. The other piece of Mc-Whorter's explanation deals with the things that are "taken for granted." This is the idea at the core of white privilege: it is a collective, implicit acceptance of whiteness as virtuous, normal, unremarkable, and expected.[3] The same goes for male privilege; all of humankind is conveniently reduced to "mankind" rather than "womankind," because maleness is thoughtlessly accepted as a baseline standard. Up until 2008, when instructed to imagine a nameless, faceless American president, without any race or gender prompt, most of us would have imagined a white man, because that is what we are socialized to expect. Given this definition, Obama's rise seems like a massive blow to white privilege and the existing racial order—the impossible has happened.

When examined from another perspective, however, the racial order appears unchallenged by Obama's rise. He was only the third black person elected to the Senate since the end of American Reconstruction in 1877. Drastic racial and ethnic inequalities, prejudice and stereotyping, and the marginalization of nonwhite people from positions of power persist today. Rigid residential segregation and the unprecedented expansion of the prison state have literally locked disadvantaged black and brown people into neighborhoods and behind bars without any chance to climb into the more stable middle class. The justice system repeatedly fails to prevent the physical destruction of black and Latino bodies; stories of brutality, harassment, and malfeasance litter the airwaves and front pages in every region of the country.

America seems lost in the fog, lurching forward and drifting backward, goaded by winds of both progress and decay. For every voice that hails Obama as the living embodiment of "hope" and "change," a dissenter insists that Obama's rise has either halted the march towards social justice or depleted our collective tolerance for even thinking and talking about race. This state of confusion, where Obama's America weeps race-heavy tears of joy from one eye and anguish from the other, is the starting point for this book, yet its aim is not to reach a definitive conclusion about whether race relations are getting "better" or "worse." Rather than measuring our racial state, we have to understand what race is, and we cannot understand race through dictionary definitions alone. Instead, we have to deal with race in action, drawing on concrete examples from our own lives that provide common ground for discussion and, eventually, understanding. President Obama's rise is an invaluable teaching tool because Obama is part of our collective experience. Scholars and journalists have studied the president to gain insight into his thoughts and actions, but this book focuses on Obama to understand how racial meaning is generated and how we might think about race more clearly.

Thinking and Talking About Race

Howard Winant writes, "The 2008 election was the first to have a viable Black candidate, but it was hardly the first U.S. election to be about race. In fact, every national election is about race."[4] From slavery to Jim Crow and civil rights, to the Southern strategy, to terrorism and immigration reform, racial politics have played key roles in candidates' campaigns and electoral outcomes. Events during Obama's campaign and first term, such as the Jeremiah Wright controversy, racial epithets and threats cast by anti–health care reform advocates, Justice Sonia Sotomayor's confirmation process, the resignation of Shirley Sherrod from the Department of Agriculture, and a host of other incidents, make navigating racial controversy a part of Obama's job description, even if addressing the ongoing catastrophe of mass racial inequality remains beyond the ill-conceived purview of contemporary presidents.[5]

"Race" is rooted in false beliefs about the validity of observed physical differences as indicators of human capacity or behaviors. Human beings build categories and make distinctions naturally. But there is no biological basis for racial categories and no relationship between classification based on observed physical characteristics and patterns of thought or behavior. Humans do not have separate subspecies or races the way some animals do, and genetic traits like skin color are inherited separately from other physical and mental traits, such as eye and hair features, blood type, hand-eye coordination, and memory. The company line among academics is that "race is socially constructed," meaning that it is an idea produced by human thought and interaction rather than something that exists as a material fact of life on earth. Social imperatives change racial categories and meanings over time, as political, cultural, and scientific developments force us to reconsider what once seemed certain. No matter the time and place, race is intimately bound with the distribution of rights and resources, and racial ideas are manifest in social inequalities.

The danger in affirming race as a social construction is that this understanding is easily distorted into the false belief that race does not exist or does not matter. This problem is compounded by exalting "assimilation" as part of the moral quest to achieve a color-blind society, where people's attitudes and behaviors are completely liberated from racial thinking and everyone is treated equally, regardless of color. The impulse towards color blindness, combined with the belief that racism is a thing of the past, results in "racism without racists,"[6] as the institutional foundation for racism remains intact despite a reduction in attitudinal antipathy towards racial others. Even if individuals no longer affirm racist beliefs, the institutions that order our social lives, such as banks, schools, and the criminal justice complex, utilize practices and policies that maintain and strengthen white social dominance. Eduardo Bonilla-Silva documents a plethora of strategies employed by those who defend themselves against the moral charge of racism, but whose actions do not interrupt institutional racism and whose beliefs clearly support the unjust racial order.[7] Those of us who are interested in racial problems walk a difficult line, explaining that although race is a product of our own making and classic, explicit racism has diminished, the United States remains in the midst of a crisis of white supremacy and racial hierarchy.[8]

It is daunting enough to face the harsh reality of race in small word counts, let alone wade through hundreds of pages of racial pontification. Talking and writing about race in everyday life is difficult, in no small part because we do not want to face the glaring racial divisions and racism right under our noses. Michael Taussig writes,

This reconfiguration of repression in which depth becomes surface so as to remain depth, I call *the public secret*, which, in another version, can be defined as *that which is generally known, but cannot be articulated*. . . . This "long knownness" is itself an intrinsic component of knowing what not to know, such that many times, even in our acknowledging it, in striving to extricate ourselves from its sticky embrace, we fall into even better-laid traps of our own making. . . . Knowing it is essential to its power, equal to the denial. Not being able to say anything is likewise testimony to its power.[9]

There is significant and useful ambiguity in Taussig's phrasing when he writes that the secret "cannot be articulated." First, this inability to articulate may refer to fear of repercussion or social disruption. In other words, we have the language to tell the secret, but we dare not do so. We may see something wrong and feel the urge to scream, "I am the only black person on this crowded commuter train to the Boston suburbs, and the only empty seat in the whole car is the one next to me! It's racism!" But we refrain out of cowardice, or because it is impolite, or because it might be misconstrued in some way. Especially in white-dominated spaces, we often avoid race-talk out of courtesy and prudence, but silence betrays us as a path to justice. Eviatar Zerubavel asserts, "The careful absence of explicit race labels in current American liberal discourse [sic] is indeed the product of a deliberate effort to suppress our awareness of race. Ironically, such deliberate avoidance may actually produce the opposite result."[10] Even when we neuter our language for the sake of an ostensibly worthy political goal, such as the elimination of racial bias or the prevention of racial insult, we suffer self-inflicted moral and political wounds by remaining quiet; and race stays on our minds.

One step removed from complete racial silence, race baiting and implicit appeals tell the "public secret" about nonwhite deviance, generating racial meaning without explicit hate speech towards people of color. Tali Mendelberg explains that the social norm of equality (color blindness) creates a national political climate that is hostile to overtly racist appeals and racial language. Instead, the injection of race into political contests takes place "under cover," as white candidates attempt to influence voter behavior in their favor by implicitly priming racial fears about nonwhite opponents. During the 2012 Republican presidential primary season, Newt Gingrich unleashed a series of rhetorical attacks designed to prime white voters' racial fears and resentments. First, he homed in on the American poverty crisis by focusing on black teenage unemployment, proposing that inner-city schools hire their own students as janitors. According to Gingrich, this plan would help the students learn work habits "so they didn't have to become a pimp, or a prostitute, or a drug dealer."[11] Weeks later, during Gingrich's march to victory in the South Carolina Republican primary election, he described President Obama as a "food stamp president."[12] These invocations of black ghetto pathology are launched into the public sphere in lieu of direct statements about blacks' inherent laziness, sexual deviance, and violent tendencies. But the racial meanings of prostituting, drug dealing, and welfare scamming are unambiguous, because the speaker attaches them to black people, rooting them in the black body, whether that body resides in the White House or the ghetto. Gingrich won the South Carolina primary, and Mitt Romney tried to reestablish the fallacious Obama/welfare connection during his 2012 presidential campaign, which demonstrates the situational effectiveness and political allure of race baiting without explicit racism.[13] By contrast, when people are made aware of these cues, the effectiveness of implicit priming is diminished,[14] and race-based mistreatment can be recognized and addressed.

An alternative reading of Taussig's public secret posits that the secret is "long known" but untellable because *we do not have the language necessary to tell it.* That is, our language is directly tied to power, and hegemonic language cannot be used to rearrange power relations; in Audre Lorde's terms, "the master's tools will never dismantle the master's house."[15] Toni Morrison explains the perils of living without language that falls outside the bounds of hegemony, as "one is obliged to cooperate in the misuse of figurative language, in the reinforcement of cliché, the erasure of difference, the jargon of justice, the evasion of logic, the denial of history, the crowning of patriarchy, the inscription of hegemony; to be complicit in the vandalizing, sentimentalizing, and trivialization of the torture black people have suffered."[16]

We are not simply banned or scared away from talking and writing about race altogether. Racial meaning is not solely engendered through silence and racial coding. The power of race lies in the fact when we attempt to address it, our efforts are undermined and obfuscated by everything from rampant misinformation to imprecise terminology, to ideas about polite conversation and appropriate settings, to a lack of conversational entry and exit strategies. In short, much racial analysis is neither epistemologically adequate nor likely to lead to insight or political progress. As Stuart Hall notes, "there is always something left unsaid about race,"[17] and Evelyn Higginbotham explains that this is because race acts as a "metalanguage" that "not only tends to subsume other sets of relations, namely gender and class, but it blurs and disguises, suppresses and negates its own complex interplay with the various relations it envelops."[18] This is akin to Taussig's warning that "even in our acknowledging it, in striving to extricate ourselves from its sticky embrace, we fall into even better-laid traps of our own making."

"Metalanguage" is a metaphor, and I do not mean to convey that race abides by a clear set of grammatical and syntactic rules, or that it is activated solely through verbal exchange. Race is not a language; it is commonly understood as a system of social classification, and it has material effects on people's lives. However, race does not act like a stable system of classification. Instead, echoing Hall, Higginbotham, and others, I insist that *race operates like a language*, because it produces and covers up meanings both simple and complex; because it signifies things beyond the obvious; because it is flexible, adaptable, and dependent on context. As Hall tells us, "race can never be finally fixed, but is subject to the constant process of redefinition and appropriation."[19] *Race is not only subject to this process; it actively shapes other knowledge systems: race redefines and appropriates vocabulary itself.*

Racially Speaking

Consider the following example: On March 2, 1996, college basketball analyst Billy Packer, who is white, referred to Georgetown University star Allen Iverson as a "tough monkey," in reference to the pint-sized guard's fearless play. Iverson is African American, and Packer was criticized for what many viewed as a racist characterization, despite the fact that he intended the remark as a compliment. Many of Packer's friends and colleagues including Georgetown's legendary (and African American) coach, John Thompson, rushed to his defense, denouncing the notion that "monkey" should be interpreted as a slur. Packer met with the Reverend Jesse Jackson in an effort to mediate the controversy and understand why people had taken such offense. Describing what he learned from Jackson, Packer offered the following: "'Naïve' is probably a pretty good word, because ever since I've been a kid I have never looked at people in terms of black and white. I'm absolutely not a racist, and anyone who has ever been involved with me knows that."[20]

The problem is not the word "monkey" itself; it is that the meaning of the word cannot be derived simply from immediate intent.[21] Packer may harbor no conscious antipathy towards black people, but is there something about Iverson's blackness that makes Packer more likely to call him a "monkey," even in praise, than he would a white player? Insisting that Packer is "racist," or obsessing over questions of intent, misses the point. The metalanguage and public secrecy of race take over the meaning of the incident. Packer's defensiveness and complete denial does not result in exoneration, as race remains an active social force and the comment is contextualized by a history of similar remarks.

Again, I have no interest in condemning Packer. In instances such as this, when people argue that "monkey" holds racial significance, they are often derided as race-obsessed warriors for self-defeating political correctness, looking for a fight. Rather than building such a case, let us interrogate the opposite position, namely, that this comment has absolutely nothing to do with race, or that it was an isolated incident. Those who make such arguments must forget, ignore, or explain away an ongoing history of associating black people with apes.[22] There is something deviant and threatening about the combination of race and gender, blackness and masculinity, that keeps this racist imagery in circulation throughout American popular culture. She who takes the nonracial position is unconvinced that the African-male-as-ape overtones of "classic" American films like *Birth of a Nation* (1915) and *King Kong* (1933) have any bearing on LeBron James's 2008 *Vogue* magazine cover photo, where the basketball genius poses, mouth agape in midscream, with an arm around the waist of supermodel Gisele Bündchen. She forgets that thirteen years before the Packer incident, another Georgetown basketball star, Patrick Ewing, was greeted by rival fans in Philadelphia with a sign reading "Ewing is an ape," and that a banana peel was thrown on the court when he was introduced by the arena's public address announcer.[23] She ignores that in 2011, Brazilian soccer star Roberto Carlos had a banana peel thrown at him during a game in Russia, another in a series of incidents in European and Russian professional football where players of African descent are subject to racial harassment.[24] Later in that same year, a spectator hurled a banana peel at black Canadian professional hockey player Wayne Simmonds during a game in Ontario, Canada.[25]

She was not watching in 2008 when news cameras captured footage of a man at a Sarah Palin rally proudly brandishing a stuffed monkey (a children's toy, not an actual monkey) with an Obama sticker taped to its forehead.[26] An enterprising toy company made a similar connection, selling a stuffed animal called "The Sock Obama"—a stuffed monkey with exaggerated red lips, dressed in a suit with a campaign button on the lapel. When pressed for an explanation or apology for their depiction of Obama, the toy company released this tongue-in-cheek statement, mockingly invoking "naivety" with eerie resemblance to Packer's self-defense: "We guess there is an element of naivety on our part, in that we don't think in terms of myths, fables, fairy tales and folklore. We simply made a casual and affectionate observation one night, and a charming association between a candidate and a toy we had when we were little."[27]

This is how the metalanguage of race works. For those who are upset, the meaning of the Packer comment is not determined by the immediate visual stimulant of Iverson's play, or solely by the context of the sentence in which the term appears. It is determined by racial history and the global reality of racism. The discourse of innate and dangerous black male physicality is a pillar of racist ideology. Especially when the context emphasizes black bodily supremacy or bodily menace, race moves through our minds like water through sand, dampening "monkey" and changing its constitution. The Packer incident was not an attack, and the word "monkey" does not hold the exact same meaning as the instances of overt racism catalogued above. But the range of explanations for why the word was spoken and why people were unnerved must take such events into account.

In many cases, racial meaning is created and halfheartedly disguised without explicitly mentioning racial categories. The man at the Palin rally with the Obama monkey did not yell racist slurs into the camera or offer a thorough explanation of how race combines with gender to solidify the monkey's racial meaning. Instead, he smugly introduced his prop as "Little Hussein," in reference to Obama's middle name. However, in the opposite case, where racial labels are overemphasized, the elements that give a racial term its meaning are also hidden. For instance, in early 2012 a writer for *Elle* magazine in France tried to compliment the Obamas for incorporating "white codes" of fashion into their clothing style,[28] thereby teaching other American blacks how to dress respectably. In this case, whiteness was named and emphasized. When someone compliments or criticizes a person of color for "dressing like she is white," the phrase holds meaning because whiteness is commonly associated with a style of dress that is available only to those who can afford to buy clothes from particular stores or designers, and choose to do so. In this way, racist associations between whiteness, wealth, status, and beauty are strengthened without words like "rich" or "classy" that force listeners to recognize how the statement moves beyond purely racial knowledge. "Dresses like he's white" becomes a shorthand phrase for more complicated intersecting indicators: the meaning of the phrase depends on silent class difference just as much as it does on the spoken racial difference.

Racial Thinking with Clarity

How can we avoid the pitfalls of racial confusion and make sure we get the meaning correct? Evelyn Higginbotham develops her theory of race as a metalanguage to emphasize the necessity of *intersectional* analysis.[29] In the case of gender, for example, this does not mean we should simply consider gender as a complement to race. Instead, we must explain how gender intersects with and transforms race, and vice versa. Barack and Michelle Obama both self-identify as black. But stereotypes of black masculinity and black femininity differ, and perception and treatment of each member of the Obama family differ accordingly. To take the example a step further, perceptions and treatment of Barack and Michelle are often different from perceptions and treatment of black men and women who are impoverished, as class, race, and gender intersect with each other to produce meaning.

Meaning is generated through difference; "black" and "white" hold separate meanings because we understand each color as different from, and in relation to, the other. We might even say that this meaning is fairly consistent in the Western world, in the sense that whiteness signifies normalcy and superiority, and nonwhiteness signifies deviance. But the normalcy of whiteness and the deviance of nonwhiteness can never be fully described in purely racial or phenotypic terms. Describing the supposedly inherent *character* of blackness, brownness, redness, and yellowness—describing precisely *how* they differ from whiteness, or the nature of the relationship between two racial signifiers—requires moving beyond the initial system of classification and beyond the list of races. Racial signifiers are based on phenotype, and therefore visuality. But the image of the racialized body, and therefore the racial label, signifies something beyond corporeality: the visual signifier has cultural, behavioral, and political implications (often grounded in false beliefs) that require categories other than color schemes and body parts to understand and articulate. The meaning of a racial term is always dependent on its intersection with knowledge that lies beyond the immediate and the visual.[30]

Some scholars interested in social justice believe that affirming intersectionality is not enough to produce effective criticism, and that the "race, class, and gender" mantra should be forsaken. Antonia Darder and Rodolfo Torres, for example, concede that race, class, and gender are interrelated, but strongly object to treating these forces as equals, because the influence of *capitalism* is unrivaled.[31] By definition, they argue, class distinctions imply material domination and inequality in capitalist society. Class groups come into being as a result of exploitation, and the social fact of class difference is rooted in labor. By definition, the capitalist and the laborer are unequal—the capitalist has more power. This is not the case where race and gender are concerned, because it is possible to imagine race and gender categories that are different from each other but whose relationships are not determined by exploitation. Orange people and green people, for example, may be considered different, but this categorical difference is not unequal by definition, because the categories are not encoded through labor as material reality. It is often considered "democratic" to celebrate racial and ethnic difference, but not class, because class difference, and poverty in particular, is engendered through exploitation and suffering.[32]

If one of the suggested paths out of the racial trap is focusing on structure and insisting on labor relations as the key to all systems of oppression, another is to focus on the cultural realm and abandon the language and epistemology of race. This strategy cannot be reduced to a willful ignorance of the ways in which race continues to matter in society. Paul Gilroy knows that racialization and racism occur, and that they are deeply injurious. But he writes that it is time for people, especially politically marginalized nonwhites, to leave racial ideas behind. Gilroy argues that even when oppressed groups reclaim their assigned racial labels to resist domination, maintaining racial solidarity and keeping those labels intact demand authoritarianism and reliance on a fascist discourse of authenticity. In addition, commercial forces have taken hold of racialized cultures, especially black culture, which results in spectacular and hypervisible black commoditization. When this happens, blackness is transformed into a commitment to pseudo-revolutionary style that has nothing to do with lived experience or productive politics for black people.[33] As an alternative to the racialized tradition, Gilroy argues, we should commit to using the notion of "diaspora" when discussing spatial and citizenship affiliations. More importantly, Gilroy suggests a commitment to "planetary humanism," an ethic grounded in rationalism and disdainful of robust collective identities.

What is the cost of following Gilroy or Darder and Torres to the hilt? Suppose I am visited during office hours by a first-year student named "James," an Asian American who announces that although he never spent much time thinking about race and ethnicity, he was moved by Barack Obama's 2008 campaign and victory. The president's story led him to think about his own identity, and his place in America. James wants to talk about his experiences with racism and sexism, and get my recommendations about classes to take, books to read, and ways to politically engage these issues while on campus.

As an educator, I have a choice to make. I could politely inform James that his so-called racial awakening is illusory, and that to truly understand himself he needs to study labor and class relations rather than race and gender, which are fruitless distractions. Alternatively, I could take Gilroy's argument to heart and tell James that I am happy to chat but that I will not talk about these topics using racial terms and categories. When he feels the need to use racial language, I tell him he can only use the word "diaspora" to talk about groups, or find another way to describe racialized subjectivity. I then move on to a compelling summation of Gilroy's view, emphasizing the need to commit to a utopian and humanistic vision, one that persists undeterred by the staunch differences between the world as it exists today and the world as we want it to be.

If I take either of these two paths, no matter how politely I make these suggestions or how persuasively I make the case for each alternative, I am at serious risk of alienating this young person. James has made himself vulnerable to me and has told me that this intellectual spark is clearly tied to personal experiences as a racialized and gendered subject, in accordance with conventional understandings of race. The events he recounts have occurred in the material world and are not figments of James's imagination. I may be sympathetic to portions of Gilroy's analysis or to the explanatory dominance of class, but if my ultimate goal is to get James to see the wisdom of other approaches, I have to validate the student's experiences first. I have to start by talking about race and ethnicity in order to explain what it means when we say these concepts are socially constructed, and show that they interact with other forces.

My choice to stick with intersectionality is driven in large part by its versatility. Emphasizing how race, class, gender, and other discourses change and depend on each other allows for a range of contact points, where thinkers of all ages can start with familiar ideas and experiences and plug into a matrix rich with possibility. Intersectionality is a compulsion to search for and highlight all the social forces that give cultural events racial meaning. This line of thinking reveals that racial oppression depends upon, and supports, all other systemic forms of social injustice, and that addressing racial problems yields benefits beyond the realms of race relations and racial inequality. Political issues from environmental sustainability to LGBT rights impact and are impacted by the racial order, and the possibilities for coalition-based social justice activism abound.

Paint the White House Black

It is difficult, then, to productively address race: Problems of *racial knowledge* stem from a climate of silence and from the inherent properties of race itself. *Racial language* often fails us or corrupts our vocabulary, and the *meaning of race* is dependent on interactions with other social forces. Subsequent chapters use topics pertaining to the Obamas to illustrate these points and solve the problems caused by inadequate racial language and murky racial meaning. The raw material for the book includes a synthesis of research from fields across the academy, readings of texts and social performances, and analysis of in-depth interviews with students.

I approach each topic with the following questions: In a narrative about racial history or an explanation of a racial phenomenon, which are the key terms and passages that contain racial meaning, even if words representing racial categories never appear? When racial terms do appear in the narrative, are they helpful? Do they actually describe social experience, or do they obscure it? Which other forces and explanations might racial language be distracting us from? Finally, if all of the research I cite in building an argument about race comes from studies designed only to analyze racial differences, what have I omitted from my explanation? None of these questions yielded answers that would downplay the importance of race relative to other factors. Rather, this sort of inquiry more fully reveals the meaning and power of race in action.

The following chapter addresses the codependence of "race" and "nation," focusing on what I call the "politics of inheritance." I begin by discussing racism and national identity, unpacking the ways race affects American nationalism and patriotism. The insidious linkage between whiteness and Americanness fuels a shameful percentage of the vitriol directed at Barack Obama. But the argument is not just about how race corrupts the meaning of nation; it is about the underlying logic of inheritance as a baleful path to political knowledge. Obama's 2008 election is indicative of the uncertainty swirling around race, as described above. But Obama's rise also points to the chaos surrounding contemporary national identity, and the waning but still formidable grip of the politics of inheritance as the core of nationalism. A close reading of Obama's 1995 memoir, *Dreams from My Father*, reveals alternative methods for arriving at both racial and national identity. I offer suggestions for forging a new American nationalism.

Chapter 3 picks up on the theme of "newness" and "futuristic" political subjects by investigating multiracial identity. Obama is frequently described as "black" rather than "multiracial," "biracial," or another term denoting racially mixed parentage. The president makes both explicit and implicit reference to his multicultural background, while avoiding in-depth discussion of multiracialism. However, the peculiar history of interracialism and multiracialism produces tropes of multiracial representation and anxieties about racial bodies that we all recognize, even if Obama does not describe them. The metalanguage of race can drown out real life experiences and turn multiracial people into symbols and objects. I move beyond multiracial iconography and build on the burgeoning literature about multiracial people by allowing them to speak for themselves. I analyze a collection of interviews with young adults who self-identify as racially mixed (biracial, multiracial, and so on); these interviews map the boundaries of multiracialism, feature discussion about Obama's racial identity, and take measure of the president's racial significance. Interviews reveal the metalinguistic challenges of race as well as the promise of intersectionality.

The fourth chapter follows from the third, as multiracial people are often depicted as one of many foreboding signs of misguided "postracialism," igniting panic about "the end of black politics." Not only does Obama's racially mixed body pose a threat, but many argue that Obama downplays his blackness by avoiding direct discussion of racial issues and deemphasizing any connections to the old guard of African American politics. It is tempting to understand this rhetorical trend as a sudden and unprecedented shift from civil rights blackness to postracial politics, or attribute it to Obama's political savvy and disposition. Instead, I call attention to research on the class divide within the black American community and the transformation of the black *counterpublic*—the real and virtual spaces where black ideologies and political organization foment. These elements reveal the shift to postblack or postracial politics as a gradual phenomenon, driven by its intersection with class, rather than an innovative campaign strategy inspired solely by Obama or any other candidate. Improving the state of black politics, an ostensibly "racial" problem (as signaled by the word "black"), requires grappling with new forms of technology and new kinds of political space. Access to contemporary tools of political communication is impacted by class inequality; the entire discussion here demonstrates the impossibility of separating race from class.

Chapter 5 returns to the foundation of intersectionality theory, focusing on Michelle Obama, whose ascendance (like her husband's) forces us to deal with intersections of race, class, and gender. Though Ms. Obama stands among the most celebrated first ladies in history, she is also subject to public representations that vacillate between timeworn racist stereotypes of black womanhood and a newer, more complicated representation: the uppity black superwoman. The superwoman image is especially insidious, as it traps black women within the confines of their success and conceals racism and sexism. Michelle Wallace is one of several black feminist scholars who explain that the fact that black women manage to survive hardship and disadvantage comes to perversely signify their mythic strength, an attribute we celebrate at the expense of actually combating oppression.[34] Michelle Obama represents a paradigmatic case of this phenomenon with a slightly different hue, thanks to her substantial privilege and power. But the chapter is not merely a history of Ms. Obama's public career or a lament of the stereotype, as her example speaks to the interventions necessary for stepping out of the shadow of such stereotypes.

The final chapter pans back, placing the book in its context and describing the future implications of thinking about race in the terms I have laid out. I also describe the power of studying celebrities and their stories, not as metaphors for our real lives but as gathering sites that bring us together. Finally, two appendixes provide additional information about contemporary racial inequality in the United States (Appendix I), and offer methodological details relevant to the interview analysis in Chapter 3 (Appendix II).

Race is a difficult concept to grasp; outbursts and silences disguise its relationships with a host of other phenomena. But ignorance, avoidance, and silence will never lead us into the clear. When race is quiet, we have to amplify and expose its web of relationships. When race is too loud, we have to settle it down to achieve understanding. The goal of the book is to use Obama's rise to talk about race sensibly, with respect for its complexity and in concert with other ideas that are important to us.

CHAPTER 2

MY (FOUNDING) FATHER'S SON

Race, Nation, and the Politics of Inheritance

> Nobody really thinks that Bush or McCain have a real answer
> for the challenges we face, so what they're going to try to do is
> make you scared of me. "You know, he's not patriotic enough.
> He's got a funny name. You know, he doesn't look like all those
> other presidents on those dollar bills. You know, he's too risky."
> —*Barack Obama*[1]

As a prompt to think about race and nation simultaneously, we might
begin with the most basic question—"What is extraordinary about
Obama's rise?"—and give the most reductive reply: "He is black."[2] This
reply is not wrong, of course, but the simple fact that Obama is black
does not explain the hysteria. The "black" in "He is black" is loud and noticeable, but it has no stable meaning because it has no context and nothing to intersect with. Obama's race makes him an anomaly, not because of
race alone but because race intersects with other, less "remarkable" traits.
Barack Obama is straight, Christian, economically privileged, and male,
and these intersecting forms of privilege link him to all previous American presidents; blackness is highlighted as that which makes him different
because of his other characteristics.

But even once we acknowledge Obama's intersectional privileges as
part of the explanation, stating "He is black" can only be the starting point for understanding the hysteria over his election. The reason
for the excitement must be clarified by explaining that the president's
blackness symbolizes something greater than his own accomplishment.
More specifically, Obama's individual triumph as a black person be-

comes a sign of the country's progress. We draw on America's shameful racial history to argue that racism is not as harsh as it once was, and the United States is one step closer to realizing its moral destiny through the redemption of black people, who were debased as slaves and excluded from the polity as one of the country's original sins. People of all backgrounds are thrilled because Obama stands as proof that the American dream still lives, and we are all stakeholders in the American ideals of freedom and opportunity. Invoking the *American* dream as essential to Obama's *racial* significance illustrates that *racial meaning is not simply "racial"*—it is bound to this country's *national* history. Just as the meaning of Obama's blackness depends on its intersection with gender, sexuality, religion, and class, so too it depends on its intersection with national identity.

The trouble is that American nationhood is in a state of material and epistemological crisis. The material component is an ongoing saga, and I'm afraid that I have nothing earth-shattering to say about a financial collapse that countless economists continue to grapple with. Instead, this chapter focuses on the epistemological component. My aim is to deconstruct what I call the "politics of inheritance," a path to knowledge that underpins antiquated understandings of both race *and* nation, as well as their most pernicious mutations, classic racism and bigoted cultural nationalism.

First, I try to explain succinctly how and why whiteness is so frequently equated with Americanness. I then home in on the politics of inheritance as the epistemic link between race and nation, where the body is taken as evidence of one's national and racial credentials and destiny. The discussion pivots with the Obama event, which exposes the tensions in the contemporary link between racial and national identity and throws the politics of inheritance into question. The cracks in the politics of inheritance are manifest not only in the fact of Obama's rise but in the president's own writing. Though Obama does not explicitly frame *Dreams from My Father* as an exportable blueprint for building identity, the memoir rejects the politics of inheritance as the basis for his ideas of blackness, Americanness, and intersectional black Americanness.

Instead, Obama's story is rooted in lived experience and the conundrum of social inequality.

The individual aside, where does this new means of self-knowledge leave the nation as a collective? The politics of inheritance is weak. Neoliberalism, in all its disdain for antiracist practice and nationalism writ large, may be the most imposing potential successor or, rather, executioner of national identity. But the country's ideological metamorphosis is far from certain, and this vacuum offers plenty of space for alternative nationhood. My efforts to fill that space, presented at the end of the chapter, are predicated on the continued disintegration of classic racism and committed to retaining some form of collective American identity as a social good.

Race, Nationalism, and Patriotism

Academics frequently approach the codependence of racism and nationalism by scrutinizing the ideology of the American dream. Jennifer Hochschild explains and critiques the American dream as a combination of the following false beliefs: opportunity is equal for each individual; society is meritocratic; and success (and failure) is individually determined and deserved. According to the American dream myth, people who fail to achieve success are deemed not only inept but dishonorable. Those who reside at the bottom of the economic hierarchy are not worthy of empathy, and there is no pressing reason to interrupt the cycle of poverty and suffering. The American dream ignores institutional racism and other forms of durable social inequality. The fact that suffering is disproportionately shouldered by black and brown Americans is considered an unfortunate, but not immoral, side effect of meritocracy.

The American dream is especially important in considering the description of Americanism in Obama's memoir, which I'll do below. For now I want to take a slightly different approach, focusing on the human body as evidence of fixed, categorical, and honorable descent. Developing this argument requires clarity on a few key concepts. "Race" is discussed in the first chapter. "Ethnicity" is also a fluid social construction, but it is not the same as race. If race depends on false beliefs about physical characteristics and biology, ethnicity refers to culture—a set of common beliefs, values, and practices (arts, language, religion) that distinguish one group from another. Often race and ethnicity bleed into each other, leading to discussion of "racial cultures." The malleability of these ideas leads many scholars to reject the distinction between race and ethnicity altogether and adopt the term "ethnoracial," especially when discussing ethnoracial politics and oppression outside the United States.

We also need working definitions of "state" and "nation" to proceed. "State" is easier to define; the term refers to a territory of people under the control of a single government that assumes the responsibility of maintaining social order and defending its citizenry. The state government is distinguished from other associations within a territory as the only collective with the power to make and enforce the law.

"Nation" is a much trickier term, but there are two central ideas. First, in the nation-state era, *nation is the identity component of statehood.* Members of the nation-state understand themselves as connected to each other, their territory, and their government, which ideally they participate in or legitimize. Nation-states contrast themselves with other national communities, such that nationhood implies relationships with various outsiders who live in different territories, answer to different authorities, and build alternative stories of self.[3] Second, *"nation" is a political claim, not a category or group of people.* The nation-state is composed of citizens and other inhabitants, but "nation" is not another word for the people who live in the nation-state. As Rogers Brubaker notes, the nation does not exist "independently of the language used to describe it. It is used . . . to mobilize loyalties, kindle energies, and articulate demands."[4]

Nationalism is the idea that the nation-state's political goals should reflect a singular, clearly delineated identity or common culture—a culture produced by a group with shared traditions and beliefs, and the only legitimate claim to authority over its constituents.[5] *Patriotism* is love for the country and its symbols. When the nationalist impulse manifests as belief in the moral authority of national culture, patriotism and nationalism can become mutually constitutive as conationals fervently insist upon the greatness of their nation or nation-state above all others.

The scholarly debate around the essence of a nation is heavily influenced by Benedict Anderson, who argues that the nation is an "imagined community" that is both limited and sovereign,[6] and modern-day nation-states are enabled by developed economies and systems of communication that connect people to each other. Even if conationals do not have similar everyday experiences, they have access to a set of common ideas and values. The beauty of Anderson's argument is that it explains how nation-states accommodate inequality and adapt to the influx of new populations. Widespread access to core ideas allows for the extension of national identity to those who were previously considered outsiders. Indeed, Brubaker affirms that one of the reasons nationalism should be retained is that it can aid in the integration of immigrant populations.[7]

There is an argument to be made that the United States is the paragon of this integrative ideal, often theorized in two ways. According to one school of thought, the immigrant nation is a "melting pot," wherein ethnoracial groups lose their cultural distinctiveness over time, assimilating into "mainstream" culture—an amalgamation of ethnic traditions and a space where ethnic identity does not impact life outcomes. Though race and ethnicity are not the same, they are often collapsed within the discourse of American multiculturalism and assimilation, and the melting pot model provides the sentiment behind Obama's famous proclamation during the 2004 Democratic National Convention: "There is not a black America, and a white America, and Latino America, and Asian America, there is the United States of America."[8] Alternatively, scholars and commentators exalt *ethnic pluralism*, arguing that ethnoracial differences remain but are equally respected and valued as part of greater American culture; American society is represented as a "salad bowl" rather than a melting pot. If America is a melting pot, ethnoracial attachment has either a negative impact on, or is irrelevant to, measures of patriotism and nationalism. If America is a salad bowl, each racial or ethnic group celebrates and maintains a sense of ethnic pride that enhances feelings of patriotism and nationalism, without any significant differences based on the group's position in the social hierarchy.

Unfortunately, as Jim Sidanius and his colleagues have repeatedly demonstrated, neither the ethnic pluralist nor the melting pot model can account for social inequality or different levels of national attachment among ethnoracial groups.[9] Instead, Sidanius advances "social dominance theory," arguing that group-based social hierarchies organize society, provide the basis of intergroup conflict, and ultimately privilege dominant group members who control resources and occupy positions of power.[10] Sidanius shows that across societies, dominant racial and ethnic groups demonstrate more robust patriotism than low-status groups. In the United States, white Americans score the highest among all racial groups on scales that measure both patriotism and feelings of national superiority, and disturbingly, patriotism among whites increases as a function of higher levels of both classical racism and social dominance.[11] This relationship between racism and national attachment does not manifest among other racial and ethnic groups.[12] Yesilernis Pena and Sidanius confirm these results in a later study, demonstrating that "the greater whites' tendency to subordinate 'inferior groups,' the greater their level of United States patriotism." These findings are contrasted with data analysis of Latino Americans' responses, which demonstrate the opposite trend, as strong support for social dominance is actually associated with lower levels of United States patriotism.[13]

It is no surprise that in 2008 the intersection of patriotism and racism affected whites' voting behavior. In their study of Washington state voters, Christopher Parker, Mark Sawyer, and Christopher Towler find that among whites, "when holding the other variables in the model at their respective means, patriotism, symbolic racism, and laissez-faire racism all decreased the likelihood of casting a vote for Obama by 35 percent, 40 percent, and 37 percent, respectively."[14] In other words, patriotism effectively operates as a form of racial discrimination within the sample. A year after Obama was elected, the same forces were at play: Eric Hehman and his colleagues confirmed that whites continued, at disturbing rates, to perceive Obama as un-American (incongruent with nationalism)—a sentiment that simply does not manifest among black respondents. Not surprisingly, whites with higher levels of racial

prejudice believe Obama to be both un-American and a poorly performing president.[15]

Clearly, people of color are capable of being just as patriotic as
whites, and many different versions of American nationalism exist. Further, nationalism and patriotism are not racist constructs for every individual white person; age, income, gender, and education level influence
these connections. But at this point, findings across a range of disci-
plines suggest a distinct and troubling relationship between racism, patriotism, and nationalism for white Americans as an aggregate group.[16]

Race and Citizenship

In his remarks at the memorial service for diplomat Richard Holbrooke,
President Obama asserted, "America is not defined by ethnicity. It's not
defined by geography. We are a nation born of an idea, a commitment
to human freedom."[17] But in contemporary nation-states, "human freedom" requires the full rights of citizenship, and denying these rights is
fundamental to the economic exploitation of people of color throughout the history of the United States, from the violent seizure of indigenous people's land and the birth of the first colony in 1607, to black
slavery, to the denial of Chinese American and other nonwhite migrant
labor rights during the nineteenth-century gold and railroad booms.
Nonwhites were explicitly prevented from becoming naturalized citizens and rendered unable to legally protect themselves from violence
and exploitation. The justification is key: *race-based denial of citizenship
is justified not solely in the name of economic exploitation or growth. It is
grounded in the belief that the "weaker" races are not fit for democratic self-
government.*[18] Racist ideologies warn that including nonwhites as part
of the citizenry undermines democracy, which is supposed to be the
essence of Americanism. Colonizers believed they had a right to exter-
minate and displace indigenous people, who were "savages" incapable
of civil behavior let alone civil politics or prudent management of the
land's resources. American slavery was cast as a paternal arrangement;
supposedly childlike African American slaves were kept in bondage and
considered property both "for their own good" and for the good of the

country, which could not be subject to the political whims of blacks as participants in government.[19]

The same biological incapacity for self-government was ascribed to Irish, Italian, and Jewish Americans, who were cast as uncivilized and untrustworthy, and exploited as urban laborers in the late nineteenth and early twentieth centuries.[20] Today we think of these groups as ethnicities within the privileged racial category of whiteness, but during these earlier periods they were described in explicitly demeaning racial language. As this bigotry was formalized through the half-baked science of eugenics—a belief in improving the human race through controlled breeding and regulation of the biological stock—it manifested in legislation. The Immigration Act of 1924 ranked racialized white ethnics according to the desirability of supposedly endemic character traits, and was ratified in order to ensure that most immigrants to the United States would be west Europeans rather than "less refined" east Europeans or Asians, many of whom were already banned by the Chinese Exclusion Act of 1882.[21] In each case, the message is that the racial group in question cannot be incorporated because its members are incapable of civility and proper participation in America's cultural and political system. When people spew venom about the danger of allowing "illegal aliens" to cross the border between Mexico and the United States, on the grounds that unsanctioned border-crossing portends criminality and disrespect for American values (violating American nationalism), we hear echoes of intolerance as old as the country itself.[22]

Nominally, the privileges of citizenship and legal rights are public matters, and ethnoracial stories and particularities are supposed to be kept private. As long as the laws conferring civil rights are on the books, the narrative goes, marginalized groups have no reason to complain. But as Alondra Nelson explains, social rights, including a general ethic of national inclusion, are rarely conferred to women and ethnoracial minorities even when civil rights are solidified.[23] Public secrecy about racial and ethnic injustice is part and parcel of the web of white privilege that defines American nationhood. As the feminist movement instructs, "the personal is political," and in practice, reconciling racial and ethnic identities with public American national identity is traumatic.[24] The suffering caused by nationalism that marginalizes the experiences of those who do not fit the ethnoracial mold is not merely overreaction or self-pity born from the neurosis of members of disparaged groups. To the contrary, objections raised by oppressed racial and ethnic minorities spring from the explicit and successful efforts of those in power to deny opportunity to people of color and link whiteness to American identity. An adviser to Republican presidential hopeful Mitt Romney provided one such example in July 2012, suggesting that the Obama White House did not understand the "special relationship" between the United States and Great Britain drawn from shared "Anglo-Saxon heritage."[25] Racial inequality and suffering can only be considered irrelevant to "the American experience" when the stories and bodies of people of color are erased from the most powerful symbols of American nationalism.

The metalinguistic influence of race on national categories and words like "American" is not speculative; it is empirically verified and theorized. *Symbolic racism* holds that white racial prejudice is no longer rooted in or expressed as beliefs about nonwhites' biological inferiority, and is not necessarily connected to conscious ideas about political and economic self-interest. Instead, negative perceptions about nonwhites are rooted in beliefs that racial minorities fail to embrace, embody, and symbolize distinctly "American" ideals, such as hard work and individual responsibility.[26] These attitudes toward nonwhites are engrained early in life, such that subjects who demonstrate evidence of symbolic racism have built implicit associations between nonwhite subjects and deviance. That is, black, brown, yellow, and red bodies symbolize a repudiation of American values, even if the explicitly racist beliefs about these groups' biological inferiority are rejected.

Symbolic racism has the added value of being most accommodating to the phenomenon of *implicit* racial bias. As documented by social psychologists, such as Mahzarin Banaji, and popularized by Malcolm Gladwell in *Blink* (2005), implicit bias does not concern conscious attitudes or beliefs. A subject may honestly believe there are no meaningful differences between racial and ethnic groups. But when tested for unconscious, implicit bias, she may still present a set of involuntary associations that reveal a grouping together of race-related ideas. Many Americans, including people of color, build distinctly pro-white patterns of association, as whiteness is grouped together with goodness and Americanness, and nonwhiteness is associated with danger and otherness. Even if someone does not consciously believe negative things about a given racial group, implicit bias can affect his or her behavior towards group members.[27]

The Politics of Inheritance

So we have a problem: the metalanguage of race has taken over ideas of nationhood. I have already highlighted, in brief, the legal racialization of citizenship to explain the American case. But the deeper explanation I want to pursue concerns the epistemology of "race" and "nation" as more abstract concepts. Anthony Smith notes, "No 'nation-to-be' can survive without a homeland or a myth of common origins and descent."[28] The tension between race/ethnicity and nation persists because the very ideas of race and nation require the construction, protection, and maintenance of narratives of common history rooted in the body. The word "nation" is derived from the Latin *natio* meaning "to be born." Both ethnoracial and national means of understanding oneself are indubitably historical, as the question "Who am I?" is resolved via "truths" about where I came from, and who came before me. Colloquial American history traces the roots of the nation back to the "Founding Fathers," men who bravely declared independence from England and authored the constitution. The nation takes a distinct bodily form. It is no coincidence that these men are referred to as "fathers" rather than nongendered citizens, that American women were denied the vote for over a century, and that the geographical territory of the country—the "motherland"—is gendered feminine and therefore in need of masculinized military protection. Our most basic conceptions of what it means to be American are rooted in the notion that we are the biological descendants of straight, white, Christian men, and the very idea of Western nationhood emerges from a white male subject position.

The *politics of inheritance* is not simply the idea that political power is inherited, as in dynastic societies. It is a political epistemology that looks to figures from the past as a source of knowledge about present-day societies and about appropriate action. Of course, studying history is indispensable for political progress, provided we are looking for evidence of specific circumstances, policies, or events that explain contemporary conditions. But the politics of inheritance is not focused on the interpretive project of empirical, document-based sociohistorical research, or on the complex social processes that shape social order. Instead, the politics of inheritance rejects skeptical, "shared and secular" *history* in favor of absolute and doggedly defended *memory*,[29] venerating notable historical figures and biological lineage to resolve questions of individual and group identity, and provide broad moral and political "wisdom" for navigating our present and future. The politics of inheritance thrives on narratives featuring recognizable human characters who embody and symbolize virtuous ideologies. In some cases, these characters have celebrated names and faces, and in others, our inheritance comes from anonymous heroes, but specific people are always remembered as exemplary historical actors. As political prudence and morality are unquestionably embodied by these visually recognizable figures, all bodies become ideological documents, all too easily read, interpreted, and categorized via implicit and explicit processes. For those invested in the politics of inheritance, social and political identities are passed down from one generation to the next, preserved in the blood. The design of descent is perhaps subject to mediation and mutation, but never to fundamental change.

Lawrence Bobo points out that the United States now stands somewhere between Jim Crow and postracialism, as long-held beliefs about race as biological destiny slowly evaporate but echoes of classic biological racism float through the enduring channels of institutional racism and inequality.[30] Similarly, Obama's election in 2008 proves that on a national scale the politics of inheritance is in peril, but not yet vanquished. In 2007, those most deeply invested in this epistemology were revealed in all their petulant, flailing, and pitiful desperation as Barack Obama's eligibility for the presidency was called into question on the false grounds that he had not been born in the United States. As recently as 2011, survey data suggested that 51 percent of Republicans still believed the falsehood that Obama had been born outside of America.[31] Those who propagate this lie are dubbed "Birthers." This is not an organized party or group of activists, rather, a decentralized collection of propagandists and zealots who spout nonsense and conspiracy theories.

Obama lived in Indonesia from 1967 to 1971, where Islam is the dominant religion. However, freedom of religion is a part of Indonesia's constitution, and Obama attended a school with students from different religious backgrounds. In June 2007, *Insight* magazine (a subsidiary of the *Washington Times*) reported that while in Indonesia, Obama attended school at a "madrassa," an Arabic word that means "school" but is wrongly associated with extremist institutions that deny the rights of non-Muslims. In response, CNN sent a reporter to Obama's school to investigate the claims, which were revealed to be completely baseless.[32] Though Birthers' claims were thoroughly debunked by legitimate news organizations, the right-wing propaganda machine stuck to its guns, as conservative talk show host Melanie Morgan suggested that Hillary Clinton might have been the source that leaked the initial madrassa report, and Fox News raised the stakes with a headline designed to prime the national security fears at the root of this racial suspicion: "Hillary Clinton Drops Madrassa Bomb on Obama."[33]

Obama released his long-form birth certificate to the public on April 27, 2011, but this and other efforts by Obama defenders become fodder for conspiracy theorists for whom belief (memory) is drawn from sources other than reason and documented evidence (history). As Chip Berlet points out, "As soon as you criticize a conspiracy theory, you become part of the conspiracy."[34] Obama is not simply suspected of being a foreigner. From the beginning of his 2008 campaign, Obama's national identity intersected with his ethnoracial and religious identity; he was cast as a dangerous and deviant foreigner, born and raised in a Muslim, Arab, and/or African country, depending on the fable. The indoctrination Obama received as a child is central to the tale, as the narrative suggests he was brainwashed by the same sort of anti-American extremists who committed the September 11, 2001, attacks. Significantly, the specific classification of Obama's ethnoracial stain (black, biracial, Arab, African) is almost irrelevant. The logic of the conspiracy theories remains constant across their infinite geographic possibilities: whiteness is the key signifier, and without it, Obama's body cannot mean "American." For committed Birthers, the actual location or documentation of Obama's birth does not matter. Obama's body is the star and crescent on the flag. It is the metalinguistic memory that speaks in silence, both to and for the conspiracy theorists. It says, "I am not like you. I am not from this land, and I do not share your heritage. I am not American."

These bogus claims are legitimized and exploited for political gain by anti-Obama politicians and commentators, and elevated to platforms and to larger audiences, such as web, television, and radio-based news outlets. Opponents of Obama, who are attached to journalistic organizations or elected by the American public, do not explicitly argue that they believe Obama has no claim to citizenship. Instead, right-wing media celebrities, such as Rush Limbaugh and Sarah Palin, stoke the flames with intimation and innuendo, stating that "the public rightfully is still making it an issue," without confirming that they actually believe Obama is ineligible to be president.[35] In February 2011, journalist David Gregory asked Republican Speaker of the House John Boehner whether "it's your job to speak up against that kind of ignorance," in reference to rumors about Obama's religious commitments and citizenship status. Boehner stated that he believes Obama is a citizen, but "it's not my job to tell the *American* people what to think. The *American* people have a right to think what they want to think." These themes were revisited during the 2012 presidential campaign, as former New Hampshire governor and Mitt Romney campaign surrogate John Sununu stated that Obama needed to "learn how to be an American."[36] With Brubaker's insistence that "nation" is used to mobilize loyalties and articulate demands, and Banaji's and Sidanius's research as sociological context, it is plain to see how Boehner and Sununu's invocations of nationalism and repeated appeals to "the American people" are informed by the metalanguage of race. Intentional or not, this is an implicit appeal to white supremacist sensibilities.

Much like the Birthers, the decentralized collection of groups who identify with the Tea Party steeps itself in a version of nationalism grounded in the politics of inheritance and interwoven with racist ideology. Racism does not comprise the whole of these groups' collective political platform—they are broadly interested in "fiscal responsibility, constitutionally limited government, and free market economic policies."[37] However, Parker finds that support for the Tea Party among whites is a clear predictor for racial resentment towards blacks and Latinos, as well as reduced support for gay rights.[38] A quick Internet search for "Tea Party racism" reveals countless verbal attacks, images, and signs about Obama, who is derided as a socialist, terrorist, or Nazi and depicted variously as a topless African witch doctor in tribal garb, Hitler, the Joker, and an ape.[39] There is an ongoing struggle within the Tea Party movement, with some factions openly denouncing and expelling others from the unregulated collective in an effort to cleanse the Tea Party name.[40] Still, multiple journalists and researchers document Tea Party representatives' hate-filled, racist propaganda,[41] as well as Tea Party representatives' penchant for using thinly veiled racial coding to disparage the president and mobilize white voters.[42]

The memory-driven political agenda of Tea Party groups is amnesiac and schizophrenic. Obama is cast both as a Nazi and as a hapless puppet of the Jewish establishment at Tea Party meetings.[43] Protestors demand that government be returned to the people at rallies funded by the same corporations that wield massive lobbying power.[44] They long for a return to the "good old days" when government interference in the lives of hard-working Americans was negligible. Yet many argue that Medicare should be preserved, and the narrative conveniently ignores the fact that the white middle-class American ideal was enabled by early and mid–twentieth century government initiatives that clearly privileged white people, such as the Federal Housing Authority, Home Owners Loan Corporation, and the GI Bill.[45]

The Tea Party's ignorance about institutional racism is not especially remarkable. But what is significant for this discussion is the way that nationalism and patriotism are manifest in Tea Party performances. As historian Jill Lepore points out, Tea Party activists' antihistorical project is especially peculiar and forlorn: a compulsive reenactment that ignores material reality and the rules of time and space, transporting present-day citizens back to the eighteenth century and acting as if the Founding Fathers walk among us today.[46] The fact that degrading visual images of Obama play such a prominent role, and that so many activists appear in Revolutionary War-era costumes, speaks to the need to symbolically represent political agendas with one's body. In order to exemplify the patriotism invoked by group names like the "Tea Party Patriots" and the "1776 Tea Party," activists dress up like white men who violently fought for a country where whiteness and maleness were prerequisites for the full privileges of citizenship.

Nilanjana Dasgupta and Kumar Yogeeswaran explain that one of the keys to Obama's success in 2008 was his downplaying racial and ethnic identification and emphasizing his public contributions to the country as a whole. This combination as a public servant of all Americans, rather than solely blacks, frames Obama as sufficiently, if not ancestrally, American, and therefore fit for the presidency. Dasgupta and Yogeeswaran also suggest that prolonged exposure to highly admired African Americans holds the potential to reduce implicit bias against blacks as a group, and further erode the already decaying notion that "American = white." The flip side of this coin, however, is that "exceptional" people may either fuel the denial of racism or be cast aside as exceptions to the rule of deviant racial/ethnic group culture.[47] So while Obama successfully negotiated a context shaped by the implicit belief that "American = white," his success does not explicitly critique the politics of inheritance, the logic at the core of racial and national identity ascription. Such a challenge emanates, however, from the pages of Obama's memoir, regardless of the author's intent.

Race, Nation, and Inheritance in Dreams from My Father

While Obama's election shows the weakening grip of the politics of inheritance on the country's collective consciousness, his book reveals the epistemology's inadequacy at the level of the individual. In the introduction to *Dreams*, Obama describes the book as "a record of a personal, interior journey—a boy's search for his father, and through that search a workable meaning for his life as a black American."[48] The book's subtitle is *A Story of Race and Inheritance*, and right from the start Obama establishes the relationship between these two ideas. It is through the interrogation of Obama's descent that he endeavors to uncover his identity. Significantly, his racial identity is not simply "black"; it is "black American," highlighting the intersection between race and nation I have established.

Obama identifies as black rather than multiracial in the text, and in trying to craft his blackness, Obama's father, Barack Sr., takes on a special role by virtue of his absence. Though Obama provides biographical details about his white grandparents and his mother, his father's life takes on mythic significance as one of many origin stories from his youth. His father's life is another account in the vein of "Prometheus and the gift of fire," and "the tortoise of Hindu legend." Later, Barack would "become troubled by questions. What supported the tortoise? Why did an omnipotent God let a snake cause such grief? Why didn't my father return?" But as a boy, Obama was "satisfied to leave these distant mysteries intact." Three sentences after these questions, Obama makes it clear to the reader that his father's life is not merely a mystery, but a "morality tale."[49]

This phrasing is significant, because "morality tales" are not simply recitations of past events, created and preserved for the sake of historical accuracy. Morality tales are prescriptive. The reason for crafting and revisiting these lessons is not only that they tell us about the past but that they provide instructions and aspirations for living one's life in the present. The politics of inheritance depends on precisely this logic: one's bodily record of the past sets demands and expectations for the present and future. In many cases, these tales reveal things that we cannot change. Obama cites the serpent from the Garden of Eden, a parable that tells us that man is a sinner—this is his nature, impervious to social intervention. We are all descendants of Adam and Eve, and they were sinners, so we are sinners. The politics of inheritance uses mythic memories of the past to anchor and organize the present. If Obama wants to cement his black identity, as a young boy he believes he must look backward, to the memory of his father, to do so.

Most of the stories the young Obama knows about Barack Sr. do not directly address race, and even though Obama conceives of his father's life as a morality tale, the details of Barack Sr.'s biography are difficult to come by until Obama is much older. However, in the same passage where Obama describes the role of his father's legend, he mentions the one race-related story he recalls being told as a child. Significantly, this story has as much to do with Obama's racial destiny as it does his national destiny. Obama's grandfather, Stanley, recounts an incident where Barack Sr. is called a "nigger" in a local bar. Instead of reacting violently, Barack Sr. "stood up, walked over to the man, smiled, and proceeded to lecture him about the folly of bigotry, the promise of the American dream, and the universal rights of man."[50] The antagonist was overwhelmed by Barack Sr.'s speech and apologized profusely, offering food, drink, and rent money to the elder Obama as penitence. As a disillusioned teenager, Obama grew skeptical of this and other origin tales, but later in life, a random phone call from someone who had been at the bar confirmed the tale as true, and he heard the same note of hope in the stranger's voice as he had in his grandfather's many years before.

This is the starting point for the book. The young Obama is invested in his father's greatness because the politics of inheritance dictates that it portends his own, and because the hope that his father provides is manifest as belief in the power of the American dream and the possibility of black dignity. Almost immediately, the reader senses Obama's suspicion of this ethic as a narrator much wiser than the young boy he describes.

Obama's skepticism and introspection weigh heavily on his interpretation of events and people, especially his father and his grandparents. Barack Sr.'s mythical aura is the starting point for the text, and Obama makes it clear that the entire Obama family has fallen under the old man's spell to some extent. Obama's white grandparents, however, are primarily responsible for raising him, and though he has deep love and appreciation for Madelyn ("Toot") and Stanley ("Gramps") Dunham, his criticism of his grandfather's worldview exemplifies Obama's questioning the politics of inheritance. In part, Obama expresses simple disbelief in the stories his grandfather tells him; for example, Barack is convinced of the veracity of the tale of Barack Sr.'s barroom speech only after a stranger validates his grandfather's story. The reader is further encouraged to perceive Gramps as someone prone to distortion and exaggeration, for Obama notes that although Gramps claims racism drove him to relocate from Texas to Hawaii, Madelyn tells Obama that Stanley's inability to find steady work prompted the move.

These lies take on added significance, because Stanley epitomizes the hopeful, and many times pitiful, American dreamer. Gramps is damned by the false economic promises of the dream, as he never fully recovers from the economic misfortune suffered in Texas, and Toot becomes the primary breadwinner in Hawaii. But the shame of Stanley's Americanness is not simply economic failure; it is ideological naivety. Obama explains:

[Stanley] was an American character, one typical of men of his generation, men who embraced the notion of freedom and individualism and the open road without always knowing its price, and whose enthusiasms could as easily lead to the cowardice of McCarthyism as to the heroics of World War II. Men who were both dangerous and promising precisely because of their fundamental innocence; men prone, in the end, to disappointment.[51]

The American dream sets believers up for disappointment and is useless as a moral compass, as it can just as easily lead to cowardice or to heroism.

Stanley is not alone in falling under the seductive spell of Americanism, as his gregarious optimism and embrace of multicultural idealism are symptomatic of "a sprit that would grip the nation for that fleeting period between Kennedy's election and the passage of the Voting Rights Act: the seeming triumph of universalism over parochialism and narrow-mindedness, a bright new world where differences of race or culture would instruct and amuse and perhaps even ennoble."[52] Obama pities Gramps for this, dismissing Stanley's idealism as "a useful fiction," and his grandfather's life as "a prop in someone else's narrative."[53] The idealized morality tale that unfolds between Kennedy and the Voting Rights Act charts no course for those born in its wake. Obama does not inherit his grandfather's ideas of America, despite (and in large part because of) Stanley's ceaseless storytelling and insistence on living as if the dream is real. The narrator steadfastly rejects his grandfather's efforts to pass down this form of national identity, one laced with premature celebrations of America's racial redemption.

Obama's conception of Americanism is not inherited from his father or grandfather; its foundation is built from his experiences living in Indonesia. The principal qualities of Americanism are not freedom and equal opportunity; they are power and privilege. Obama describes a scene in Indonesia where his mother bears witness to an impoverished local woman, shuffling through the streets of a wealthy neighborhood, begging for change. Obama writes as if reading his mother's thoughts, as she reflects on "*Power*. The word fixed in my mother's mind like a curse. In America, it had generally remained hidden from view until you dug beneath the surface of things; until you visited an Indian reservation or spoke to a black person whose trust you had earned. But here, power was undisguised."[54] At this moment in the text, America's defining characteristic is its ability to disguise social inequality and present an air of civility, social equality, and dignity, especially when one hovers among the privileged class. Obama's understanding is clearly intersectional, informed by the race of the American in question, as blacks and American Indians have knowledge of Americanism that disrupts the normalcy of white privilege.

Obama's mother, Ann, tries to reject white American privilege and endeavors to pass on a critical worldview to her son. But in the end, she succumbs to practical considerations when it comes to claiming national identity.

She had always encouraged my rapid acculturation in Indonesia: It had made me relatively self-sufficient, undemanding on a tight budget, and extremely well mannered when compared to other American children. She had taught me to disdain the blend of ignorance and arrogance that too often characterized Americans abroad. But she now had learned, just as Lolo had learned, the chasm that separated the life chances of an American from those of an Indonesian. She knew which side of the divide she wanted her child to be on. I was an American, she decided, and my true life lay elsewhere.[55]

At this point in the text, Obama is still a child, and this is where he develops his sense of what it actually means to be American. American-ism is not defined by the myths and aspirations of his father and grand-father, which Obama explicitly casts doubt on when they are described twenty-five pages earlier. There is no such skepticism as the narrator describes his mother's awakening to the true meaning of "American." Readers are left with the impression that Obama is sympathetic to this understanding, in large part because it is based on his own life experi-ences and encounters with American privilege rather than the myths and memories of older family members. Though this understanding is informed by Obama's mother, there is no reaching back to a morality tale about his mother's personal life as means to understand the mean-ing of "American." Instead, Obama simply perceives the material reality of American privilege in a foreign land.

Obama first starts to craft his personal meaning of blackness through similar means, as he refers to his own experiences rather than a black identity seamlessly inherited from his family. This construction of black identity takes shape despite the best efforts of Obama's mother, who fuses the dignity of black political struggle with the personal quali-ties of Obama's father. Ann tells Obama that he inherits his "brains" and "character" directly from Barack Sr., and she decides that Obama will follow his father's example, leading a "tough" and "principled" life. Obama describes his mother's insistence on these points as a subject in which "I had no choice. It was in the genes." These edicts are directly followed in the narrator's description by Ann's efforts to instill black pride in her son. She brings him books about the civil rights movement and recordings of Mahalia Jackson, emphasizing the black American liberation struggle to motivate Obama as a student with opportunities derived from the racially encoded sacrifices of others. "To be black was to be the beneficiary of a great inheritance, a special destiny, glorious burdens that only we were strong enough to bear."[56]

Obama does not reject these sentiments outright, but they are re-vealed as inadequate material for understanding blackness, because life experiences direct him toward different meanings. When Obama reads a magazine story about a black man who tried to pull off his skin, it leads him to reflect on other cultural phenomena that challenge his mother's version of heritable black dignity.

I began to notice that Cosby never got the girl on *I Spy*, that the black man on *Mission Impossible* spent all his time underground. I noticed that there was nobody like me in the Sears, Roebuck Christmas catalog that Toot and Gramps sent us, and that Santa was a white man.

I kept these observations to myself, deciding that either my mother didn't see them or she was trying to protect me and that I shouldn't expose her efforts as having failed. I still trusted my mother's love—but I now faced the prospect that her account of the world, and my father's place in it, was somehow incomplete.[57]

Obama does not deny the history of the black liberation struggle, reject the notion that he should lead a principled life, or denounce the inheritance cast upon him by Ann. But the politics of inheritance proves insufficient when Obama encounters the social reality of race. Obama's struggle to build an honorable black identity intensifies through his teenage and young adult years. At various times, Barack turns to black literature, global politics, and popular culture as building materials to construct a more radical and politically progressive blackness than the one prescribed by his mother and bequeathed to him by his father. Though he gradually moves away from the idealized blackness passed down through the morality tale that is his father's life, he does not fully reject the obligations of inheritance until his sister, Auma, visits him in New York and recounts her relationship with an often hostile and bitter Barack Sr. Now a young man, Obama flatly admits that his father's lessons and legacy take on different meaning from those of Gramps and his mother's partner, Lolo, not just because Barack Sr. is absent but because he is black. He writes, "It was into my father's image, the black man, son of Africa, that I'd packed all the attributes I sought in myself, the attributes of Martin and Malcolm, Du Bois and Mandela."[58] When Auma describes Barack Sr.'s disappointment and how the old man had fallen on hard times, Obama uses all the phrases we might expect to describe his epiphany, telling readers, "The king is overthrown. . . . The emerald curtain is pulled aside. . . . Whatever I do, it seems, I won't do much worse than he did."[59]

Auma's visit prompts Obama to travel to Kenya, to meet extended family and visit his father's homeland and final resting place. Upon his arrival, he finds it exceedingly difficult to negotiate his commitments, because "family seemed to be everywhere," and poverty noticeable.[60] In the United States, Obama writes, he "had been able to translate those feelings into politics," but in Kenya, "a commitment to black empowerment" and "faith in democracy" would not procure jobs or put food on his family's table.[61] Obama interprets this problem as another iteration of his personal conflict in the States, wherein economic success and stability distance those who succeed from their less fortunate brethren. Again, the politics of inheritance fails to provide a road map, as "no one here could tell me what my blood ties demanded or how those demands could be reconciled with some larger idea of human association."[62]

In the epilogue to *Dreams*, Obama recounts his final days in Kenya, including a visit to the home of a family friend, Dr. Rukia Odero. Rukia has much to say on the romanticization of Africa, acknowledging that there is "something different about this place,"[63] but generally lamenting both African and European desire for "an unblemished past."[64] She opines that clinging to a politics of inheritance that looks backward to a false past for solutions to contemporary political problems is especially damning for Africans, who build mythic morality tales of African history in order to cope with the pain of economic, cultural, and physical violence suffered at the hands of European colonizers. Nostalgia is tempting but politically poisonous, and inheritance-based cultural nationalism is counterproductive for Kenya and its neighbors. Rukia is reluctant to provide a solution but suggests a piecemeal, pragmatic approach to reconciling cultural and political conflicts in postcolonial African nation-states.

To recap what we can glean from these events: from a very young age, Obama's intersectional racial/national identity is shaped by the myth and memory of his absent father. Obama is led to believe that Barack Sr. embodies dignified and honorable blackness in combination with the highest principles of the American dream. To say Obama's *idea* of black American identity is shaped by his father is not enough; instead, he is explicitly and implicitly told that such identity is his *personal destiny* because he is his father's son. As he ages, Obama becomes increasingly skeptical about the utility of his father's life as a morality tale. Blackness, Americanness, and black Americanness assume meanings that widely diverge from the ideals passed down by his family. More specifically, Obama's encounters with social inequality run counter to the ideas his family would have him inherit. He sees blacks marginalized and degraded by mainstream American culture, laments institutional racism, and identifies self-doubt as a chief enemy of the black liberation struggle. The United States is a democracy, with the potential to evolve. But when Obama perceives Americanism in the real world, it is defined by privilege, both white Americans' relative privilege living as expatriates in Indonesia, and his own privilege relative to black family members in Kenya.

Not only does the politics of inheritance provide inaccurate conceptions of race and nation; it cannot provide a path forward out of widespread political marginalization and poverty. My reading should not be interpreted as a suggestion that we steadfastly ignore family history. Obama's book illustrates that there is much to be gained from untangling the ties that bind us to our relatives and ancestors. But self-knowledge as a social and political subject must flow through other channels than inheritance. Rather than pursuing social justice in Chicago through a form of inheritance-based cultural nationalism, Obama opts for community organizing on the basis of material concerns. Familial obligations cannot instruct Obama as to how to conquer the economic challenges facing postcolonial Kenya or the African continent more broadly.   *Dreams* clearly reveals the politics of inheritance as insufficient for understanding one's individual social identity, defining group boundaries and organizing communities, or furnishing guidelines for pursuing social justice. But insufficiency is not complete abdication. If we take Obama's 2008 campaign rhetoric and his second book, *The Audacity of Hope* (2006), as evidence, we have no choice but to recognize Obama's attraction to the hopeful versions of Americanness offered by his father and grandfather. In *Dreams*, Obama identifies the other active ingredient of his hope formula, harvested at his spiritual awakening in Trinity United Church of Christ in Chicago. If there is one place in the text where the skeptical narrator, an older, wiser Obama with the gift of perspective, is seduced by the politics of inheritance, it is here, at the moment of revelation.

And in that single note—hope!—I heard something else; at the foot of that cross, inside the thousands of churches across the city, I imagined the stories of ordinary black people merging with the stories of David and Goliath, Moses and Pharaoh, the Christians in the lion's den, Ezekiel's field of dry bones. Those stories—of survival, and freedom, and hope—became our story, my story; the blood that had spilled was our blood, the tears our tears; until this black church, on this bright day, seemed once more a vessel carrying the story of a people into future generations and into a larger world. Our trials and triumphs became at once unique and universal, black and more than black.[65]

This version of hope is different from those passed down by the Dunham family. It is not the steely, principled, and dignified resolve of black liberation workers, nor is it the wide-eyed idealism of opportunity and equality conjured by the American dream. However, this passage clearly relies on the politics of inheritance as means to describe Obama's transformation; it is an embodied morality tale manifest through recognizable historical characters who carry their story through the blood "into future generations and into a larger world." But if this is dissimilar from other examples, it is distinguished too by its lesson: the unique is universal. This is not a description of an individual destiny or personal calling, nor is it a descent-based elucidation of group boundaries. It is a politics of inheritance that renders each subject and body empathetic and universal rather than ethnically, racially, or nationally specific and loyal. This is the best-case manifestation of a flawed epistemology, and sadly the least common, both in *Dreams* and in waking life.

Away from Inheritance, Toward a New National Identity

Obama's rhetoric often emphasizes reconciliation and the subjugation of racial/ethnic identity to national solidarity. One might speculate as to whether Obama truly believes that racial and ethnic divisions are trivial, but the discussion here is not about what Obama "really thinks" American nationalism should be. Rather, it illustrates that troubling connections between normative white masculinity and American nationalism endure, and it suggests that regardless of his actual beliefs, Obama's election and memoir are anomalies in the symbolic construction of racial and national identity. More bluntly: I do not care about Obama's conscious or "true" beliefs about the politics of inheritance. The point is that *Dreams* is fertile ground for illustrating and interrogating the concept, and Obama's election in 2008 points to its demise.

Where do we go from here? How do we more fully eschew the notion that "American = white," and transform criticism of the politics of inheritance into a productive alternative for national affiliation? One response might be that we should simply reject all forms of nationalism, and the recent traction of neoliberalism as a political ethos may cement this path, taking the choice out of our hands altogether. The essence of neoliberalism is the belief that the uninterrupted pursuit of self-interest yields optimal market efficiency and prosperity. As individual state economies are more fully integrated into a single global economy, capital flows more easily to those spaces where it is treated well, allowed to multiply, and likely to be reinvested. Therefore, state intervention in economic affairs is an anathema; if economic development is restricted by state laws, corporations will simply leave one nation-state and move to another, thereby crippling the labor market in the abandoned territory, and ruining the economy.

We can see how problematic this is for distinctive national identity. If the neoliberal state is realized, the political goals of all states are the same: allow individuals to make self-interested decisions and maximize overall growth. Such goals bear no connection to collective identity or cultural belief systems, including those with ethnocultural bases. If neoliberalism has any culture to speak of, perhaps it is most closely approximated by cosmopolitanism. However, cosmopolitanism is far from neutral or virtuous, as it often requires, as prerequisite, forms of privilege reserved for those with the technological and economic means to participate in global society.[66] The starting points for contemporary cosmopolitanism are Western economic dominance and white privilege.

Federal economic policy has taken on an increasingly neoliberal hue since the Reagan administration. Unfortunately, this is not an appropriate course of action for building a strong national culture, nor has it increased economic stability. Two indisputable outcomes of these policies over the past thirty years are an unconscionable concentration of wealth at the very peak of the class pyramid, and an unwillingness to punish corporations for irresponsible and unethical practices that cripple the economy. This is not an argument for absolute socioeconomic equality as a realistic or desirable political goal. But a nation that reveres acute economic prosperity while turning a blind eye to inequality will never optimize its potential for national solidarity and pride. One percent of the American population accounts for one quarter of the nation's income and 40 percent of total wealth. This top 1 percent has seen its income rise by 18 percent during the past decade, as middle-class income falls.[67] As of the end of 2011, 46.2 million Americans were living in poverty, accounting for the highest percentage of the population (15.1 percent) since 1993.[68] In addition, social mobility between classes has steadily declined; those who begin with economic disadvantages are increasingly unlikely to move up the ladder.[69]

The social and cultural differences between the haves and the have-nots inhibit our ability to look at those who are less fortunate than we are and see ourselves. Without this mutual recognition, when the chips are down and the nation-state is in crisis, disparate social groups will not trust each other enough to bond together and make collective sacrifices for the good of the whole. Bob Herbert and Joseph Stiglitz are two of the many commentators who have urged America to view the 2011 protests and violence in Egypt and Libya as warning signs about the implications of allowing the wealth gap to continue to widen.[70] It is true that the state has difficulty equitably redistributing wealth, and an outright rejection of capitalism cannot be taken seriously. The market is not evil, but it is inherently political. It cannot be isolated from formal political institutions such as property rights; it needs the state to discourage corporate actors from wild risk-taking and speculation; and it needs governments to serve as lenders of last resort when catastrophe strikes: the state must play a role.[71] All forms of durable nationalism depend on the just distribution of economic resources and equal opportunity as the foundation of social stability.

Stable societies enhance communication amongst their citizens rather than engendering spatial and cultural segregation, and this is where linguistic/cultural systems and the politics of inheritance exert their influence. If neoliberals' operating assumption is that cultural beliefs are romantic and extraneous peculiarities of human life destined for extinction, history suggests otherwise. Cultural communities value their belief systems and traditions, and they need the legitimate authority structure to protect cultural practices so long as they do not infringe upon others' rights. Culture matters, and nation-states cannot ignore it. Moreover, some cultural belief systems, like racism and bigoted cultural nationalism, impinge upon civil rights and sound economic decision-making. Prejudice and discrimination in the housing and labor market, for example, are long-standing and severe cultural problems with demonstrable economic effects. The state is obligated not only to make these practices *illegal* but to advance an alternative cultural ethos that explains to its citizenry why the practices are *wrong*. Invoking nationalism as means to encourage collective disavowal of prejudice and discrimination, rather than pretending institutional racism does not exist, is a shrewd and sensible move for any government.

Americanness must enhance bonds within and between ethnoracial communities. This requires increasing the volume of symbolic representations of Americanism that challenge straight, Christian, white male normativity, and performing these representations in public rather than forcing marginalized ethnic and gender groups to cultivate their American identities privately. Steps in this direction include erecting statues and monuments of women, openly queer, non-Christian, and nonwhite historical figures, using nonbodily objects to represent national events, and rethinking the privileges accorded to Western European religious traditions when the government designates holidays.

Epistemologically, the new nationalism moves away from the politics of inheritance and the provincial, "great man" model of historical pedagogy, towards versions of American history that emphasize collective action. Refusing to adhere to the politics of inheritance is not the same thing as forsaking one's ancestry or discrediting the chronicles of family history. Indeed, there is nothing wrong with preserving such history and remembering those who have passed on. The utility and distinctly political impact of these memories is what is at stake. When we obsess over pinpointing the precise location of our true "roots," imagine morality and belonging as embodied and exemplified by historical figures, and map their choices and destiny onto our own, we handicap ourselves in the struggle to harness the winds of social change.

As for teaching beyond the "great man" model of history, I am not arguing for antihistorical nationalism, and I acknowledge the utility of biography. However, biographies must be crafted with an eye toward explaining social processes and the relationship between context and agency rather than glorifying their subjects' unique talents and personal influence on historical events. Further, I am not advocating a full-fledged embrace of patchwork multicultural history, where groups are sharply delineated and we strive to tell an equal number of "ethnic" stories from each designated community. Rather, focusing on collective action and networked social processes as the fuel of American history forces recognition of the ways different forms of oppression and resistance intersect with one another. The Civil War was about slavery, and therefore it was about race. Yes, Abraham Lincoln issued the Emancipation Proclamation. But the Civil War was also an upheaval caused by the global transition from agrarianism to industrialized capitalism, and by the countervailing winds of Enlightenment liberalism and colonialism blowing across and between all corners of the Atlantic world. Black slavery in America continued well beyond 1865, and other forms of slavery persist within our national borders today. American slavery is and has been rooted in sexism and rape culture, just as it is rooted in racism. United States history is fundamentally intersectional, and when it is transfigured into a linear sequence of biographies, acts, and arguments, its lessons are lost.

The new American nationalism is not about the right to be happy and successful. It is about disdain for intolerance and about honest self-examination and a tradition of collective action in the name of equal opportunity. It is activated by the reality of injustice and inequality, which spurs the government and its citizenry to action. None of this is possible when we ignore the severity of contemporary racism or treat it as an unfortunate accident. Responsible interrogation of America's history and present reveals purposeful, gruesome, and shameful injustice. Staring the beast in the mirror squarely in the eye is frightening, and it is not easy to feel proud when faced with something horrific. James Baldwin writes, "I love America more than any other country in the world, and, exactly for this reason, I insist on the right to criticize her perpetually." This relentless self-confrontation is central to the American creed, and the embodiment of American freedom. It is the epitome of patriotism.

CHAPTER 3

"MUTTS LIKE ME"

Barack Obama, Tragic Mulattos, and Cool Mixed-Race Millennials

> Malia is allergic, so it has to be hypoallergenic. There are
> a number of breeds that are hypoallergenic. On the other
> hand, our preference would be to get a shelter dog, but
> obviously, a lot of shelter dogs are mutts, like me.
> —*Barack Obama*[1]

Shelby Steele, author of *A Bound Man: Why We Are Excited About Obama and Why He Can't Win* (2008), is unconvinced that Obama's rise signals the potential for any sort of new nationalism or a fresh approach to race. Steele is a scholar, journalist, and political commentator with a twenty-year career as one of America's preeminent self-described black conservatives.[2] His political beliefs grow from his understanding of power, which is rooted in the governing group's ability to claim innocence and therefore moral authority and self-righteousness. According to Steele, prior to the civil rights movement white Americans cast themselves as innocent and righteously empowered in the name of democracy. During the movement, however, blacks reclaimed their innocence by demonstrating that whites were in fact guilty of unjustly subjugating and degrading black people. This tactic led to concessions from whites and empowerment in the form of civil rights legislation. Steele believes that, sadly, blacks' strategy for empowerment has not changed.

Portions of Chapters 3 and 4 were previously published in Michael P. Jeffries, "'Obama Studies' in Its Infancy," *Du Bois Review: Social Science Research on Race* 7, no. 2 (2010): 403–15.

Blacks keep blaming whites for their problems and holding tight to an outdated notion of black solidarity as they make political demands, in the hope that further concessions will be granted. Steele admits that he played on "white guilt" as a teenager and young adult,[3] but he identifies this phase in his life as a mistake, and details his ideological enlightenment. Instead, blacks (and other oppressed racial/ethnic groups) should assume personal responsibility for their actions and progress as individuals based on merit; this is the only way America will heal its racial divide and the only way that blacks will ever be truly liberated.[4]

Steele, like Obama, was born to a white mother and black father, and for this reason he compares the president's struggle to arrive at a comfortable racial identity with his own journey. *A Bound Man* begins with reflections on Obama's psyche, casting the president as a man who spent much of his life haunted by race. Steele believes Obama knows that traditional conceptions of race fall woefully short of capturing our life experiences, and due to his mixed parentage and biography, Obama seems to represent a rejection of common knowledge. However, Steele argues that while Obama the symbol embodies a break from racial/political tradition, Obama the politician forfeits his chance to learn from his multiracial upbringing and abandon hackneyed models of identity politics. Steele posits that Obama penned *Dreams from My Father* to defend himself against the inevitable criticism that he is not authentically black. For Steele, Obama's defense takes the form of a desperate quest to embody something close to black authenticity. Obama's community organizing in Chicago, rejection of his white girlfriend, and dogged skepticism of blacks who encourage him to assimilate are examples of his yearning for a "real" black identity. This is the bind Obama finds himself in; his multiracial identity situates him so far from authentic blackness that his desire to embody it is inevitable, yet Obama lives with the constant knowledge that he cannot expunge those parts of himself that invalidate the black authentic ideal.[5] Steele fears Obama will never have the gumption to pursue the correct political course and bring about a new racial future, because to be convincingly black Obama has to cling to the past and "exaggerate black victimization in

America. And he has to argue for public policy that responds to the exaggeration rather than to the reality of victimization."[6] Obama's *personal* struggle as a multiracial subject has dire *political* implications.

Steele's views about racial politics are deeply flawed. Nowhere in these rants against collective identity and white guilt does he acknowledge that oppressed groups organize around stigmatized identities as means of self-defense when patterns of mistreatment are either legalized, socialized, or both. Mutual recognition among group members is often a precursor to political consciousness, coalition building, and activism, and this activism is often undertaken not only in the name of group pride but in the interest of greater social justice. Moreover, tomes of empirical evidence suggest that institutional inequality and mistreatment (racism, sexism, and so on) are legitimate problems rather than self-serving multiculturalist fabrications. As for whites' collective guilty desire to see a qualified black man become president, there is evidence that whites' establishing moral credentials by endorsing a single person of color may cement their racial bias and allow for future mistreatment of nonwhites.[7] But desire to earn the moral credential was less than overpowering for most whites at the time of the 2008 election: Obama did not win a majority of white votes. Skepticism about Obama and his intentions is certainly within the bounds of legitimate inquiry, but *A Bound Man* seems strangely out of touch with reality.

Despite these errors, Steele's argument is important because it suggests that the predicament of multiracial identity is not just a personal struggle to find oneself; it is closely tied to broader issues in American racial politics. This chapter features data from in-depth interviews with young multiracial adults to investigate connections between the president, mixed-race identity, and America's racial landscape. Previous studies focus on multiracialism with attention to family dynamics, personal life experiences, and political activism. While I include data about respondents' understandings of themselves, I am especially interested in how multiracial people view Obama. The president serves multiple roles in this investigation, eroding the boundaries between the personal and the political. He might well be a reference point as respondents construct their identities, but beyond this, Obama's very public biography has the potential to shape political discourse about racial identity and racism at the national level.

I begin with an explanation of how multiracialism fits into the metalanguage and intersectionality framework; this is followed by a brief history of American interracialism and multiracialism. After laying the historical and sociological foundation, I turn to multiracialism specifically as it pertains to Obama. I draw on conversations with forty-nine self-identified multiracial respondents between the ages of eighteen and twenty-three years old, who sat with me and talked at length about their life experiences, impressions of Obama, and American racism and race relations. Respondents hold favorable opinions of the president, take pride in his success, and believe that Obama's rise provides some benefits for multiracial people. However, respondents assert that Obama is widely viewed as black rather than multiracial by the American public, and his political career and racial identity are greatly constricted by racism and racial norms. Respondents also insist that racism remains an urgent social problem, despite the excitement generated by Obama's victory.

Multiracialism and the Metalanguage of Race

Recall Evelyn Higginbotham's initial theory of race as metalanguage, as explained in the first chapter. When race is too loud, it covers up the meaning-making process and conceals its interplay with other social forces. When race is too quiet, it appropriates other knowledge systems, silently lending meaning to concepts and words that are not essentially racial.

Thinking about race as metalanguage alerts us to the fact that race cannot be understood as a set of static categories that correspond to distinct identities and experiences. When two or more categories are combined, conventional ways of thinking about race can only produce another categorical label, "biracial" or "multiracial." Qualifying for the ascribed label is not dependent on individual experience or the way a subject is treated; it is driven by the aforementioned racial logic of inheritance. The label is automatically invoked because of who the subject's parents are, rather than the subject herself. Labeling someone "multiracial" or "biracial" does not mean that her daily experiences proportionally reflect her parents' racial mixture.

Here, race is too loud. If we take the language literally, we might expect biracial and multiracial people to have the racialized experiences common to two (bi) or many (multi) groups. But in reality, multiracial people taken together have a dauntingly diverse range of social experiences and identities, because of the ways race intersects with ethnicity, gender, class, region, and many other factors. Sometimes multiracial people share experiences with members of "traditional" racial groups. Other times they share experiences with fellow multiracials, and there are many cases where they conceive of their experiences as unique and separate from any group identity. Those who choose the multiracial label may choose it selectively, and have wildly differing views about how consistently to apply it and what obligations and connections they share with fellow multiracials.

If the compulsion for racial categorization and the ascription of a stable multiracial identity exemplifies the loudness of race as metalanguage, Kimberly DaCosta's analysis of multiracial families provides an equally impeccable example of how the metalanguage of race silently lends meaning to nonracial ideas. She writes,

The invisibility (and rarity) of multiracial families, which essentially reflects a breaking of family bonds across racial categories, owes its genesis to the very tight *relatedness* between American notions of race and family. This tight relationship is born of two processes—what I call "the racialization of the family" (how racial premises came to be buried in our understanding of family, in which genetic/phenotypic sharing is coded to signify cultural sharing, intimacy, and caring) and "the familization of race" (how it came to be that members of the same racial group feel a kin-like connection and how that familial understanding is used politically).[8]

This is a perfect illustration of the metalanguage of race: "family" silently carries racial meaning, even when race is quiet and we avoid the explicit use of racial categories to describe how we are related. Just as

Higginbotham discusses the racial encoding of a phrase like "good hair," DaCosta highlights the racial encoding of words like "brother" and "sister," colloquial terms that normally indicate shared descent, as well as more politicized invocations and indicators of solidarity and shared experience, in cases such as religious/spiritual fellowship, or shared national/ethnic descent.[9] When DaCosta writes that multiracialism "reflects a breaking of family bonds across racial categories," her point is that multiracial families and multiracial people illuminate and amplify the metalanguage of race as it quietly it does its work. Multiracial people and the caring, closeness, and codependence of multiracial families excavate the subterranean assumptions we make about who can love, depend on, and care for whom. To recognize their anomalous presence is to be forced to remember how stringently interracial relations have been policed and prohibited by law. This is not to say that the mere existence of multiracial people and families is revolutionary or politically progressive, but rethinking race, challenging assumptions, and recognizing "natural" and "inherited" racial divisions as products of oppression is a necessary first step for political change. Race mixing is not just an epistemological problem that shows us why conventional understandings of race are wrong; it is a social and political problem that the United States has struggled with since its birth.

History and Tropes of Interracialism and Multiracialism

Xenophobia and legalized racial and ethnic discrimination are global phenomena, but the prohibition of interracial marriage in religious and civil law is uniquely American. Werner Sollors points out that "even the word used to describe interracial sexual and marital relations, *miscegenation*, is an Americanism . . . coined by two New York journalists in an 1863 pamphlet, [as] a political hoax designed to hurt abolitionists and Republicans who were invited to endorse it." It is an invented word, difficult to translate into other languages, "derived from Latin *miscere* and *genus.* . . . [It] faintly echoes the term for the European class mismatch, *misalliance*, and replaced *amalgamation*."[10] From the time the first laws against miscegenation were established in the colonies of Virginia and

Maryland in 1661, the purpose was to prevent blacks and whites from getting married.[11] Of course, black-white sexual relations were commonplace in American slave society, as white male slave owners routinely raped enslaved black women for pleasure and further propagation of their labor force. The children of these encounters posed no legal problem so long as the law stated that the child followed the legal status of her mother. But a society dependent on strict social and labor separation between blacks and whites could not sustain itself if the two groups were allowed to marry and produce offspring that disrupted the rules of the polity and the economy.

Intermarriage between whites and American Indians was banned shortly after the first black-white miscegenation laws, and as increasing numbers of Asians immigrated to America, the states most heavily affected by these demographic shifts forbade Asian-white marriages as well, in order to prevent family formation and naturalization. Laws about unions between whites and Mexicans were policed differently. Maria Root highlights California as an example of a state where white-Mexican unions were legalized, as Mexican women could inherit their family's land, which provided economic incentive for white men to partner with them. However, as was the case with other racial groups, the racist and sexist sanctity of white womanhood was compulsively protected and Mexican men could not marry white women.[12] In all cases, the purpose of the law is not merely to prevent any and all interracial contact; it is to preserve the idea of whiteness and protect white supremacist patriarchy.

Despite legal efforts to discourage white-nonwhite partnerships and avoid the difficult question of what to do with offspring who fall between racial categories, the multiracial citizen became a powerful social symbol and trope in the American literary imagination. The condemned word for black-white multiracial subjects is "mulatto," an outdated term at the center of what is now a thick field of literary studies. "Mulatto" had been a census category since 1850; the 1890 Census included categories for mulattos, quadroons (one-fourth black), and octoroons (one-eighth); and multiracial options remained in place until the 1930 Census, thus formalizing the "one-drop" rule, where one drop of black blood in one's ancestry means the subject must be classified as black.[13] Hazel Carby explains, "historically the mulatto, as narrative figure, has two primary functions: as a vehicle for an exploration of the relationship between the races, and at the same time, an expression of the relationship between the races. The figure of the mulatto should be understood and analyzed as a narrative device of mediation."[14] This role as a bridge between the races and explorer of racial frontiers is rarely a happy one. From its earliest appearance, the "tragic mulatto" is characterized by the tortured existence she leads, stuck between two worlds that reject her, just as Steele describes Obama.

The tragic mulatto is not merely a historical artifact or a figment of the literary imagination. In 2009, a year after Obama was elected president, justice of the peace Keith Bardwell refused to preside over the marriage of Beth Humphrey (white) and Terence McKay (black) in Louisiana. Bardwell explained, "I've had countless numbers of people that was born in that situation, and that they claim that the blacks or the whites didn't accept the children. And I didn't want to put the children in that position."[15] Anecdotes such as the Bardwell case are reflected in sociologist Erica Chito Childs's recent work, which documents the fact that the "problem" of multiracial children continues to crop up as a reason for everyday Americans' opposition to interracial marriage within their families. Chito Childs argues that in many cases, whites like Bardwell who oppose interracial marriage employ the discourse of concern for multiracial children as means to cloak traditional racism and avoid explicitly admitting that they are uncomfortable with nonwhites.[16]

The tragic mulatto was initially crafted in a social context where laws against black-white interracial marriage were constitutional and commonplace in most of the states in the union. The seminal moment in the legal history of interracial marriage in the United States is the Supreme Court case of *Loving vs. The Commonwealth of Virginia* in 1967. In 1958, Mildred Loving (black) and Richard Loving (white) were legally married in Washington, D.C.; they returned to Virginia only to be arrested at their home and have their marriage declared illegal. After a series of appeals, the Loving case made its way to the Supreme Court, which ruled unanimously that state laws against interracial marriage prevent the pursuit of happiness, therefore violating the Fourteenth Amendment of the constitution. Approval of interracial marriages rose sharply in the thirty years after the *Loving* decision, especially among those with higher incomes and educational attainment, and in 1997 a significant majority of both blacks and whites expressed approval for the first time.[17]

Between 1990 and 2000, the number of interracial marriages in the United States increased by 65 percent, and such marriages accounted for 7 percent of the national total. That growth rate is slowing, as mixed-race marriages increased by only 20 percent from 2000 to 2010, and they now constitute roughly 8 percent of marriages nationwide.[18] These are important trends, because much of the canonical literature on racial and ethnic assimilation points to intermarriage as a key indicator of how integrated a society is.[19] Canonical assimilation theory can be problematic in that many models posit white ethnic assimilation as the norm, trivializing the ways that racism and immigration differences shape acclimation to American culture for nonwhite ethnoracial groups. But the idea I want to retain is that the more assimilated a racial or ethnic group is, the less impact a group member's racial or ethnic origins have on social experience and life chances at attaining socioeconomic status. Along with status attainment, residential integration, and the decline of linguistic differences, intermarriage breaks down group boundaries and turns racial and ethnic identification into more of a private choice than a publicly mandated ascription—these are the conditions described in the "melting pot" version of American nationalism in the preceding chapter.

Where are we now? Here are the data from the 2010 Census on mixed-race marriages, organized by four categories: Asian, black, white, and a final category comprising all remaining races and race combinations (Table 3.1). Data on Hispanic marriages are collapsed into these figures, as the census allows Hispanics and Latinos, which are comprised in an ethnic group, to identify as any race (white, black, American Indian, or Asian). A person who writes in her own race is included in one of the remaining races and combinations.[20]

TABLE 3.1. Mixed-race marriages

	White wife	Black wife	Asian wife	ARRRC[1] wife
White husband	50,410,000	168,000	529,000	487,000
Black husband	390,000	4,072,000	39,000	66,000
Asian husband	219,000	9,000	2,855,000	28,000
ARRRC[1] husband	488,000	18,000	37,000	568,000

1 ARRRC = all remaining races and race combinations
Data source: U.S. Bureau of the Census. Current Population Survey, 2010.

Again, approval and incidence for interracial marriage has risen steadily since the *Loving* case, but perhaps the most striking feature of these data is the extent to which they demonstrate the durability of racial divisions in America: ninety-two percent of Americans choose a marriage partner from within their racial group, and the choice to partner with someone of a different background is clearly impacted by beauty standards congealing from intersections of race, class, and gender privilege. As noted above, restrictive marriage laws from the seventeenth through the twentieth centuries were implemented with the express purpose of protecting white supremacist patriarchy. In the preceding chapter I note just how far the country is from a high assimilation/ integration "melting pot" version of American nationalism. If interracial marriage is a key indicator, the United States seems to be moving in that direction, but we are leagues away from the assimilationist ideal.

The story is mixed (pun intended), as interracial marriages continue to rise, but racial hierarchy and patterns of endogamy persist. Of special note is the "all remaining races and race combinations" category, which suggests the need to reexamine the boundaries of traditional monoracial identification. The recent history of multiracial American identity provides just such an opportunity.

Multiracial Americans in the Twenty-First Century

David Parker and Miri Song point out that the landscape of research on multiracialism carries an air of scrutiny and negativity, as if the condition of multiracialism brings inevitable suffering and pathology.[21] But new studies in multiracialism are less dependent on the tragic mulatto trope. Kim Williams's *Mark One or More* (2006) details the years leading up to the 2000 Census, when a small group of decentralized, poorly funded activists advanced a persistent argument for including a multiracial category for racial identification on the census. Adopting the mantra of Maria P.P. Root's "Bill of Rights for Mixed Race People" (1992), organizations led by and largely composed of white middle-class mothers of multiracial children—such as the Association of Multiethnic Americans, Project RACE, and A Place for Us—argued that racial self-identification is a civil right that government cannot deny. These groups capitalized on a rare political opportunity and the inherent weakness of the Office of Management and Budget (OMB), which administers the census but operates with little autonomy and authority, is subject to frequent turnover, and is ill equipped to manage political pressure. Through persistent letter writing and eventually testimony before Congress, key figures in the small but insistent multiracial category movement were eventually appointed to the United States Census Advisory Committee in 1995. Ultimately, these efforts fell short, and no multiracial category was added to the racial and ethnic identification section of the census. But for the first time, respondents were allowed to mark one or more races.[22]

Williams's account highlights the divisive and highly politicized nature of racial and ethnic categorization on the census. The census is more than a list of United States citizens. It is a government database used to determine how to allocate funding and human resources for schools, libraries, public works projects, and other elements of the infrastructure. Additionally, the census is used by civil rights advocates to demonstrate the prevalence of racism and discrimination, and force the government to act. This was an indispensable tool during the civil rights movement, and in 1977 OMB Directive 15 established four racial categories and two ethnic options for collecting these data: American Indian or Alaskan Native, Asian or Pacific Islander, Black, White, and Hispanic/Non-Hispanic. Multiracial category advocates, however, argued that the concerns of other racial groups and government agencies charged with allocating resources were secondary concerns; the individual's right to choose her identity and the parent's right to identify her child as multiracial, are paramount.[23]

Given the use of the census as an antiracism tool, it is not surprising that National Association for the Advancement of Colored People president Kwame Mfume and others expressed deep concern about advocates' efforts to create a multiracial category; if African Americans chose to identify as exclusively multiracial, the official count of black Americans would be depressed and the reality of racism and discrimination against blacks would be obscured.[24] The psychological and cultural complement to this argument, advanced by Molefi Asante, is that those who are committed to establishing a multiracial identity category are motivated by their desire to escape the stigma of blackness (or protect their children from it) and move up the racial hierarchy. For Asante, the desire to be classified as biracial, mixed, or multiracial is evidence of antipathy toward blacks or of black self-hatred and denial.[25] This may be an extreme view, but Asante's suspicions are not completely baseless. Herbert Gans urges us to consider the possibility that demographic and socioeconomic conditions in the United States are redrawing the color line from the space between white (normal) and nonwhite (deviant), to the space between black (deviant) versus nonblack (normal).[26] David Gallagher provides further evidence for this possibility, as his study of interracial relationships suggests that for whites there is a significant difference between bringing home a partner who is black and bringing home someone who is Asian or Latino. It is possible that the racial status quo is being reorganized and white dominance is unchallenged by absorbing multiracial Asians and Latinos.[27]

Multiracial people are not a "new" phenomenon, but the 2000 Census carries tremendous symbolic value as the starting point of the new millennium and the racial bellwether of things to come. DaCosta points out that despite the fact that a multiracial category was not established, the multiracial category movement was a watershed moment, because arguing for government recognition of the nonexistent category actually creates and legitimizes the group in the minds of the activists, the government, and the American public.[28] In 2000, seven million Americans, accounting for 2.4 percent of the population, marked more than one racial category on the census. In 2010, nine million Americans marked more than one race, an increase of 32 percent in ten years, accounting for 2.9 percent of the total U.S. population. As is the case with the data on interracial marriage, it is important not to exaggerate the prevalence of this population, for monoracial identification on government documents remains the preferred option for fully 97 percent of all Americans. However, some researchers estimate that the multiracial population could account for over 20 percent of all Americans by the year 2050.[29] As part of "Race Re-mixed," a series of articles in the *New York Times* on multiracial Americans, Susan Saulny highlights noteworthy elements of the 2010 data set:

- The multiracial population is overwhelmingly young, and among the races, American Indians and Native Hawaiians and Pacific Islanders are the most likely to report being of more than one race. Blacks and whites are the least likely.

- Among American children, the multiracial population has increased almost 50 percent, to 4.2 million, since 2000, making it the fastest-growing youth group in the country.

- The number of people of all ages who identified themselves as both white and black soared by 134 percent since 2000 to 1.8 million.

- The most common racial combination is black and white. Ten years ago, it was white and "some other race"—a designation overwhelmingly used by people of Hispanic origin, which is considered by the government to be an ethnicity, not a race.

- In the South and parts of the Midwest, the growth has been far greater than the national average. In North Carolina, for instance, the multiracial population grew by 99 percent. In Iowa, Indiana, and Mississippi, the group grew by about 70 percent.[30]

These details speak to the notion that mixed-race identity is flourishing,[31] especially among young people, and catching on in regions that are not traditionally associated with liberal political culture. This has significant implications for the "tragic mulatto" trope in multiracial discourse, as the young, cool, and futuristic multiracial emerges as a competing, though equally inadequate, representation of mixed-race subjectivity. Such a shift complements DaCosta's findings about the use of multiracial subjects as streetwise, rebellious, and unconventional symbols of the cool new economy, with no connections to the actual experiences of multiracial subjects.[32] The iconography of mixed-race fashion models and spokespeople often reinforces white supremacist beauty standards by fetishizing mixed-race bodies as uniquely beautiful, so long as they are impeccably groomed according to middle-class beauty standards, well dressed, and relatively light skinned. The commoditized coolness and sexual exoticism of these bodies are derived from their intoxicating hint of color; just enough forbidden and dangerous racial difference to give consumers a buzz, but not enough pure blackness, brownness, or yellowness to make them feel sick or threatened.

The rapid circulation of these cutting-edge, futuristic bodies complements the seductive and harmful discourse of postracialism as the new, utopian state of racial and family relations in America. In her prescient critique of the mixed-race textbook industry, Michele Elam first highlights the importance of rendering mixed-race people intelligible to the eye, particularly through the digital photograph montages and collages of parents and their multiracial children that fill the pages of such texts and accompany a number of campaigns designed to normalize multiracialism. However, "these images work together to codify anew the already iconic status of the heteronormative unit [where heterosexuality is assumed and privileged] at the expense of other family formations." Interracial marriage and multiracial offspring become "palatable under cover of conservative 'family values,'" and "interracial marriage is rehabilitated as a model for the American Way."[33] More troubling, stylized mixed-race publications and studies that position themselves as "ahead of the times" rather than "in the times" risk failing to properly historicize miscegenation panic and the history of mixed-race people.[34] When such imagery serves as proof that America is living in its own mythic, melting-pot future, inequality and diversity are erased, as is a history fraught with racism and rape as tactics of exploitation and eugenic improvement in Western societies.

However, these pieces of the puzzle are useless without attending to the actual meaning of multiracial identity for those who choose it. One of the defining patterns in research on multiracial identity is that multiracial individuals report their racial identities inconsistently and use racial identity as a fluid construct.[35] For instance, someone of mixed heritage may identify differently at home versus at school, or provide different answers to a survey's identification questions depending on whether the focus is on parental ancestry or personal identity. There is no specific wording in a question that results in *all* multiracials identifying as multiracial. Friendship groups, school environment, region, and family dynamics intersect with race in myriad ways to produce a racialized sense of self. Due to this highly specialized variation, no clear set of beliefs, values, or group boundaries currently define multiracials as a "group." Instead, multiracial identity is defined by its flexibility.[36]

Though rigid, all-encompassing boundaries of multiracial group identity are impossible to sketch, Natalie Masuoka's recent work elucidates important trends in multiracial self-identification and political ideologies. Masuoka uses a data set that does not simply target individuals who have already identified as multiracial. Instead, the survey takes respondents who were previously identified as monoracial (Asian, black, white, native American, or other), asks them about parental ancestry, and then asks if they identify as multiracial.[37] Two key findings emerge. First, blacks and Latinos are more likely to self-identify as multiracial than whites, lending support to fears that insistence on bounded categorical multiracial identification on official documents would depress the count of these groups. Second, ideologically speaking, multiracials fall somewhere between monoracial whites—who are less Democratic, less aware of racialized experiences, and less likely to support race-based policy solutions than all other racial groups—and monoracial blacks, who show the strongest measures across these three criteria.[38]

Rather than providing a quantitative analysis of survey data sets, the remainder of this chapter examines multiracial identity through one-on-one, in-depth interviews with forty-nine self-identified young multi-racial adults. (The first letter in the abbreviation following each interviewee's name indicates the mother's race, and the second letter indicates the father's race. For example, the combination "AW" indicates that the respondent has an Asian mother and white father, and "WA" that the respondent has a white mother and Asian father. See Appendix II for complete set of abbreviations.) The results of my study are not prescriptive and should not be taken as universal truths about what all multiracial people think. However, the interviews stay true to the mission of this book, illustrating how racial meaning is made and providing a platform for the voices of multiracial people as they reflect on Obama's role in contemporary and future racial politics.

Obama and Racial Identity

Everyone who was interviewed mentioned that Barack Obama is predominantly viewed as black rather than multiracial. Respondents offer this opinion without being prompted and also in response to a question specifically about Obama's mixed-race background. Despite the fact that Obama is almost always identified as black rather than as a person of mixed heritage, respondents emphasize that they perceive him as multiracial or as simultaneously multiracial and black. Neil (WA) explains, "I perceive him as biracial. . . . I don't even know how he sees himself. . . . He probably identifies more with being black because of like his immediate family. Michelle Obama and everything. And I guess the way that society pegs him. But I don't necessarily believe in that."

The ideas in this quotation are widely shared, and in making this point, multiracial respondents lay claim to racial knowledge and interpretation that separates them from most Americans. Only one of the forty-nine respondents did not know about Obama's multiracial background at the time of the interview. When I asked respondents where they learned about Obama's multiracialism, they report reading a news story about it or reading *Dreams from My Father*. Some respondents believe that the public knows about Obama's mixed heritage but discounts it, and others believe that Obama's multiracialism is simply unknown to the majority of Americans.

Though respondents who support Obama are quick to note that Obama's multiracialism has no bearing on their opinion of him as a government official, they are pleased by Obama's rise and public visibility as a cultural figure. Parsing Obama's "coolness" is a difficult task, because on many occasions the word "cool" is used to express general approval rather than characterize something as new or hip. In most cases, the coolness described by respondents does not contain the most problematic elements of the cool new millennial trope, because respondents do not explicitly endorse beliefs about unique mixed beauty or the irrelevance of racism as they discuss Obama's rise. In others, respondents build narratives dangerously close to the cool new millennial archetype.

If they're like, "Oh, he's the first black president," I'm like, "Well, it's cooler than that. He's only half black." (Helen, WA)

Going to Brazil this summer and how they talk about race, what they care about racially, and how everyone there is just so mixed. I loved it, it was great. I think that hopefully that's where America will go. We'll all just become that mocha race. It will be great, cool. (Nika, WA)

These quotations are far from representative of the sample, but they are important pieces of the interview data. There are equally important passages critiquing the cool new millennial idea, especially from female respondents who are angered by the fetishism of "exotic" multiracial women's bodies. In sum, data show that multiracial subjects are entangled in, critical of, and occasionally seduced by the discourse that turns multiracial bodies into cool new millennials at the expense of actual experience.

It could be that Obama is considered cool because he is perceived as black, given the long history of commoditized black bodies as brands signifying sleekness, danger, and sexuality. Melissa Herman finds that despite personal awareness of their multiracial background, multiracial black youth are commonly perceived as solely black by observers and are subject to the traditional stigma attached to monoracial blacks.[39] Social identity results from the reconciliation of the subject's idea of herself with her experiences and interactions in society.[40] It is not surprising, then, that so many multiracial blacks "choose" to identify as solely or primarily black rather than multiracial. Mixed-race identity is not the same choice for all subjects and may not always aid people of African descent as they build the best identities they can for navigating American society. Traces of these explanations for the relationship between blackness and multiracialism reside in respondents' interpretations. Some respondents suggest that Obama's public racial identity is in part an individual choice because he actually identifies more with black people, and in part a social construct built by the media and other forces. In particular, the pressure to construct an appealing political image weighs heavily on respondents' analysis of Obama's identity choice and ascription.

Probably whatever he said in public, in a public forum, has been vetted by the campaign people, so maybe they thought it was better that he be African American. I mean, maybe that's better than being mixed, to some people. Maybe they think, oh, it's fine if black people keep to themselves and marry each other, but not if they marry someone white. (Gina, AW)

You know, he always talked about his mother and his grandmother, who died right before he was elected. And so, he doesn't reject the white side, but I think he tries to play it down a lot, which he's almost forced to. (Claire, BW)

That's a little disappointing, that at this stage in America that you have to still pick one side, you have to still "one drop" yourself like that. But on the other hand, I don't think it's necessarily his preference. I think he's kind of doing it for his career. I mean, would he have had that much support? You know, would everyone have raved as much if he was the first mixed president as opposed to the first black president? I don't think so. (Talia, WSA)

Respondents do not believe that Obama rejects his mixed heritage outright, and a few take no issue with calling the president exclusively "black" rather than multiracial, if that is what he prefers. But in general, respondents do not discuss the ways that blacks' choice to identify as multiracial may pose a different set of challenges than it does for nonblacks, due to legal, institutionalized disadvantages initiated during slavery and Jim Crow. Many believe Obama is complicit in deemphasizing his multiracial identity for the sake of the campaign, or allowing it to be subsumed in the wave of public assumption about his race. With respect to Obama's political circle, the president's handlers choose to emphasize blackness, not necessarily because they naturally view Obama as such but because it is politically expedient. However, when asked why the American public places Obama squarely within the category of blackness rather than multiracial, respondents describe a natural or subconscious tendency to view Obama as black for three key reasons.

First, Obama is commonly understood as black simply because he is clearly not white. Ho, Sidanius, Levin, and Banaji find that both Asian-white and black-white biracial individuals are more likely to be perceived and classified according to hypodescent (assigning a child of mixed parentage to the lower status group) than placed in the "white" category.[41] In addition, the threshold for perceiving black-white biracial subjects as white is higher than it is for Asian-white biracials, supporting Herman's findings. Whiteness is the most privileged and protected racial category. It is the normative and expected racial category for American presidents, and respondents construct a clear boundary between whiteness and all other classifications.

I guess when you look at the past forty-three, forty-four presidents, they all look the same. And he's the only one that looks different, and so it's sort of that kind of line in the opposites of this and that. And I mean, it is also what he looks like. He looks more black than he does white or anything else. And so, although I would say he doesn't look completely nonmixed race, but I mean, it's just, it's harder to tell. (Laney, BW)

That stands out to a lot of people, like "oh, all of our other presidents have been white" . . . I think that people can see that he's black, and it's harder to like, see that he's multiracial, or that he's biracial. And people don't think of that as an issue as much, because I don't think that they've had to really face it before, but I know that like in my life, I face it every day, and that's who I am, so I notice that first. (Helen, WA)

Each of the two above quotations overlaps with the second major reason Obama is subject to hypodescent and categorized as black: because of the way he looks, especially his skin color.

He was raised by his white mother. His father wasn't there. But, because he's darker, he would be considered black, and I wouldn't be? Even though, I'm the opposite situation? And so, I just found that interesting. But he was, I mean, he deserves to, like, no one is going to deny that he's black. (Claire, BW)

People who are half black, it seems like no matter how integrated they are with like other communities, it always seems like the black side, like, dominates everything about them. Like, they don't consider other parts of his life, or like, his situation, they just see that "oh he's African," because he has dark skin. (Joanne, WA)

Finally, respondents argue that the language for talking about the complexity of multiracialism is inadequate, which makes fashioning oneself as black a convenient choice. A large collection of respondents note that it is simply "easier" to think and talk about Obama as black, as exemplified by the following comments.

For him, I don't think there is really a way to reflect on being just half white, but rather to reflect on the mixed part of his identity, more than just the African American part of his identity. (Steve, WB)

I found it really interesting when he just marked black on the census. I almost feel that, or I wonder if that was a public gesture. I mean, it also could be due to the fact that we don't have an option on the census for, at least a little easy checkbox for identifying as multiracial or multiethnic, or however you identify mixed. But I don't even think that would, I mean, as a category, it doesn't make sense either, because that encompasses so many different experiences. (Dora, AW)

I think that he probably has a really, you know, deep and complex understanding of how being multi [multiracial] feels. And yet I think being the president of the U.S., he needs to kind of give it a more simplified form. Like he can't just say, he can't give a whole speech about what it means to be multi. You know? And I think he has kind of resorted to being this, "the first black president." (Mira, AW)

These excerpts highlight the metalinguistic problems of race described in the first chapter. Steve says there is no readily available way for Obama to reflect on his multiracial identity; Dora says there is no readily available category that captures multiracial identity; and Mira says there is no readily available way to speak about multiracial identity. Rather than dealing with all the complexity and intersectionality of race, making oneself racially intelligible to the American public requires playing by categorical rules that disguise the interplay of race with other social forces.

A few of the preceding quotations highlight respondents' disappointment about Obama's racial identity choice and public perception. This sentiment is not universally shared, but it is a well-grounded theme in the interviews. Conventional logic might lead us to interpret this disappointment as a clear boundary of multiracial identity. In many cases, racial solidarity and the rewards of racial group identity demand consistent and public claiming of the identity in question. If this is a firm boundary erected by multiracials, or an important shared cultural value among these respondents, we should expect to see sanctions against any person who fails to uphold the value of consistent and public identification. But research suggests that this sort of identity claiming is not central to multiracial identity, and respondents' treatment of Obama supports such findings. Respondents are saddened, disappointed, and even slightly angered by Obama's refusal to insist on his multiracial identity, but they do not reject him as a multiracial person. On occasion, the sadness and anger are directed at Obama himself, but more frequently they are expressed as disappointment in social norms. Respondents' sadness and disappointment are tempered by thoughtfulness about their own inconsistency with respect to the way they racially identify.

I was personally a little bit offended by it [Obama choosing "black" on the census], and then when I was in Shanghai and people, I knew that they were constantly thinking I was white. All of a sudden, there were a couple of times when I referred to myself like, "Oh, yeah, people always think I'm some white girl," and then it kind of progressed to toward the end of my trip there were a couple of times when I referred to myself as white, which I don't ever do. So, then I kind of was like, "OK, maybe I'll cut Barack some slack," and realize that if people are constantly dividing you one way, you're going to start to identify with that categorization. (Alena, AW)

He justified it [choosing black on the census] by saying that because people have always seen him as black, therefore he feels black, and he identifies with black people. That's cool and all. But are you, OK, so are you being fraudulent by emphasizing this? It's not really part of your identity, just for the campaign? Or are you suddenly rejecting it for the political implications of being black? I don't know. I felt like he was picking and choosing. I guess I do the same thing. Like, picking and choosing, depending on the purpose for his benefit, which I do, too, but I feel like mine doesn't mean as much. (Patricia, WA)

These excerpts are important because they highlight respondents' stream of consciousness about this issue. Their empathy is unprompted by any question from the interviewer or suggestion that their own reported identity management techniques mirror Obama's. Instead, this is self-generated recognition of the flexibility and inconsistency of their own multiracial identification, and Obama's behavior helps them understand their own. Despite the common perception of Obama as solely black and the president's somewhat limited personal veneration of his multiracial identity, respondents describe him as "a pretty good representation of what it means to be a multiracial American" (Ruth, WL), and someone who "struggled with his identity . . . that a lot of people can relate to" (Leanne, BLW).

Multiple respondents report identifying as different races depending on social context, the wording of a given question, and the person asking about their identity. One respondent identifies as black, Latina, and multiracial all in the course of the same interview. This flexibility and inconsistency are not indicative of a rejection of multiracialism, as many respondents engage in social and political activity on the basis of their multiracial identity. It does mean that commitment to exploring and affirming multiracial identity does not require strict categorization and does not foreclose on the possibility of alternative racial identification.

The Impact of Race on Obama's Career

Respondents advance the notion that Obama's racial identity attracts attention that is "both positive and negative" (Emma, WA). The most forceful statements about the impact of race on Obama's career focus on racism against Obama and the pressures associated with being the first president of color. In other segments of the interview, respondents speak at length about the ways their experiences are shaped by instances of alienation from both whites and nonwhites who question their racial authenticity. However, when Obama is impacted by racism, it is driven by the fact that he is black, or that he is not *white*, rather than a sense that he is not black enough. Again, a clear boundary emerges between whiteness and nonwhiteness—this time when describing instances of racism. The comments below illustrate respondents' support for theories of symbolic racism, as explained in the preceding chapter.

The idea of being American, like, it doesn't mean you have to be white. People obviously try to misuse his whole race thing, or be like, oh, he's actually like a terrorist, which is also stupid. (Krista, AW)

As far as like the extreme conservatives, like Tea Party candidates, I don't know, the "Muslim," disparaging campaign, that he's like, not American. I think that wouldn't be possible if he was white. (Carl, WB)

I mean my feelings about the Tea Party are just, they just make me angry basically. But yeah, I think that at least some part of the reason why they're, like, rallying and they're so angry is because he's black, even if they're not going to admit it. Even if they don't know it consciously. (Leanne, BLW)

As much as they might deny it, there would be no Birthers if Barack Obama were a white man, and there would be no people calling to see his birth certificate and questioning if his pastor had led him down the path to hating America. And there would be no one questioning if he was a Muslim. (Louis, WA)

I mean, all this Birther crap. Like if Obama was white, would he have people claiming, you know, he was born in Kenya? Or that he's a secret Muslim. I think that's sort of, those types of things root from a degree of xenophobia and racism. (Damon, WA)

Respondents are attuned to the racism suffered by Obama, specifically manifest as the connection between whiteness and American nationalism. The Tea Party and Birthers make frequent, unprompted appearances in the transcripts as groups that levy absurd racist attacks against Obama and raise respondents' ire. The meaning of Obama's race is undeniably intersectional: religion intersects with race and nationality as part of the stigma that Obama's opponents attempt to attach to the president. Obama is able to overcome these issues, in part because he projects a nonthreatening version of blackness that approximates the white bourgeois leadership ideal.

He comes from, I think, the same sort of background that I do, where he had the privilege of going to a upper-middle-class schooling system, that sort of thing, where he ended up going to Harvard, and he was on a success track. It's interesting to watch how he dresses and how he handles himself when he's doing any kind of political thing, because it's always been my opinion that he can't do anything too black, whereas people would have trouble accepting him. So he was a good candidate, because he wasn't too black. He came from a heritage that was only half black, and he went to a proper school, and he went through that sort of thing. If you notice, he never has a shape-up [popular element of black men's hair style]. I've only seen him [with a shape-up] once, and I was so surprised. (Wayne, WB)

I thought it was a little weird that he chose to kind of like ignore his biracial identity, because I feel like it definitely has played a role, like he doesn't look like just a black man to me, I think he looks very mixed and to me. I mean, everyone sees with different eyes and it depends on your perspective, but I've even heard people say, you know, the way he talks is white, or something like that. And like some of his features are not like what people think of when they think of a black person. So I think that that probably helped him because we live in a mostly white country, not mostly, but lots of racist people. (Renee, WB)

Though Obama's biracial background does not result in his widespread identification as a multiracial person, his mixed heritage combines with schooling, phenotype, and speech style as qualities that respondents believe mediate racism and garner acceptance from whites.

These are not the only reasons Obama appeals so broadly to the American public, as respondents mention Obama's height, family life with Michelle, and charisma as universally appealing features. But the point is that Obama's racial identity performance is dissonant with the most widely available and reviled stereotypes of blackness, because of the way race intersects with other factors. Wayne's description of Obama's "upper-middle-class" schooling is a classic example of class intersecting with race to reduce the perceived threat of black deviance.

Obama's Impact on Racial Conditions and Racism

Respondents are critical of many of Obama's policies, but they overwhelmingly support Obama relative to the other candidates in the 2008 election. They describe feeling lucky and excited when Obama won, and a few acknowledge Obama's status as a trailblazer who disproves stereotypes and can be a "new beginning" (Ariel, AW) who "opens doors" (Wayne, WB) and "forces a lot of Americans to kind of accept different races into their lives now that they know that their president is not a white person" (Dawn, WME). However, Obama's actual stance on racism and other racial issues is not one of his defining characteristics. Though respondents may like to see Obama talk about race more often, such discussion is not a central feature of his political career or his job as president, in large part because his hands are tied by the expectations of the office.

I feel like he has a really good grasp on race, but I don't know necessarily how he feels about it himself. And I feel like it's almost a little bit of a taboo topic, like he should be talking about it. It's not necessarily something a president talks about, because they've all been white before him. (Robin, LB)

He's definitely shied away from it, in my view. . . . You think about the sort of situation that's going down and the way . . . the media and then different political adversaries to Obama are playing off of paranoia. Something, like a slip like that [saying the wrong thing about race] could be pretty bad for him politically. (David, WL)

Just as political considerations may contribute to Obama's self-framing as black rather than multiracial, the pressures of the presidency discourage risk-taking when it comes to racial discourse, recalling the notion of public secrecy from Chapter 1. The fact that Obama shies away from discussions of racism rarely leads respondents to condemn him, but racism and racial inequality remain urgent political issues for the sample. When asked to describe or speculate about Obama's impact on America's racial history, they stress that racism remains a serious problem.

Obama is good, a good unifying kind of moment, but it shouldn't distract from the other things. And I don't think it's a Barack Obama problem, but I just think that in general, people are resting on the laurels of past achievements in race relations. And a lot of people I know today, they're like [disapprovingly] "Oh, racism's not a problem. There's no racism." It's just more subtle. Or if it's not more subtle, it's just something people don't think about. (Steve, WB)

I think it's supposed to communicate that we're all much more open-minded, and there isn't even racism anymore, and that the problems are solved. So then obviously, I don't really think that's true. (Kathy, WB)

I don't know if it's like a pessimistic view, but I don't see racism ever going away. . . . I don't want to create like a stereotype of Southern people, but if you go deep down in the South, it's still really, there's still a lot of backwards thinking there. And I don't see that going away ever because you have children. You instill these views and these opinions in your children and yet, if they end up staying in the same area, then they're not going to learn. (Lynn, WB)

I don't want to harp on this, but like I feel like it [Obama's victory] was sort of detrimental, because it's just, other people, like particularly conservatives, can say "look, we've already reached it" [the end of racism]. (David, WL)

Recent studies suggest that Obama's election may actually inhibit the fight against racism, as the 2008 election has resulted in the belief that we have reached the end of racism, decreased perceptions of racial discrimination against blacks, and amplified concerns that antiwhite bias is now a more pressing social problem than traditional racism.[42] Despite the fact that multiracial subjects are often cast as representatives of the new, postracial future, this cohort rejects postracial idealism.

Finally, respondents have mixed opinions about Obama's specific impact on the multiracial community. As mentioned, many respondents are pleased that Obama was elected, because his negotiation of racial identity mirrors their experiences. But this is a separate question from whether Obama's celebrity influences behavior or discourse when it comes to multiracial issues. Some students say there have been more conversations, both in the media and on college campuses, about multiracialism in the wake of Obama's ascent. In many cases, those conversations take place at group meetings in multiracial student organizations, and multiple respondents suggest that these organizations are revitalized nationwide by Obama's election. Ruth (WL) explains, "I think he's just a point of pride for a lot of multiracial people, and that he's sparked more visible ongoing dialog. Like, the *New York Times* has their series right now on 'race remixed,' and things like that, that wouldn't have happened had it not been highlighted in the election season."

Other respondents notice no real uptick in conversations about multiracial issues among their friends, or multiracial people they know, or in the public sphere more broadly since Obama first rose to prominence. Assessing a trend using these interviews is a challenge, as arriving at college presents the first opportunity for many of these respondents to engage issues of multiracialism with any formality or regularity. Due to the age range of the sample, enrollment in college coincides with Obama's rise as a public figure, making it difficult to separate the impact of each event on awareness of and changes in multiracial discourse. The interviews do not suggest that Obama is considered a leader or icon of a surging and explicitly political movement, either for institutionalized multiracial categorization or social identity.

Multiracial Voices and Politics

In this summary of interracialism and multiracialism in the United States, I have investigated young adult students' perceptions of Barack Obama as means to interrogate the symbolic boundaries of multiracial identity. The sections of this discussion complement each other and speak to three broad questions: How is Obama perceived by this cohort of multiracial respondents? How do perceptions and interpretations of Obama and his career inform the character and contours of multiracial identity? And how do these data add to research about multiracial views on race and racism?

To begin, the president is not cast as a political savior or a widely accepted representative of all multiracial people, as he is most commonly known in the country as black rather than multiracial. Respondents' recognition of Obama's multiracialism in spite of this fact is a commonly shared understanding that sets them apart from the American public. Obama's emphasis on his blackness at the expense of his mixed racial heritage disappoints and annoys some respondents, but they still view him favorably, celebrate his visibility, and relate to his experiences.

One of the key findings is that a grounded and durable boundary between whiteness and nonwhiteness emerges as the basis for respondents' understanding of racism. Respondents assert that unfair criticism of Obama grows from the racist belief that only white bodies can be legitimate representations of the American citizenry. To be clear, there is no evidence that any of the respondents harbor feelings of antipathy towards white people en masse. Whites are well represented in respondents' friendship networks (as the saying goes, "Some of their best friends are white!"); forty-five subjects report European ancestry; and many of them insist on recognizing and appreciating all branches of their family trees. However, the racism Obama encounters and the stumbling blocks along the road to racial progress are rooted in white privilege and white supremacy. The problem is not an amorphous racial discord more or less evenly distributed among, and damaging for, all racial groups; these findings are important because they allay concerns that multiracial people, especially those of Asian and Latino descent, will automatically accept white normativity, float towards the top of the racial hierarchy, and abandon blacks socially and ideologically. However, with a few exceptions, there is a lack of consideration of the ways American institutional and legal history and the stigma of blackness impact the challenges and choices multiracial blacks are faced with.

In support of previous research, multiracial identity is revealed as a flexible and fluid construct for respondents who choose it. Many respondents cherish opportunities to raise awareness about multiracial subjects and gather together to share experiences. When asked about identifying themselves on official documents, respondents express the collective desire to expand the range of options available and/or choose more than one racial category. But there is no evidence of rigorously policed multiracial group boundaries, nor is there insistence on a single, officially recognized multiracial category. Respondents acknowledge the diversity and complexity of multiracial experiences, which is discordant with the assumption that clearly delineated shared practices and values define ethnoracial cultures and group identity. The flawed logic of racial categorization does not resonate with respondents' experiences, so at present their multiracial group-ness does not fit well within available racial schema.

One of the limitations of this study is that socioeconomic elites and people from the northeast region of the United States are overrepresented. The field of multiracial studies would greatly benefit from work that focuses on the experiences of people from other class statuses and regional groups, especially considering aforementioned demographic data suggesting multiracial population growth in the South and Midwest. Another issue is that the sample is insufficient for comparative analysis, which might follow up on Natalie Masuoka's aforementioned findings about ideological differences among multiracials that correspond to specific racial and ethnic backgrounds. Finally, one of the underlying assumptions of this chapter is that popular-culture phenomena are valuable symbolic material for people building their identities and ideologies. Some respondents suggest that Obama's rise leads to an uptick in multiracial student group activity and increased attention to multiracial issues in the public sphere. Quantitative survey and discourse analysis are needed to confirm these possibilities.

Those who identify as multiracial face two pressing needs at the moment. First, multiracial people need to continue to fight for platforms for discussing their experiences among themselves and bringing multiracial stories to the American public. Demographic trends suggest that the multiracial population will continue to grow, and as more young people claim this identity, we should expect multiracial student groups and organizations to sustain themselves for longer periods of time. Off campus, anecdotal evidence suggests that multiracial artists and writers who produce material about their experiences have access to more platforms than ever before, as the Internet provides venues that complement events in the material world, such as the Mixed Roots Film and Literary Festival. The notion that only multiracial people care to hear these stories is disproven by the success of books like *Dreams from My Father* and *The Girl Who Fell from the Sky* (2010), a novel by Heidi Durrow that survived nearly fifty rejections by publishing companies to become an international best seller.[43] As these narratives gain greater exposure and multiracial diversity is fully exposed, mythic and politically disingenuous representations like the tragic mulatto and cool new millennial tumble down the well of obscurity.

The second pressing need for multiracials is to integrate storytelling with goal-oriented activity, namely, educating others about racial meaning and racial injustice, and ending racism. With respect to racial meaning, revisiting the census category debate provides a unique opportunity to educate others about the differences between racial and ethnic identity and the stakes of checking racial and ethnic boxes. There is substantial disagreement about the utility and justification for a single multiracial category, and little evidence that institutionalizing the category is an optimal solution. Multiracial people argue that their range of experiences renders a single category inadequate, and social justice groups express legitimate concern about the impact of a multiracial category on antidiscrimination law. David Hollinger provides a sensible alternative where the census is concerned: recognize that race and ethnicity are in fact different concepts, and separate color (race) and culture (ethnicity) into clearly distinct categories with two questions. Initially, the official document might ask if "you have physical characteristics that render you at risk of discrimination, and if so do those characteristics make you black, red, yellow, or brown?" The follow-up question is, "Do you consider yourself to be a member of any of the following ethno-racially defined cultural groups?"[44] Hollinger acknowledges that the questions are imperfect, but in each case respondents could check as many boxes as they see fit, and space would be available for write-in answers. This is a much more flexible method that gets at the core of the issue for people whose ascribed race does not match their beliefs and practices.

Explicitly antiracist labor must be intertwined with the epistemological and ontological wings of multiracial activism. Race is political by definition. It organizes society and influences rewards, penalties, integration, isolation, prosperity, and suffering. Politicizing multiracialism requires dissecting narratives to find common ground; goals that all group members can agree on despite their divergent experiences. Insisting on institutional accountability for race/ethnicity/gender discrimination, performing community service that mediates the debilitating effects of class/race segregation, and working with other groups to ensure ongoing dialog about racial injustice are three activities that are well within the capability of most multiracial student groups. Multiracial people in their postcollege years may not have easy access to a close-knit network of multiracial activists, but they do have the ability to marshal their resources toward the same political goals. Identity alone is neither a curse nor a blessing, but when it moves us to act against injustice, it becomes a virtue.

CHAPTER 4

POSTRACIALISM RECONSIDERED

Class, the Black Counterpublic, and the End of Black Politics

> I never bought into the notion that by electing me,
> somehow we were entering into a post-racial period.
> —*Barack Obama*[1]

After President Obama's first State of the Union address on January 27, 2010, MSNBC anchor Chris Matthews, lavishing praise on the president's command of the moment, infamously gushed, "It's interesting: he is postracial, by appearances. I forgot he was black tonight for an hour."[2] According to many, this is the greatest of all Obama's superpowers: the ability to coerce the public into a euphoric hallucination, transporting followers into a world where he is cleansed of the stain of blackness and seems just as presidential as the bourgeois, Christian, straight white men who preceded him. Matthews's compliment demonstrates that white privilege still functions, as he has to deracialize Obama to communicate just how well Obama meets expectations for what a president looks and sounds like. If others share Matthews's enthusiasm, voters "forgot Obama was black" long before the State the Union. By many accounts, this postracialism was the chief reason Obama was elected in 2008, rather than the economic collapse or the nuts and bolts of voter mobilization, fundraising, or opponents' mistakes.

In this chapter I seize upon postracialism, not merely to argue that such thinking is a mistake but as a classic example of the empty loudness of race. "Postracial" is a racial term, but without historical specific-ity and intersectionality it has no meaning at all; or rather, it has too many meanings to be intelligible.

Two drastically different understandings of "postracial" guide the analysis. In the first instance, the term refers broadly to social condi-tions; the postracial society is one where racism is vanquished or where the impact of race on one's life chances is insignificant. Not surprisingly, these claims are briefly explained and summarily dismissed—the entire book after all is about the ways race continues to shape life outcomes and the meanings we attribute to our social world.

Alternatively, "postracial" refers to the style and strategy employed by the Obama team, whereby the candidate and president avoids speak-ing about racial issues and calls as little attention as possible to the fact of his nonwhiteness. This sort of postracialism or deracialization is often lamented as "the end of black politics," meaning the end of an era where black politicians achieved success through prioritization of race-based civil rights causes and demands for social justice. There is a far more interesting conversation to be had about postracialism in this second sense, and this is where my efforts are directed.

The central theoretical frame for this investigation is the idea of the *black counterpublic*: a semiautonomous sphere of political dis-course maintained by and for black Americans. More broadly, the black counterpublic is any virtual or material place in which black political discussions occur, and it is also the umbrella term for the universe where ideas about black politics reside. Black ideologies are produced within black counterpublic spaces (churches, the black press, political organiza-tions, and so on), and this process is vital to black American political life because, historically, it is tied to black political action and advocacy.

Today, the black counterpublic is unstable, and this instability is the first mover in the chain that shakes and scrapes itself into a cacophony of postracial noise. President Obama's success exemplifies the reduced role of the traditional counterpublic in black American political life. His "postracial" style is a symptom rather than a cause of black counter-public disintegration. The root causes of black counterpublic evolution, and by extension the fad of postracialism, are the intersections of race with class and technological development.

These changes have both positive and negative consequences. On one hand, when black political discourse leaks out from black counterpublics into the broader public sphere, race-talk can emerge as a viable weapon against racism. Moreover, traditional counterpublics have been replaced or supplemented by new spaces, especially on the Internet, that perform many of the same functions. On the other hand, race-talk alone is insufficient means for combating racism, and although new strategies and technologies facilitate political exchange among blacks and other marginalized groups, there is little evidence that this evolution alone combats social inequality.

Postracialism as the End of Race

Postracialism is a direct descendant of color blindness. If color blindness is somewhat aspirational in nature, prescribing blindness as the path out of present racial trouble and towards a righteous future, then *post*racialism asserts that we have traversed the treacherous wilderness and arrived at a valley, renewed with racial innocence. Postracial ideology is supposedly legitimated by changes in race relations and racial attitudes, as well as historical events, such as Obama's election.[3] The shift is not only temporal, from a time when we wished for color blindness to a time when it is achieved; the change switches the unit of analysis, from *individual* behaviors and aspirations (one's choice and will to lead a color-blind life) to *social* facts (the new collective racial reality which all individuals must accept). As was the case in previous racial epochs, the new racial rules suggest that the individual who stubbornly continues to affirm the pervasiveness of race makes a moral and political error by rejecting color blindness as the righteous path. Unlike during previous eras, postracialists argue that she who repudiates color blindness makes a more fundamental error, because she clings to the past and cannot come to grips with society as it actually is.

Writing in the *American Prospect*, Courtney Martin explains many white Americans' investment in postracialism, despite the fact that it requires ignoring contemporary racial truths. "Post-racialism goes hand in hand with the notion of a 'bootstrap' nation, one where your race doesn't determine your station in life. If there is no more race—this thinking goes—white people can stop apologizing. Admissions counselors and conference planners can stop strategizing. We can wipe the racial slate clean and start over."[4]

As discussed in the first chapter, affirmation of color blindness seems like a moral and sensible political act, no matter a person's racial or ethnic background. But given the depth of racial inequality and the power of racism, the fact that the idea of the "postracial" ever became a catchphrase stands as proof of the privileges enjoyed by those who operate from nonracialized subject positions. For people of color who live each day as racially marked subjects, the notion that one or two elections could eradicate those experiences is patently absurd.

A slightly different take on postracialism does not deny the existence of race-based inequality and racism, suggesting rather that the racialized outcomes we see are actually postracial because race is no longer doing the work of stratification—class is. William Julius Wilson's *The Declining Significance of Race* (1978) is often cited as an exemplary text in this regard, but those who do so misunderstand Wilson's argument. Wilson does *not* argue that race is irrelevant, only that the black underclass faces a more difficult set of challenges than other blacks. More specifically, the American economy has changed from a plantation economy with racial caste oppression, to an industrial economy with interracial class conflict and Jim Crow oppression, to a late twentieth- (now early twenty-first-) century corporate and information-processing economy. In the present epoch, the influence of class inequality is unchecked by an American government that fails to intervene on the erosion of the middle class and the widening gap between the haves and have-nots.[5]

Those who misuse Wilson's work wash history clean of intersectionality. Class privilege is translated and maintained between generations. Due to slavery, discriminatory banking and home ownership policies, unequal access to quality education, and the expansion of the prison system, blacks in America have not had equal opportunities to build solid financial foundations and pass them on to their children. These are economic issues, rooted in labor, property, and education, but Wilson is quite clear that it is completely impossible to explain why class stratification in America looks the way it does without talking about race. This is not just a matter of historical accuracy: it is a contemporary sociological issue. As Wilson argues in *The Truly Disadvantaged* (1987) and *More than Just Race* (2009), present-day residential segregation is disconcerting not simply because ghetto residents are all poor, or because ghetto residents are all black or Latino. Instead, the intersection of class and race-based segregation produces the dire sociological and cultural outcomes we see in these communities. So postracialism defined as "the end of race" cannot be affirmed when it morphs into an argument about the preeminence of class inequality, because in America the meaning of social class is inextricably linked to race. And there is an alternate meaning.

Postracialism as the End of Black Politics

Matt Bai's August 6, 2008, article in the *New York Times Magazine* illuminates the generational divide in black American politics. The distance between public figures like Obama and stalwarts like Senators John Lewis and Charlie Rangel is a matter of actual lived experience rather than mere preference for one political style over another.

Black leaders who rose to political power in the years after the civil rights marches came almost entirely from the pulpit and the movement, and they have always defined leadership, in broad terms, as speaking *for* black Americans. They saw their job, principally, as confronting an inherently racist white establishment, which in terms of sheer career advancement was their only real option anyway. . . . This newly emerging class of black politicians, [sic] seek a broader political brief. . . . They are just as likely to see themselves as ambassadors *to* the black community as they are to see themselves as spokesmen for it. . . . Their ambitions range well beyond safely black seats.[6]

The elimination of formalized racial barriers results in expanded career options for black politicians. The fear among the old guard is not only

that their deeds will be forgotten but that if black politics is fully absorbed into the mainstream, black elected officials will no longer feel
compelled to advocate on black citizens' behalf.

In the wake of the 2008 election, numerous scholars and writers
have grappled with this panic about postracialism, or deracialization,[7]
and the end of black politics. However, perhaps the most cited academic
piece on deracialization was published fifteen years priorly, in 1993, by
Joseph McCormick and Charles Jones, whose research was spurred
by the rise of presidential hopeful Jesse Jackson Sr., New York mayor
David Dinkins, Virginia governor Douglas Wilder, and other late 1980s
black politicians who cast themselves differently from their civil rights
era predecessors.[8] Jackson's case is especially relevant, as he sought the
Democratic nomination for president in 1984 and again in 1988, when
he won thirteen Democratic primaries and caucuses. Jackson wrestled
mightily with the tension between articulating a universalist or multicultural vision of race and preserving the version of black politics he
forged during the civil rights movement. It is generally agreed that Jackson's second, more successful campaign was deracialized in comparison
to his first, but ultimately Jackson's model remained too closely tied to
traditional black politics. In September 2007, long before the Obama
campaign was in full swing, political scientist Ronald Walters correctly
predicted the major differences between Jackson's campaigns, which
were tethered to traditional black politics, and Obama's, which was not.
Walters makes four key points:

1. Jackson's campaigns were "motivated essentially to empower the Black
   electorate: Obama's motivation as presented in his campaign an-
   nouncement is to respond to the national desire for new leadership."

2. Jackson's campaigns were "dedicated to foster immediate social
   change as well as win votes: Obama's campaign style is in the mode
   of a traditional voter-appeal mobilization, with no substantial side
   benefit offered for supporters or unique groups of supporters."

3. Jackson utilized "collaboration with the Black civic culture to affect voter registration as well as voter turnout: Obama's campaign

stops do not feature the element of voter registration; rather, he is competing for the electorate as configured." This lack of collaboration with black civic culture is critical to the larger argument in this chapter about the black counterpublic.

4. Jackson's policy focus "was a vehicle for the assertion of Black interests: Obama's policy aims, although liberal to progressive, are more universalistic and lack concentrated attention to the Third World or issues that are associated strongly with underrepresented American groups." In other words, Obama's campaign is less racial than were Jackson's.[9]

Gwen Ifill picks up on these themes in *The Breakthrough* (2009), using Obama's rise to tell a story about the generational divide within black politics and, more specifically, among black political elites. Ifill avoids the term "postracial" as a buzzword, but the breakthrough is the deracializing shift in strategy away from an emphasis on black identity and building support from a black base. The new generation emphasizes skillful navigation of both the black and white worlds, and broad appeals capable of captivating a multiracial electorate.

Ifill is careful not to cast Obama as a trailblazer. She depicts black political elites and commentators as an interconnected community that is aware of the shift as it is happening, rather than something that was taken by storm and forever changed by Obama's innovation. Figures like Colin Powell, Shirley Chisolm, Jesse Jackson, and Douglas Wilder illustrate the internal ideological differences among prominent black political figures.[10] It follows that Senator John Lewis would have difficulty choosing between Obama and Hillary Clinton during the primary,[11] and that professor Eddie Glaude questions the civil rights generation's hesitance to relinquish the torch.[12] *The Breakthrough* is not a story about Obama inventing an entirely new dish; it is about a cauldron of ideology and activism that has settled at a new temperature and taste.

Moreover, in the same breath as her statement about the Obama team's commitment to protect their candidate from race-based scrutiny, Ifill acknowledges a series of racially tinged episodes, including Obama's

March 2007 "Joshua Generation" speech in front of black clergy at the historic Brown Chapel A.M.E. church in Selma, Tim Russert's questions about Louis Farrakhan at the Democratic primary debate in February 2008, Obama's Father's Day 2008 speech at the Apostolic Church of God on the South Side of Chicago, and the Jeremiah Wright controversy. So while Ifill establishes that the overall strategy was to deemphasize race, she is attentive to the myriad instances in which deracialization either failed or was not pursued by the Obama campaign. This lends credence to the notion that deracialization is situational rather than absolute, as racial themes and appeals may be both authored and avoided by the same politician during a single campaign, depending on the context of a given speech or event.[13]

In a slightly different approach to postracialism as the end of black politics, Manning Marable argues that Obama does not erase his race or deny his African descent. Instead, the president melts his blackness into a more palatable multicultural story of self that emphasizes the American dream. Immediately following Obama's election in 2008, Marable, like Walters, predicted a decidedly moderate agenda from the president, given Obama's predilection for pragmatism and compromise. More pointedly, the electoral triumph of a new generation of pragmatic black leaders, winning favor from white voters and distancing themselves from civil rights era ideology (even if the leadership style remains), is evidence of disturbing class stratification among African Americans and Latinos. In many ways, the new leadership elite are "out of touch with dire problems generated by poverty, unemployment, and mass incarceration."[14] This emphasis on the class divide and Marable's conviction about the danger it portends are the starting points for a more robust discussion of changes in black American politics.

Race, Class, and Black Politics

Class standing is dependent on some combination of employment level, income, and education. For the purposes of this section, in order to be counted as middle class or higher, one must work as an entrepreneur, professional, manager, business owner, office worker, civil servant, or salesperson. Those who reside in the working class or lower typically perform service industry jobs that emphasize repetitive tasks and manual labor. The black middle class did not reach 10 percent until 1960, but by the turn of the twenty-first century, roughly 50 percent of black Americans worked in middle-class jobs.[15] Viewed through a broad historical lens, this seems like an indicator with a positive trajectory, but recent trends in blacks' economic standing are cause for serious concern. During Bill Clinton's presidency in the 1990s, the black American poverty rate reached its all-time low, at 22.4 percent, but it is now rising.[16] As of 2010, over one quarter of all black Americans, 25.8 percent, are living below the poverty line; in comparison, the Hispanic poverty rate is 25 percent, the Asian rate is 12.5 percent, and the white rate is 9.4 percent.[17]

The recent increase in the black poverty rate becomes even more significant when we consider the ways that black class standing differs from that of whites at all levels of class stratification. The black middle class is far less stable and less prosperous than the white middle class. The most crucial reason for this, highlighted by Dalton Conley, Melvin Oliver, and Thomas Shapiro, is that black families have far fewer financial assets, such as financial securities and fully owned residential property. Even when comparing black families and white families at the same income level, black families on balance have less total wealth—assets that may appreciate in value and provide protection against market downturns.[18] Racial oppression and discrimination have prevented blacks from accumulating the sort of wealth that can be passed down from generation to generation. Mary Pattillo-McCoy's seminal study of black middle-class neighborhoods shows that when blacks do become homeowners, their property values are depressed by racial segregation, which results in perceptions from nonblack buyers about neighborhood prestige and safety and about proximity disadvantages, since black middle-class communities border economically depressed black communities. By and large, white middle-class communities are insulated from these possible sources of property depreciation.[19]

Clearly, wealth and residential segregation intersect with race and change the meaning of "middle class." But even when class is measured strictly in terms of employment, occupational segregation and the racial-ization of specific jobs and industries maintain the black-white wealth gap. The black middle class is overly reliant on public sector jobs, which have lower returns for education than do private sector jobs and do not provide networks for recruiting, as they often serve poor and working-class people rather than populations with social network ties to additional income opportunities. Blacks who do work in the private sector often perform jobs that are restricted to satisfying the consumer needs of minority clients or other niche groups; prestigious and "race-less" leadership positions are often reserved for white men.[20]

Just as the meaning of "middle class" changes thanks to its intersection with race, so too does the meaning of "poverty." As mentioned above, William Julius Wilson outlines the grave effects of concentrated poverty and racial segregation within black neighborhoods. Specifically, blacks' isolation from the legitimate economy, lack of access to decent schools, and high rates of residential turnover in poor black communities result in neighborhoods where social order is more difficult to police and cultural norms may deviate substantially from the habits most conducive to improving one's economic standing. Blacks are increasingly concentrated in positions of *extreme* poverty, including stints of impoverishment that last longer than those for whites. Far more often than is the case for whites, black poverty is permanent over the life cycle and intergenerationally transmitted; Patrick Sharkey finds that "more than 70 percent of black children who are raised in the poorest quarter of American neighborhoods remain in the poorest quarter of neighborhoods as adults, compared to 40 percent of whites."[21] Large numbers of blacks are unemployed or underemployed for long stretches of time, which creates a substantial social and economic chasm between middle-class blacks and those at the bottom of the socioeconomic distribution.[22] Again, even though middle-class blacks reside several financial notches below middle-class whites, the social and financial gap between middle-class blacks and blacks who are disproportionally subject to extreme poverty is massive, especially considering that only fifty years ago, 90 percent of blacks resided in the same class stratum.

How does the class gap among blacks, a relatively new phenomenon, influence black politics? As Michael Dawson argues in *Behind
the Mule* (1995), the defining characteristic of black political life is that
before reaching conclusions on political issues, blacks think about both
their individual preferences *and* the benefits for blacks as a whole. Over
the last half of the twentieth century, despite the class chasm, blacks
remained politically homogenous in many ways, voting for electoral
candidates as a unified group and affirming a range of political ideologies with a conspicuous absence of mainstream conservatism. Dawson
documents and analyzes this paradox, calling attention to blacks' sense
of linked racial fate, the notion that the fate of the most fortunate is tied
to the fate of the least fortunate. As long as racism abounds, blacks from
all class locations feel the impetus to affirm its salience as a political issue
and endeavor to counteract it.[23]

However, Dawson also argues that despite these commonalities,
black politics has undergone a sea change in the twentieth century. Fredrick Harris and his colleagues demonstrate that the growing gap in the
black community between the financially stable and the impoverished
most certainly depressed black civic participation during the final quarter of the century—where participation is broadly construed as activities
from voting and organizing for a political party to attending Parent-
Teacher Association meetings and leading Boy Scout troops.[24] The decline in overall political activity is complemented by emerging, if not
pronounced, differences in policy support, as privileged blacks offer less
support for economic redistribution, affirmative action, and government
assistance to black people.[25] This is not simply the result of the class gap
itself; it reflects the state of the real and virtual spaces where black politics happens. Increased black inclusion in white public spheres, state-
sponsored attacks on black political organizations, class cleavages, and
the economic deterioration of urban communities (extreme poverty)
explain why the black counterpublic we once knew no longer exists.[26]

Here is where the metalanguage of race does its work, as race shouts
over its complex interplay with other social factors. If black politics is
"dead," the explanatory dominance of postracialism suggests that it died

simply because race is no longer relevant. But Dawson's research forces us to attend to how black counterpublics actually function, rather than simply deciding whether we have moved past race. This focus produces a far more nuanced interpretation of Obama's rise, and a better explanation for why postracialism and deracialization emerge as campaign strategies.

The Public Sphere, Black Counterpublics, and Safety

Jürgen Habermas develops the idea of the public sphere to distinguish between the state, the market, and civic discourse. The public sphere is evoked when citizens who are not state officials discuss issues of political import; more colloquially, the public sphere is that expansive space where political talk resides.[27] In Habermas's model, bourgeois men who discuss politics are the only group that matters politically, because they are property owners and by extension the only group capable of or suitable for political life.[28] In response to the exclusionary practices of bourgeois male public spheres, marginalized groups create their own discursive spaces, called "counterpublics," to talk politics. Nancy Fraser describes these "subaltern counterpublics" as "parallel discursive arenas where members of subordinated social groups invent and circulate counterdiscourses, which in turn permit them to formulate oppositional interpretations of their identities, interests, and needs."[29]

The black counterpublic, or black public sphere, is *semi*autonomous because while discourse produced by black political agents is safe from the gaze of white onlookers, the matters discussed engage issues from mainstream discourse.[30] Black ideologies are produced within black counterpublic spaces, and these ideologies are vital to African American political life, Dawson argues, because they influence black political action. Dawson's version of the black counterpublic relies heavily on its institutional foundation. Not only do organizations define and prioritize the political issues that matter most to African Americans, but historically institutions, such as black churches and newspapers, "provided an environment which closely linked political debate to political action."[31] In the late twentieth century, the black counterpublic deteriorated, not because black Americans grew disinterested in politics or stopped talking about political issues but because the institutional base of the black counterpublic eroded for the reasons mentioned above. Dawson argues that today's black counterpublic bears little resemblance to its historical precedents, if it exists at all.[32]

In *Barbershops, Bibles, and BET* (2004), Melissa Harris-Perry does not deny the institutional deterioration that Dawson highlights, though she argues that the black counterpublic survives as ordinary black Americans continue to carve out spaces safe from white surveillance and develop black ideologies. These ideologies are not invented by politically shrewd black elites and then disseminated to the passive black masses. Instead, people give meaning to political happenings and develop belief systems and collective interests through "everyday talk."[33]

Dawson and Harris-Perry are foundational researchers in black counterpublic theory; their work is indispensable to the field. However, taken together, their research presents a paradox. Dawson argues that the counterpublic is on the verge of extinction, because black political institutions are weak and they do not perform the political functions they used to. Yet Harris-Perry shows that black people continue to talk about politics among themselves and in the company of nonblacks. Both authors confirm that black ideologies continue to matter in American politics. Even if the number of institutions has dwindled and their effectiveness has waned, a variety of organizations and collectives exists to serve and mobilize black constituencies, directly influencing state action. The black church, in particular, remains a force in black civic life and political mobilization.[34] So if the black counterpublic has not disappeared altogether, what exactly has changed?

Harris-Perry describes black counterpublics as "safe racial spaces."[35] A distinction is in order between racial safety as construed in black counterpublics during and before the civil rights movement, especially in the American South, and racial safety thereafter. As Houston Baker notes, "without romanticizing or minimizing the brutal realities of America's deep South apartheid, it is still possible to acknowledge that racial segregation in the United States both resuscitated and gave birth to a remarkable black southern public sphere."[36] The idea that the black public sphere emerges within a segregated society speaks to the fact that early to mid–twentieth-century black safety is, in part, a physical safety, born out of necessity in conditions where blacks were frequently victims of legal and illegal terror campaigns against people of color. Blacks were not considered full citizens, and gathering together to have political conversations necessitated a space where people felt safe from persecution.

In her study, Harris-Perry points primarily towards emotional and ideological safety. Safety is a feeling of comfort and validation; when an everyday black person enters the black counterpublic, she can say things without the worry that her beliefs and statements will be received with suspicion or disgust, as they would in mainstream discursive spaces. This safety depends on ideological content. It is a safety in knowing you are in the company of others who understand race to be a central dimension of political life rather than an anomaly or afterthought. Harris-Perry is careful to point out that the African American counterpublics are internally contested and "vulnerable to exclusionary practices."[37] So the claim is not that *any* given black person will *always* feel comfortable in *every* black counterpublic space. Still, black counterpublics have operated on the premise that there will be no surveillance, interference, or mediation from nonblack political actors or authorities.

Today, technological and commercial developments inhibit black political actors from cultivating the safety necessary for black counterpublics to operate. Marshall McLuhan's work on media technology and the public sphere challenges both Habermas's theory and, indirectly, the notion of stable subaltern counterpublics. McLuhan seeks to explain communication, social order, and social change. In Habermas's model, societies change as an organic result of publicly contested ideas about democracy, justice, and the good life. McLuhan rejects this idea. His most influential claim is that "the medium is the message,"[38] meaning that the technology we use to communicate with each other is what changes our social world. The content of each media transmission, or public sphere discussion, is almost irrelevant. What matters is that each new phase of media technology forces us to adapt and relate to each other in new ways.

These adaptations change social relations. In 1962, more than a generation prior to the advent of the World Wide Web, McLuhan envisaged a "global village" without the time and space barriers that keep people disconnected, where data sources and archives are collapsed and streamlined into a universally accessible electronic network.[39] This new means of relating to one another is not a utopian vision, but it has specific implications for those who wish to isolate minorities and marginalized groups from public culture: that can no longer be done.[40] It also means that minorities will have a more difficult time protecting themselves from surveillance.

In the past two decades, black counterpublics have been revealed to outside audiences and in many cases sold to the public. For instance, the film *Barbershop* (2002) offered the opportunity to see the black counterpublic in action and stirred up significant discussion in the public sphere about the political discussions in the film, as characters openly debated, and in some cases disparaged, the accomplishments of famous men and women in the history of black American politics. Many African Americans were displeased at the way the film trampled black discursive taboos, first by criticizing leaders of the civil rights movement (even in the service of comedy), and second by abandoning counterpublic safety, pulling back the curtain, and allowing nonblacks to see and hear such criticism. As Jesse Jackson noted shortly after the film's release, many blacks felt "the filmmakers crossed the line between what's sacred and serious and what's funny."[41]

Another example of the exposure and commercialization of the black counterpublic is hip-hop music and culture. Rap music can be a formidable critical force because of its emphasis on narrative, ghetto reporting, and rhetoric, and Dawson, Gwendolyn Pough, and others note the ways in which hip-hop constitutes a black public sphere.[42] Hip-hop remains a relevant black counterpublic site and serves as a tool for identity construction, but it is certainly mediated by its commoditization. Corporate investment in hip-hop in the late twentieth and early twenty-first centuries has resulted in increased instances of "puerile" and objectionable lyrical content.[43] Not only are the musical performances commoditized and their content compromised, but the conversation inspired by the content of hip-hop and the moral panic that surrounds it have been packaged and broadcast as a series of town hall–style talk shows on Black Entertainment Television's *Hip-Hop vs. America* (2007) series. These television specials certainly elevate the popular discourse about hip-hop, acknowledging its diversity and complexity. But in terms of counterpublic safety, every household with cable television can tune in to the debate between black public intellectuals, journalists, members of the clergy, and hip-hop stars as they talk about the politics of race, class, and gender in hip-hop culture.

More recently, CNN capitalized on the counterpublic-gone-town-hall format with the introduction of the *Black in America* and *Latino in America* series, which debuted in 2008. Each series contains episodes that range from panel discussions to documentaries highlighting issues pertinent to black or Latino communities, and the television programming is complemented by digital content available at CNN.com. In addition to the articles and short videos posted on the website, there is ample space for readers to reply to the content on the site, which prompts visitors to "join the conversation" and reply to the question, "What did you think of 'Black in America'?" Website visitors can either leave comments on the site itself or continue the conversation offline with the aid of CNN's tools for parents and educators, which amount to discussion questions that encourage engagement of the issues presented in the television series.[44] Again, the openness of these spaces forces us to reconsider the notion of safety in counterpublics designed for marginalized racial and ethnic groups.

Jeremiah Wright and Obama's "A More Perfect Union"

A classic case of the breakdown in counterpublic safety occurred during Obama's 2008 election campaign, in the form of the Reverend Jeremiah Wright controversy. On March 13, 2008, ABC News aired privately captured footage of Wright, Obama's pastor for more than twenty years at Trinity United Church of Christ in Chicago, delivering sermons with controversial rhetoric about America's moral standing. All of this is made possible by the rapid advancement and widespread availability of video recording technology and file sharing. Two sound bites gained special notoriety. In the first, during a sermon delivered by Wright on September 16, 2001, in the aftermath of the September 11 attacks, Wright exhorts, "America's chickens are coming home to roost." In the second clip, Wright exclaims, "God damn America!" during a 2003 sermon while discussing the ways that various governments, including the American government, have murdered innocent people and dehumanized their own citizens.

Each quotation was irresponsibly ripped from its context, and a number of commentators cast Wright as fundamentally angry, bigoted, and unpatriotic.[45] Pundits at all locations on the political spectrum wondered whether the revelation would submarine Obama's candidacy. If his opponents could convince the public that these excerpts exposed Obama as a stereotypical angry black man at heart, it would surely pose a problem for his electoral prospects. The transcript of each Wright sermon reveals each excerpt as a small piece of a more sophisticated criticism of America's claim to moral authority, considering the American government's numerous human rights violations. In the first instance, during the 2001 sermon, Wright is actually quoting former United States ambassador Edward Peck, who first suggested that America, unfortunately, was reaping what it had sewn. The passage is excerpted below in full, as it fully illustrates Wright's criticism:

I heard Ambassador Peck on an interview yesterday. Did anybody else see him or hear him? He was on Fox News. This is a white man, and he was upsetting the Fox News commentators to no end. He pointed out—did you see him, John?—a white man, he pointed out, ambassador, that what Malcolm X said when he got silenced by Elijah Muhammad was in fact true, America's chickens are coming home to roost.

We took this country, by terror, away from the Sioux, the Apache, the Arawak, the Comanche, the Arapaho, the Navajo. Terrorism—we took Africans from their country to build our way of ease and kept them enslaved and living in fear. Terrorism. We bombed Grenada and killed innocent civilians—babies, non-military personnel. We bombed the black civilian community of Panama with stealth bombers and killed unarmed teenagers, and toddlers, pregnant mothers and hard-working fathers. We bombed Gaddafi, his home and killed his child. Blessed be they who bash your children's head against the rocks.

We bombed Iraq, we killed unarmed civilians trying to make a living. We bombed the plant in Sudan to pay back for the attack on our embassy—killed hundreds of hard-working people—mothers and fathers, who left home to go that day, not knowing they'd never get back home. We bombed Hiroshima, we bombed Nagasaki and we nuked far more than the thousands in New York and the Pentagon, and we never batted an eye. Kids playing in the playground, mothers picking up children after school—civilians, not soldiers. People just trying to make it day by day. We have supported state terrorism against the Palestinians and black South Africans, and now we are indignant? Because the stuff we have done overseas is brought back into our own front yards.

America's chickens are coming home to roost. Violence begets violence. Hatred begets hatred, and terrorism begets terrorism.

A white ambassador said that, y'all, not a black militant.[46]

Over the past forty years, few speeches on the topic of race have garnered as much attention as Obama's public response to Wright, "A More Perfect Union," delivered in Philadelphia on March 18, 2008. In the speech, Obama denounces Wright's comments without specifying precisely which portions of the sermons he objects to, or explicitly addressing the sound bites themselves. He does not meet Wright's social criticism head on, or condemn news organizations for taking the excerpts out of context. Instead, Obama chides Wright for constructing an oversimplified version of America, one that ignores the country's capacity to change and ignores the nation's progress with respect to issues of racial injustice. He states that Wright "expressed a profoundly distorted view of this country—a view that sees white racism as endemic, and that elevates what is wrong with America above all that we know is right with America. . . . As such, Reverend Wright's comments were not only wrong but divisive, divisive at a time when we need unity; racially charged at a time when we need to come together to solve a set of monumental problems."[47] According to Obama, change, rather than unrelenting racism, is the essence of the American creed. He diagnoses the social and political divide between blacks and whites, and enumerates the responsibilities of each group. Blacks must insist upon dignity and equal treatment, recognize that their struggle is endemically linked to the struggles of all Americans, and affirm personal responsibility within their own communities. Whites must recognize that black folks' problems with racism are not figments of the black collective imagination, that it takes a serious political commitment to undo America's legacy of racial injustice, and that racial groups are not in zero-sum competition with each other for political resources.[48]

The first thing to note is that these explosive events, including perhaps the most formative speech on race in the past forty years, transpired over the course of what is frequently called a "postracial" or "deracialized" campaign. Does "A More Perfect Union" deviate from previous iterations of America's racial strife? Absolutely. But the metalanguage of race erases complexity and disallows any careful investigation of how and why this speech reflects and shapes the racial order. Instead, because this version of racial discourse and race relations deviates from the historical example, the overly simplistic explanation cast upon the public is that we have "moved beyond race," even when race takes center stage.

Second, while Obama takes great pains to distance himself from Wright without completely disowning his former pastor, he does not discuss or question how and why the private footage from inside the church made its way to the evening news. No doubt, these choices are largely motivated by political expediency, but Obama's other writing suggests that he has lost faith in the power of such institutions as major engines for change. In *Dreams from My Father*, Obama's disenchantment with the traditional black counterpublic is palpable as he describes his frustration with political organizing through black religious institutions in 1980s Chicago. The following excerpts exemplify this disenchantment.

Neither his [Rafiq's] organization nor his mosque, I had discovered, could claim a membership of more than fifty persons. His influence arose not from any strong organizational support but from his willingness to show up at every meeting that remotely affected Roseland and shout his opponents into submission.

What held true for Rafiq was true throughout the city; without the con-
centrating effect of Harold's campaign, nationalism [specifically, the black nationalism of the Nation of Islam] dissipated into an attitude rather than any
concrete program, a collection of grievances and not an organized force . . . the
Nation's active membership in Chicago was considerably smaller . . . a base that
was rarely, if ever, mobilized around political races or in support of broad-based
programs.[49]

[The Reverend Phillips] wasn't sure, he said, how much longer the church
would continue to serve that function [circulate information, values, and ideas
within the black community]. Most of his better-off members had moved away
to tidier neighborhoods, suburban life. They still drove back every Sunday, out
of loyalty or habit. But the nature of their involvement had changed. They hesi-
tated to volunteer for anything—a tutoring program, a home visitation—that
might keep them in the city after dark. They wanted more security around the
church, a fenced in parking lot to protect their cars.[50]

Would the Christian fellowship between a black school administrator, say, and
a black school parent change the way schools were run? . . . And if men like
Reverend Wright failed to take a stand, if churches like Trinity refused to engage with real power and risk genuine conflict, then what chance would there
be of holding the larger community intact?[51]

Obama sees the foundation of traditional black counterpublics
eroding before him, thanks to class divisions and weak organizational
culture. His choice to attend law school rather than remain embedded
in black institutions on the South Side of Chicago cannot be attributed
to a single driving factor, but this anecdotal evidence certainly suggests
Obama's disillusion with traditional forms of black political organization. Each breakdown in black counterpublic safety and strength carries
different stakes, but at the very least, these instances demonstrate that
such spaces are no longer shrouded from the white gaze, nor are they
viewed as the undisputed path for politically inclined black Americans
who wish to effect social change. Alterations in the protective capacity
and safety of the black counterpublic carry both positive and negative
consequences.

The Benefits of Exposing Black Counterpublics

While public fervor over the racial significance of Obama's campaign had been building for quite some time, "A More Perfect Union" is a landmark moment in race discussion in the public sphere. This is the moment that the idea of "a national conversation on race" came into fashion in the mainstream media. In his article covering the speech in the March 18, 2008, edition of the *Washington Post*, entitled "Obama's Road Map on Race," Eugene Robinson writes, "I believe he might have pulled off something that seemed almost impossible: He not only ventured into the minefield of race and made it back alive, but he also marked a path for the rest of us to follow."[52] Robinson not only affirms that Obama's ideas about race are valuable, but he celebrates Obama's willingness to address racial issues as an example that ordinary Americans can and should aspire to. Without the breakdown of black counterpublic safely and the release of the Wright footage, the national conversation on race would not have been jumpstarted.

In the months after "A More Perfect Union," a deluge of articles echoed Robinson's theme. A few days after the election ended, the *Wall Street Journal* published an article entitled "Election of Obama Recasts National Conversation on Race," suggesting that Obama had already changed the terms of racial discussion in America.[53] Readers are alerted to the possibility that for some Americans Obama signals the birth of the postracial era in American history, despite a quotation from an Obama advisor explicitly affirming the president's belief that race still matters. The article elucidates a divide between Obama's stance and interpretations of the election as an opportunity for white Americans to publicly renounce their race-based guilt. Two months later, in January 2009, the *New York Times* published a story called "Talk About Race? Relax, It's Okay." This story features quotations from a racially and ethnically diverse collection of New Yorkers as pieces of a greater argument about the ways Obama provides Americans with a comfortable starting point for discussions of race, because his personal background connects him to multiple racial and ethnic communities.[54] On February 29, 2009, the national conversation on race went global, as National Public

Radio (NPR) hosted a live forum entitled "How Does Your Country Talk About Race?" featuring contributions from invited guests and call-ins from NPR listeners around the world.[55]

Roughly one hundred days after Obama's term began, the *New York Times* ran two articles within a week of each other, suggesting not only that the nation had taken the call to talk about race to heart, but also that race-talk was improving race relations. The first report, published on April 27, 2009, features the results of a 973-person survey conducted by the newspaper and CBS News. According to the poll, two-thirds of Americans reported that race relations are now good, and the percentage of blacks that expressed that sentiment doubled from July 2008 to April 2009. The article makes no claim that these results indicate the demise of prejudice, as the writers note that half of the black respondents believe whites still have a better chance to get ahead than blacks in America. But the anecdotal evidence is decidedly upbeat, as interviewees offer statements such as, "people of different races [are] being kinder to each other," and, "[Obama's] openness and acceptance have helped others be more open and accepting."[56] A May 2, 2009, article, "Voices Reflect Rising Sense of Racial Optimism," picks up on this theme, noting that people in all regions of the country are "expressing an invigorated sense of openness toward people of other races," and featuring similarly themed quotations from sources of various racial and ethnic backgrounds.[57]

Of course, this newfound "openness toward people of other races" does not constitute full-fledged antiracist practice. Despite a marked attitudinal decrease where racial prejudice is concerned, the shift in principle has not resulted in a shift in policy, and government remains disappointingly inactive in the mission to correct racial inequality and injustice. Still, talking about race does yield some demonstrable effects, as the alternative (silence around racial issues) houses implicit racial dictums and insults.

As mentioned in the first chapter, Tali Mendelberg explains that racial messages are silently embedded within political campaigns. In a society where explicit racial insults are deemed politically incorrect, not only because they are insulting but simply because race is not an acceptable topic of conversation thanks to the norm of equality, candidates silently prime racial stereotypes and fears in order to gain advantages over non-white opponents.[58] The canonical instance of this is the Willie Horton advertisement, employed in 1988 by presidential hopeful George H.W. Bush. Viewers' fears of black crime and black male sexual savagery were primed by Horton's photograph and the accompanying story about his early release from prison and the repeat sexual assaults that followed. More recently, Tennessee congressman Harold Ford was implicitly cast as devious playboy with an appetite for white women in a commercial funded by the Republican National Committee in 2006.[59] The anti-Ford advertisement features actors posing as everyday Tennesseans asked to respond to the possibility of Ford's election. It opens with a picture of a black woman who says, "Harold Ford looks nice, isn't that enough?" As the commercial proceeds, a young, excitable white woman appears twice, first exclaiming, "I met Harold at the playboy party!" and later whispering into the camera, asking Ford to call her. The obvious racial subtext in both of these cases is grounded in the long-proffered racist myth of black males as hypersexual beings bent on violating white women.

Newt Gingrich's and Mitt Romney's efforts to connect Obama to stereotypes about blacks and welfare during the 2012 campaign certainly fall within this tradition, as noted in Chapter 1. But during the 2008 presidential campaign, the racial subtext contained an especially strong ethnoreligious component, as the contest played out in the context of America's ongoing "War on Terror." One of the lynchpins of the McCain campaign was the notion that Obama lacked the foreign policy experience and mettle to deal effectively with Muslim extremists. The questions raised by McCain about who "the real Barack Obama" is constitute a veiled suggestion that Obama lacks "American" credentials, a criticism that exemplifies the race and nation connection discussed in Chapter 2.[60] Considered as a whole, these appeals cast Obama as "anti-American" in a time of war, especially when compared to McCain, an unambiguously white military hero who served his country in battle and in Washington. For example, a 2008 advertisement funded by the

Pennsylvania GOP features multiple clips of the Reverend Wright yelling "God damn America!" and "U.S. of KKK," before asking viewers to question Obama's "judgment" rather than his Americanness or racial fitness for the presidency.[61]

Instead of dealing with these attacks in counterpublic spaces, Obama took race-talk to the public sphere, delivering "A More Perfect Union," which spurred even more discussion. While talking about race is insufficient means for combating racism, it is a necessary first step, even if the impetus for discussing race is a breach of counterpublic safety. The exposure of black politics to the American mainstream hints at the political potential of technological advancements in mass communication.

Technology, Public Spheres, and Political Organization

Unlike many of his African American predecessors, Obama's career and campaign were not launched from a firm black counterpublic base. The Obama campaign used MyBarackObama.com as a platform for both campaign chatter and political organizing and mobilization. When this platform was conceived, Obama was a marginal candidate for the presidency, millions of dollars and supporters behind the front-runner for the Democratic nomination, Senator Hillary Clinton. From the start, however, the website operated differently from its predecessors and differently from traditionally defined counterpublics. The Obama-sphere is an open, absorbent, and adaptable discursive space, linked to grassroots activism. It allows for easy entry and exit, and various levels of commitment, obligation, and attachment for those who enter.

According to the Pew Research Center,

- 74 percent of Internet users engaged the 2008 campaign online. This constitutes 55 percent of the adult population; the first time that more than half of voting-age adults report using the Internet for political action during an election.

- 60 percent of Internet users went online for news about politics or the campaign in 2008.

- 38 percent of Internet users talked about politics online with others during the campaign.

- 59 percent of Internet users used one or more of email, instant messaging, texts messages, or Twitter to send or receive political messages.[62]

The potential of the Internet to revolutionize politics lies in the possibility of (1) reducing distance between citizens and government by eliminating mediating individuals and institutions, (2) serving and politicizing a more massive audience thanks to the breakdown of time and space constraints, and (3) bolstering community building among citizens by providing space for communication and the discovery of shared interests.[63] Unlike those who trumpet the possibility of a new and improved era of American democracy ushered in by the Internet, Bruce Bimber predicts "accelerated pluralism" with increased "issue-group formation and action" but without a qualitatively different or improved political experience.[64] He explains, "the anticipated effects of expanded communication are limited by the willingness and capacity of humans to engage in a complex political life. While the Net will certainly change the informational environment of individuals, it will likely not alter their overall interest in public affairs or their ability to assimilate and act on political information."[65] Increased information does not necessarily lead to increased political action, and community building has never been a guaranteed outcome of advances in communicative technology.[66]

Political scientist and technology expert Omar Wasow argues that Obama is America's "first internet President," noting that "On YouTube, nearly four times as many people watched official Obama [2008] campaign videos as clips of John McCain (about 96 million to 25 million)," and "on Facebook, Obama has 2.4 million 'friends,' versus McCain's 623,000."[67] Barriers to political participation can be conceived in terms of resources, as citizens often lack the time, money, and civic skills to participate. In the United States, access to and use of the Internet is distributed unevenly, as people of color and economic disadvantage lag behind whites and those of middle-class standing. In recent years, however, the digital divide has shrunk, as African Americans and Latinos, including those at the bottom of the class hierarchy, are going online at an increasing rate.[68] As mentioned, one of the reasons the Internet holds the potential to change habits of political participation is that it operates with less restrictive time and space constraints than other political tools. The sheer scale of Obama's Internet presence stands as evidence that Internet-savvy political actors can reach a mass audience without demanding too much time and money from participants.

Skeptics acknowledge that the Internet can reach more people in less time than other outreach methods, but the crux of Bimber's critique is the problem of turning information into political activity. Wasow argues that perhaps the shrewdest tactic of the Obama campaign was pairing online outreach with grassroots activism. Through MyBarackObama.com, the campaign "guided online enthusiasts to reach non-techies" through the use of voter databases, e-mail recruitment, online wizards for hosting campaign events, and scripts, neighborhood lists, and instructional videos for canvassing.[69] Translating political information into action is dependent, in part, on what sort of information is being transmitted. In this case, the information guides volunteers towards political activity. The campaign realized that a strong online presence was not enough on its own, and employed the Internet as a means to generate ground-level activism.

A final point of skepticism regarding Internet politics concerns the potential to build political community. From the beginning, Obama conceptualized his campaign as "a vehicle for people to get involved, use their talents, *feel connected to something larger than themselves.*"[70] Anecdotal evidence from the campaign suggests that the Obama team achieved this goal, as volunteers gained a sense of connection to each other, self-esteem, and feeling of closeness to the candidate.[71] MyBarackObama.com is a hub for this sort of evidence, as the Obama campaign frequently posted testimonies from volunteers who participated in campaign events, using these testimonies as encouragement for others looking to get involved. One such testimony, posted on June 28, 2008, reads, "This is giving us an opportunity for a real sense of community. When you work on this campaign, you experience that. . . . I love being around people who are working for the same goal. We all feel connected already—even people we don't know—we all feel connected in support of this man who is a true inspiration."[72]

Conversation at MyBarackObama.com continues after the testimonies, campaign videos, and news articles posted by website operators. In a fashion similar to the comments section at CNN's "Black in America" website and other comments sections at digital news outlets, MyBarackObama.com visitors post poems and quotations, pass on information about other websites, discuss Obama's stance on policy issues, and comment on his relationships with other politicians. In sum, the site dispenses information about the candidate, instructs people how to transform information into political activity, and gives people space to talk about politics; it performs all the functions of an effective counterpublic, exempting the notion of safety. In addition to the discursive activity within the Obama-sphere, the campaign meaningfully impacted political discourse in the greater public sphere.

Implications of the Evolution of Counterpublics

The most disturbing element of the move away from traditional black counterpublics to more permeable and transient discursive spheres is that there is no guarantee that this transition will improve the material conditions of racially degraded or otherwise marginalized people's lives. With respect to Internet counterpublics, the first issue is that those who are politically marginalized and disengaged are likely to remain disengaged, regardless of the medium through which political information flows.[73] Second, although there is evidence that the race and class gap in Internet access across the United States is decreasing, online content remains stratified. The wealthiest media companies dominate the online content we see, not only because generating content costs money but because search engine results and link patterns are strikingly similar among the major competitors, as users are ushered through a disturbingly low number of paths to information.[74] Internet politics is largely directed by political elites, which was certainly the case during Obama's 2008 campaign.

Another drawback of Internet-based political spaces is that they do not always produce civic discourse or lead their participants to political action. Where discourse is concerned, Obama's political fame has brought the wrath of a number of reactionary political groups prone to violent, sensational, and apocalyptic rhetoric. When race makes its way into the public sphere, the results are often combustible, and anti-Obama factions have certainly garnered their fair share of airtime and web traffic in recent years. As for political action, MyBarackObama.com was successful because it was explicitly created to provide instructions and encouragement for grassroots activism among its visitors. Unfortunately, much of the political chatter on the Internet leads to polarization and petty arguing rather than organization and mobilization.[75]

More fundamentally, celebration of counterpublic evolution can mask the fact that the root causes of black counterpublic deterioration have not been addressed. At bottom, Dawson's study of black ideologies is about the intersection of class segregation and race segregation as a double helix that destroys black institutional life. Today, black Americans continue to lag behind other racial groups according to measures of education, public health, employment, incarceration, and the accumulation of wealth. The symbolic representation embodied by Obama and other public figures may lead to more discussions of race, but even if these discussions imply a shift in public sentiment away from antiblack prejudice, they are not assured to result in policy changes and other interventions on racial inequality.

Political Talk and the Intersection of Race and Class

This chapter engages the phenomenon of postracialism. The word "postracial" establishes a binary, two distinct sets of sociopolitical circumstances: either something is racial, or it is not. Understanding race as metalanguage demands that we reject this false binary and search for the complex interplay of race with other forces. As a first step, I reject the most rudimentary understanding of "postracial" and confirm that race still exerts its influence on life chances and social experiences. Even if "postracial" is used to indicate the supremacy of economic class as a determinant of life chances, class dynamics are fundamentally intersectional, as transgenerational economic advantages cannot be understood without considering racial history, and today the meaning of "middle class" and "poverty" changes depending on one's racial categorization.

Alternatively, the notion of postracialism is applied to the contemporary campaign strategies of modern-day black American politicians, who have employed deracialization as a key tactic for roughly twenty-five years. However, the strategy of avoiding explicit racial appeals and issues that are racialized in popular political discourse should not be misread as evidence that race does not impact political campaigns. Moreover, black politicians have been unable to completely avoid race as a topic of conversation. Obama is upheld as the apotheosis of the postracial candidate, yet it was his campaign that produced one of the most salient racial controversies and speeches in modern electoral history, thanks to the media's excerpts of Jeremiah Wright's sermons.

The most helpful way to understand the constellation of social forces that gives way to the inadequate idea of postracialism is to focus on institutional changes in black political life. Something is different, but the change is not simply that race no longer matters. Instead, race intersects with class and technological innovation to produce new rules for the production of black political discourse, as institutionalized counterpublics safe from surveillance are increasingly endangered. Economic segmentation among blacks, extreme poverty, the erosion of black neighborhood life, and the digital revolution have moved black political discourse online and out into the open. What do these developments portend for black and mainstream politics going forward?

Though subaltern groups can no longer assume safety from surveillance, there is no reason to believe that these collectives will simply stop producing critical political discourse. These criticisms grow from lived experiences and resultant political consciousness, and as long as unjust suffering continues, critical traditions in black public spheres and other spaces will remain. However, the once natural links between discursive production and political mobilization have been severed, because the old model of institutional leadership and political socialization has disappeared. For this reason, marginalized groups that wish to make a political impact must ensure that their political chatter is tied to instructions for transforming talk into action. It is difficult to imagine, but the Obama presidential campaign began in 2007 as a clear underdog without a broad ground game. But the campaign team was able to use social media and the digital realm not only to *connect* like-minded people but also to *instruct* them, telling followers how to get involved and be political.

A second concern: Dawson notes that one of the reasons black counterpublics deteriorated during the latter half of the twentieth century is that black political leaders are increasingly absorbed into the mainstream, and we should expect much of the same with respect to black political commentators, as networks and websites like CNN and MSNBC boast a roster of commentators and contributors with a decidedly multicultural flavor. The aforementioned Melissa Harris-Perry's politics show on MSNBC is one such example; it is a landmark program, not only because Harris-Perry stands as one of a select group of black women who are television hosts for shows that discuss politics but because the show is the first of its kind that features a tenured professor as the main talent. It would be absurd and counterproductive to simply demand that these commentators, pundits, and political laborers withdraw from corporate news media and go back to the counterpublic. However, we cannot have a situation where *all* the cultural and political workers with leadership potential from these groups are constantly competing with each other for slices of corporate news media airtime, at the expense of expanding the pie and creating new spaces controlled by and for marginalized groups. In other words, advocates for marginalized groups must have an entrepreneurial orientation, a willingness to occupy platforms of varied scale, such that their career goals are not tied to the whims of decision makers at corporations with little investment in the communities these leaders represent.

A related concern springing from the new rules of political communication and organization is that inequality in the digital realm is ignored or underestimated. Large news media corporations considerably influence the content we view on the Internet, just as they influence television programming and print journalism. The digital age holds great democratic possibility, but it is not yet realized, both because the most powerful corporations control the information flow and because access to the Internet is still circumscribed by intersecting race and class inequities. The solution to this problem is the punch line for the chapter: the political discourse that is actually being produced has to change, and the interaction of race/ethnicity and class must be emphasized.

Based on current trends in campaigning, a return to explicit racial appeals and racial framing of policy issues is unlikely. However, the traction gained by the 2008 Obama campaign, thanks to the candidate's framing of the financial crisis, demonstrates that appeals to voters' economic sensibilities are quite effective. As John Edwards found out in 2008, running a campaign focused on the "War on Poverty" may not be a wise strategy in the early twenty-first century. But the fact that voters are receptive to candidates who emphasize economic issues presents an opportunity not only to talk about class inequality but to explain how race and class oppression intersect with each other, injure groups from across the class spectrum, and weaken the national economy.

The financial crisis and housing market crash of 2008 is an intersectional phenomenon that perfectly illustrates these dynamics. As explained above, blacks and Latinos are more financially vulnerable than whites, not only because employment incomes are lower for nonwhite groups but because they do not have large wealth reserves. Where those reserves do exist, they most often take the form of residential property. In other words, black and brown wealth is disproportionately concentrated in home ownership rather than stocks and bonds, or commercial property. The housing crisis and economic recession disproportionately impacted the most vulnerable segments of both the middle and working classes, many of whom were black and Hispanic. As a result, from 2007 to 2009, the net worth of black and Hispanic American families decreased by over $200 billion; the wealth gains made over the last forty years were swiftly erased. The fifteen years prior to 2007 saw the largest growth in home ownership ever recorded among blacks and Hispanics, but this home ownership was enabled by overreliance on subprime mort-gage loans (those with a high chance of default), often with exorbitant interest rates; the collapse of derivative markets created around these loans is one of the main causes of the financial crash.[76]

The housing market and economic crisis can be summarized through the lens of race and ethnicity: blacks and Hispanics are more financially vulnerable than whites as a result of institutionalized racism and historically engendered inequality. Financial vulnerability, lack of previous mortgage experience, and limited educational attainment, in combination with residential segregation and documented discrimina-tion in the housing and mortgage markets, makes blacks and Hispanics easy targets for subprime lenders.[77] These mortgages are then quickly bundled and sold by the initial lenders in the derivative marketplace, and the initial lenders absorb none of the risk for giving out such ill-fated loans in the first place. When families who are stretching to make ends meet default on these loans, their assets, including their homes, are seized, the housing stock plummets, and the credit market freezes, bringing the economy to a standstill. Predatory lending practices aimed at exploiting the financial vulnerability of working- and middle-class black and brown people eventually destroy the entire economic system. One would think that lenders might learn their lesson and interrupt this cycle of intersectional race/class oppression after the housing mar-ket crash. But as the United States economy emerges from recession, the same lending patterns are repeating themselves. In 2009, whites were nearly twice as likely as blacks and Hispanics to receive prime mort-gages, and blacks and Hispanics were two to four times as likely to re-ceive subprime loans.[78]

The intersectional dynamics of this problem need to be explained to the public and addressed. The financial collapse was not caused purely by discrimination against blacks and Latinos, or by subprime loans alone. But the event cannot be fully understood without recognizing the intersection of race and class-based inequality and the resultant dual housing market, in which too many vulnerable black and brown fami-lies are teetering on the edge of collapse. When they fall, a domino effect takes down the whole structure. If we believe that an educated citizenship builds the strongest democracy, we should treat the public with the respect it deserves and amplify intersectional explanations for contemporary class inequality. Trumpeting postracialism denies intersectionality, panders to anti-intellectualism, cheapens political discourse, ignores the lessons of history, and prevents us from solving social problems.

CHAPTER 5

THE PERILS OF BEING SUPERWOMAN

Michelle Obama's Public Image

Obviously, black women have not been reflected, at so many
different levels. Our images are limited to such a small number of
things that we're just delighted to see ourselves in a broader sense.
—*Michelle Obama*[1]

Jacqueline Kennedy Onassis passed away in 1994. Five years later, a Gallup poll identified her as one of the eighteen most-admired American women of the past fifty years.[2] During her lifetime, Ms. Onassis revolutionized the role of the first lady, making over the White House as a social center and a hub for the latest décor. She was often cast as the epitome of style and grace, retaining her own personal designer to keep her flush in her signature with dresses, gloves, and low-heel shoes. Though her charisma equaled that of her husband, after President Kennedy's death Jackie receded from the public spotlight, marrying a Greek shipping mogul and moving on to a successful second career as an editor for Doubleday Books. She is remembered fondly and frequently, and people need not speak her name to do so. Any time a female celebrity wins over the media with the right smile, or the perfect dress, her legacy echoes in the distance. Jackie is considered by many to be the paradigmatic icon of American femininity, defined by a mix of physical beauty, refined taste, and earnest dedication to her family through joy and tragedy.

Gender norms and inequalities are undeniably central to female celebrity in American popular culture. In the case of Ms. Onassis, for exle, her reserved, nonthreatening mannerisms and skillful navigation of the domestic sphere facilitate her enshrinement in the pantheon of honorable femininity. Onassis's public image poses little threat to patriarchal ideals, and our collective obsession with themes related to her physical appearance speaks to the primacy of the male gaze and continued objectification of women. However, in Ms. Onassis's case, white privilege operates in its customary silence, concealing itself within the discourse of beauty and public affection. Conversely, Ms. Obama's race was an issue from the moment she stepped into the spotlight.

This chapter details America's relationship with Michelle Obama as means to investigate representations of black womanhood. Public representations of Michelle Obama vacillate between overlapping, timeworn racist stereotypes of black womanhood, and a newer, more complicated racist construction: the uppity black superwoman. The superwoman image is especially perfidious, as it paradoxically traps black women within the confines of their economic success, concealing larger patterns of racism, sexism, and class inequality.

I begin with a brief history of the first lady, a role that continues to evolve and is subject to the influence of the women who occupy the post. Next, a more thorough explanation of intersectionality theory is paired with discussion of stereotypes of black femininity, and the idea of the uppity superwoman is introduced. As Michelle Obama's public career is charted, I argue that the criticism she is subject to does not simply draw upon classic stereotypes of the deviant black superwoman, but adds a new layer to the issue, given the sociological situation of black women in America, who are often cast as a privileged group relative to black men.

Public fascination with and celebration of first lady Michelle Obama are largely motivated by how flagrantly she debunks racist and sexist stereotypes. Ms. Obama defends herself from these attacks and disrupts the discourse of uppity black superwomanhood by constructing a decidedly down-to-earth public image, emphasizing her role as "Mom in Chief" and claiming her sexuality. I conclude by providing further suggestions for ameliorating these issues and breaking free from the limitations of traditional representations of black womanhood.

The Role of the First Lady

Presidential scholarship is more than just celebrity gossip. We study the president because he or she has the power to alter the course of history. The scrutiny with which we investigate the public and private lives of these figures is justified by the notion that understanding their belief systems and personalities helps us understand the decisions that impact the country and the world. While it is beyond dispute that numerous first ladies have publicly and privately influenced the office of the presidency, the first lady has no prescribed governmental power, at least formally speaking. Without a clear sense of precisely what the position is or how these women influence the course of history, the scale often tips in favor of superficiality or disregard. First ladies are largely ignored by historians, and texts dedicated to their lives focus largely on social or biographical elements of the woman in question rather than providing systemic analysis of the position as a whole. The result of this is a tradition that focuses on a relatively short list of women who occupied the White House, with the aforementioned Jacqueline Kennedy, Eleanor Roosevelt, and Hillary Clinton as the three women who have received the most journalistic and scholarly attention.[3]

Robert P. Watson identifies the key challenges in studying this group of public figures. First, there are a small number of cases, which encompass significant variation in historical and social context, so quantitative data sets are difficult to produce. Where qualitative data are concerned, the rhetoric and writing of the first ladies themselves must be considered legitimate source material. Unfortunately, the amount of written material pales in sheer comparison to the resources available for studying their male counterparts. The few materials that are available are often viewed with heavy skepticism by researchers, who must take into account the ways in which texts released by the White House are monitored and constructed in order to create a particular public image of the president and his administration.[4]

These research barriers, combined with the lack of clarity about the function of the office, should motivate scholars to focus more intensely on the topic rather than ignore it. It may be impossible to evaluate the first lady in the same way we measure the performance of other public figures, but it is possible to undertake structured studies of the position rather than fixating on one or two charismatic figures. Anthony Eksterrowicz and Kristen Paynter draw on Watson and others in developing a typology of first ladies based on their autonomy and influence on the White House. In examining first ladies up through Hillary Clinton, they argue that we have passed that time in American history when first ladies were expected to be silent partners, and moved increasingly in the direction of an "independent/integrative model." In this arrangement, "a first lady can develop a public policy agenda independent of the president's and still rely on a partnership, either professional or personal, to help in the implementation of such an agenda."[5] The first lady's influence is drawn from her professional qualifications rather than solely from her relationship with the president, and the office of the first lady is increasingly intertwined with that of the president.

Another element of the first lady's evolution is her emergence as a public speaker. Eksterrowicz and Paynter are quick to point out Eleanor Roosevelt's seminal influence on this aspect of the position, as the first spouse to speak at a national convention and hold regular press conferences.[6] The opportunity to address the public provides an additional avenue for researchers who wish to formalize the study of the first lady, as the tools for analyzing rhetoric are well established among scholars in communication and political science. Shawn Parry-Giles and Diane Blair undertake this task with a discerning eye and call our attention to several key findings, which deserve to be quoted at length as they directly pertain to contemporary first ladies, including Michelle Obama:

Historically, most women who moved their political activity from the nongovernmental sphere of volunteerism to a legislative space were, without fail, criticized for overstepping the boundaries of the position. Such public advocacy, nevertheless, helped bring social welfare issues to the political spotlight such that the most recent congressional testimony by a first lady received bipartisan applause; the *Washington Post* praised Laura Bush for having a "brain [that was] full of data and statistics and opinions." First ladies' benevolent discourse not only assisted in eroding some of the negative sentiment over women's rhetor-ical-political activities, but also constructed a public and empowered role for U.S. women.[7]

There is no doubt that first ladies are constricted by gender norms, and the issues they bring to the pulpit are directly influenced by "re-publican motherhood principles."[8] Parry-Giles and Blair go as far as to suggest that many of the contemporary first ladies consciously mimic the performance of those who came before them, in that many of the actions and initiatives they undertake during their time in the White House fall in line with the tradition of benevolent volunteerism estab-lished by their foremothers.[9] The rhetorical turn is crucial, however, be-cause it publicizes and politicizes this tradition of benevolent volunteer-ing and mothering through public speech. The ultimate outcome, as detailed above, is the erosion of the separation between the public and private spheres, and a new model for women's citizenship.

There are cases where first ladies are clearly attached to particular policy initiatives, and we can trace the successes and failures of their legislative efforts, though they themselves are not legislators. Eleanor Roosevelt's efforts during the implementation of the New Deal are well documented; she lobbied on behalf of numerous legislative acts that were passed during her husband's term. More recently, Hillary Clinton was appointed as cochair of a special task force on health care reform at the outset of Bill Clinton's first term, in 1993. Ms. Clinton was involved in a number of related causes prior to her appointment to the task force, and established herself as an explicitly political force from the fist mo-ment she arrived at the White House. However, when the plan put forth by her and her colleague, Ira Magaziner, was defeated in Congress, the backlash was severe. Democrats subsequently lost control of Congress in 1994, and critics pointed to the ambition and divisiveness of Hillary's plan as a reason for the defeat. Clinton then reinvented herself as less of a policy wonk, releasing her book about childcare, *It Takes a Village* (1996), and slipping back into a more motherly public persona.[10]

So even in the case of Clinton, where we can study the presidential spouse as a policy-maker, *the first lady functions as a symbol, first and foremost*. Acknowledgment of the primacy of this symbolic role does not downplay the agency of the women who occupy the office, nor does it constitute an endorsement of the function of the office as it currently stands. Rather, it is to highlight the peculiarity of Michelle Obama's job as one that demands that she serve as a symbol and sign without a robust set of guidelines outlining her nonsymbolic responsibilities. Michelle Obama's standing as the predominant symbol of American womanhood is constantly modulated by the metalanguage of race. A national survey conducted in late 2011 by the *Washington Post* and the Kaiser Family Foundation attests to Michelle's favorable standing with the American public and women in general. Three-fourths of white women and two-thirds of white men reported a positive impression of the first lady. But data also suggest that Michelle's life and public standing are intensely important to black women, who identify Ms. Obama as someone who is familiar to them and who believe that the first lady shares their values and understands their problems, at rates that approach 90 percent, far higher than white respondents.[11] Prevailing representations of black womanhood in America need to be addressed in order to understand Michelle's intersectional social meaning.

Intersectionality and Controlling Images of Black Women

Black feminism is a social movement and intellectual tradition produced by two conjoined forces. First, black women resist their own oppression, advance social criticism, and work for change in the name of social justice. Black feminism is no more and no less than this fact, and we need not make reference to other traditions in order to know it when we see it. Second, the intellectual and political community that explicitly identifies as "black feminist" is constructed with reference to the inadequacy of mainstream, straight, white, bourgeois feminism. Black women and other women of color have historically been excluded from positions of authority in mainstream feminist organizations. Perhaps more importantly, the theories and strategies of mainstream feminism have proven inadequate. For example, if traditional feminism directs women to go into the workforce and embrace their sexuality as two tactics to achieve empowerment, these tactics are at odds with black women's experiences, as generations of black American women have been forced to work and have been denied claims to Puritanical white femininity by the fabrication of black sexual deviance. When feminism—defined as the goal of ending sex and gender oppression—does not prioritize intersections of race, class, sexuality, and other social markers, it falters.[12] If endeavors towards sex and gender justice place too much emphasis on equity and fail to destabilize supposedly monolithic male/female sex and gender categories, they must be reevaluated or paired with more complex criticisms and strategies.[13]

Intersectionality is the cardinal theoretical contribution of black feminism, and it is introduced early in this book without the benefit of a close reading of its initial formulation. In her seminal article "Demarginalizing the Intersection of Race and Sex" (1989), Kimberle Crenshaw presents the concept by highlighting flaws in the treatment of race and sex discrimination by the American legal system. She writes, "in race discrimination cases, discrimination tends to be viewed in terms of sex- or class-privileged Blacks; in sex discrimination cases, the focus is on race- and class-privileged women."[14] This poses two problems. First, there is the obvious epistemological problem; the uniqueness of black women's oppression cannot be comprehended because race and gender are viewed as autonomous discourses and identity markers. This epistemological failure results in a second, material problem: the inability to administer justice. With false understandings of identity in place, an offense can only be registered and corrected when the plaintiff is someone who is already privileged and who can demonstrate that if not for race, *or* class, *or* gender—if not for this one, clearly identifiable source of injustice—she would be treated fairly.[15] Those who are mistreated along multiple axes have no means of redress in court.

Crenshaw warns that the solution to this problem is *not* to insist that every time a black woman is oppressed the oppression is completely unique and unrelated to traditional notions of race and gender oppression. She explains that at times, black women may be victims of traditionally conceived racism and sexism, where discrimination is similar to that of either black men or white women. At other times, these more commonly understood forms of racism and sexism may be layered upon each other, producing a double burden. And finally, there will be occasions when these forces operate in concert to produce specific experiences.[16]

When Crenshaw discusses those forms of discrimination and oppression considered to be traditional, she highlights the fact that they are actually intersectional, by explicitly naming traditional sexism as a particular race/gender intersection: white women's experiences. The fact that some forms of racism are normalized is a function of the way we privilege specific intersections (those dependent on white or male experiences) rather than others. This position should not be taken to its extreme; I am not arguing that every single instance of discrimination or oppression is like a snowflake—totally unique—because there are an infinite number of intersections that influence each subject's identity, and thus each subject's experience. To the contrary, there are patterns in intersectional oppression, and they are manifest in the prevalence of a limited number of compulsively repeated stereotypes and representations of black womanhood.

In her masterpiece, *Black Feminist Thought* (1991), Patricia Hill Collins catalogues four classic racist representations, or "controlling images," of black womanhood.[17] These representations are not entirely separate from each other, for they often overlap and operate in conjunction with one another to restrict and denigrate black womanhood. The first controlling image is the black woman as mammy, a representation born during slavery that romanticizes black women's experience as domestic laborers in white households. The mammy is submissive and obedient to her white masters, loves the white family as if it were her own, and is essentially asexual.

Second, black women are represented as emasculating matriarchs. Scholars have long documented the importance of black women as stewards who contribute economically to black households and therefore exert a different sort of power from that of white American female homemakers. In the 1960s, however, this history was distorted, as black mothers were recast as all-powerful, unfeminine, and at worst, castrating tyrants of the black family. The touchstone moment in this controversy was the release of Senator Daniel Patrick Moynihan's report "The Negro Family: A Case for National Action" (1965).[18] The report argues that the observed uptick in black single-mother households leaves black families especially vulnerable to sustained poverty and problems with child socialization. Without stable employment for black men and women, these trends are likely to continue and yield specific cultural pathology within black families, as black parents are unable to assume traditional roles for their children to emulate. In other words, employment and family structure are linked, and we need to pay attention to both the structural and cultural elements of racial inequality if we wish to improve socioeconomic outcomes for African Americans. The stereotype is built when undue causality is attributed to cultural pathology, and the impact of labor inequality and racism on life outcomes for African Americans is ignored. Black behavior subsumes structure, and the matriarch's hostile demeanor and authority undermine the authority of black men, which causes black familial pathology.

The third controlling image is the black woman as welfare mother. "An updated version of the breeder woman image created during slavery," Collins explains, "this image provides an ideological justification for efforts to harness Black women's fertility to the needs of a changing political economy."[19] This image is grounded in the stereotype of black laziness and blames black mothers for failing to pass on a work ethic. They are prone to having children but do not want to work, and become a strain on the government and the economy. The black welfare mother sees herself as a victim and is constantly complaining rather than working hard to improve her situation.

Finally, black women are represented as jezebels or whores, characters defined by their hypersexuality and predatory orientation towards men. The jezebel originates during slavery to justify white male rape of black women, an indispensable tool of psychological terror and economic exploitation in the American political economy.

These representations are technologically and historically specific and constantly in flux. When they appear in contemporary society, they manifest as updated descendants of their prototypes. The jezebel, for example, remains relevant as a frame for historicizing "video ho" and groupie culture in hip-hop and pop music videos. Matriarchs make frequent appearances in hackneyed situational comedy shows and movies, such as Martin Lawrence's "Big Momma" film franchise. African American slavery is no more, but the smiling, obedient mammy can still be found as the trademark label of Aunt Jemima's syrup and pancake mix; and "baby momma" has become a ubiquitous catchphrase as black vernacular is adopted to mollify and transform the single-welfare-mother stereotype into a colloquial term for the mother of unwanted children, or more playfully, the mother of one's children, or simply a romantic partner.

Each representation centers on the racist notion that black women are sexually deviant.[20] The best-case representation is an asexual, non-threatening caretaker who worships the white family and poses no threat to civility. If she is not a mammy, the black woman is an angry, bitter creature, whose disgusting sexual mores result in personal debasement, the erosion of the black family, and the corruption of the nation-state. As these stereotypes and insults spin on the axis of black women's sexuality, Lisa Thompson's insistence that "conservative sexual behavior is the foundation of the performance of middle-class black womanhood" cannot be overstated.[21] Adopting a politics of respectability is not a new political strategy for black Americans, but the centrality of black women's bodily performance and the denial of sexual agency is elemental to black middle-class women's respectability in a way that it is not for financially stable black men. White women and black men may be able to craft a middle-class image that celebrates their attractiveness or sexuality and allows space for sexual agency. But Thompson argues that in literature, politics, and popular culture, black women's bodies are so rigorously policed that the complete negation and concealment of the body and sexual self is often the only option for black ladies in the public eye. Making it to the middle class does not simply absolve black women of their supposed sexual deviance. Instead, it raises the stakes should they find themselves under scrutiny for their bodily appearance or sexual behavior. The intersectional challenges of being what Thompson calls a "black lady" are especially pertinent to Michelle Obama's status as a cultural icon.

Michelle Obama and Stereotypes of Black Womanhood

Michelle Obama is repeatedly subject to mutations of the racist archetypes explained above. Some of these offenses have flown under the radar. When Fox News ran a caption reading "Outraged Liberals: Stop Picking on Obama's Baby Mama!" during a segment about conservative attacks on Ms. Obama during the 2008 presidential campaign, dissenters objected, but the incident did not become front-page national news.[22] In another incident, Republican congressman Jim Sensenbrenner suggested that Ms. Obama's campaign against obesity could not be taken seriously because she had a "big butt," invoking a classic stereotype of black women's bodily (and sexual) abnormality.[23] Roughly one month after the Sensenbrenner gaffe, Kansas House Speaker Mike O'Neal was publicly embarrassed by the revelation of an e-mail in which he referred to the first lady as "Mrs. YoMama."[24] Relatively speaking, however, these are small blips on the radar screen of racism directed towards Michelle; other controversies, however, became landmark moments of the Obamas' public career.

The dominant classic stereotype applied to Michelle Obama is that of the angry (and emasculating) black woman, which the first lady has explicitly discussed and critiqued. The circulation of this stereotype is complemented by public fascination with any and all conflict between Barack and Michelle Obama, especially those instances reported by Jodi Kantor in her 2012 book, *The Obamas*. Kantor's text focuses on the Obamas during the 2008 campaign and the early days of Barack's first term. Kantor recounts Michelle's frustration with Barack's political career in Chicago, which required then senator Obama to spend long hours apart from his family, and describes multiple disagreements between the first lady and the president's aides. In an interview with CBS News, host Gayle King asked Michelle to respond specifically to the reports of tension between the first lady and the president's staff. Ms. Obama insisted that she had "never had a cross word" with President Obama's first chief of staff, Rahm Emanuel, and that she was almost completely disconnected from the president's staff and all activities in the West Wing of the White House. In accounting for the fact that the relationships described in Kantor's book were deemed shocking or controversial, Michelle explained, "I guess it's more interesting to imagine this conflicted situation here and a strong woman and—you know? But that's been an image that people have tried to paint of me since the day Barack announced, that I'm some angry black woman."[25]

Indeed, Michelle Obama is correct, as the history of this accusation began in earnest on February 18, 2008, at a rally in Milwaukee, Wisconsin. At the event, Ms. Obama proclaimed, "For the first time in my adult lifetime I am really proud of my country. And not just because Barack has done well, but because I think people are hungry for change." The quotation was widely circulated, and the following day, during a rally in Brookfield, Wisconsin, John McCain's wife, Cindy, retorted, "I don't know about you—if you heard those words earlier—I'm very proud in my country."[26] The gauntlet was thrown down.

Two days later, on February 20, Ms. Obama clarified her comments, stating that she has always been proud of her country and specifying that her initial remarks were about pride in the political process rather than America as a whole.[27] This explanation might have sufficed, if not for the events of the following week. On February 26, Michelle's senior undergraduate thesis was released to the public by Princeton University. Written in 1985, Ms. Obama's thesis features interviews with current and former black Princeton students. The paper describes her experience at Princeton, where she frequently felt alienated from and disregarded by white students and faculty. In the text, Michelle concludes that even if she were to continue to integrate herself into white society, she would always remain on the margins.[28] However, when the thesis was released to the public, it was distorted by opponents of the Obama campaign, such as Fox News host Sean Hannity, who erroneously claimed that the thesis advocates that blacks "join in solidarity to combat a white oppressor," misattributing a statement from one of Michelle's respondents for a sentiment held by Ms. Obama herself.[29]

In concert with Michelle's comments from the previous week, the thesis provided ample ammunition for opponents of the Obama campaign to level accusations about her suitability as a first lady and, by extension, Barack's patriotism. The form that these attacks take is especially significant for the purposes of this discussion: Michelle Obama is cast not simply as unpatriotic but as bitter, threatening, and angry. Perhaps the most infamous example of Ms. Obama's characterization as a black female deviant is the much-publicized controversy surrounding the cartoon illustration of Barack and Michelle Obama on the cover of the June 21, 2008, issue of the *New Yorker*. The image, intended as a satirical statement about the absurdity of accusations that Mr. and Ms. Obama are anti-American radicals, is an example of a cartoonist, Barry Blitt, and an editor misevaluating the impact of releasing an image into the public sphere. After the controversy ensued, Blitt publicly stated, "I think the idea that the Obamas are branded as unpatriotic [let alone as terrorists] in certain sectors is preposterous. It seemed to me that depicting the concept would show it as the fear-mongering ridiculousness that it is."[30] But ultimately, the satire was either misunderstood by too many people or deemed an insufficient excuse for producing yet another image of Obama as terrorist.

Blitt's cartoon depicts Barack and Michelle standing and facing one another in the center of a circular, colonial-style room. Barack stands on the right side of the drawing, and in the background, to his right and behind him, a framed portrait of Osama bin Laden hangs on the wall. A fireplace, complete with the American flag engulfed in its flames, appears beneath the bin Laden portrait. Obama is dressed in sandals, a tan thobe, and a white kufi, again poking fun at the false belief that he supports Muslim extremism or is a Muslim in disguise. Barack and Michelle are engaged in a "fist bump," or "dap," a congratulatory maneuver analogous to a handshake or high five, wherein two people gently bump their fists together in celebration. This depiction is a tongue-in-cheek reference to the events of June 3, 2008, when Barack Obama became the presumptive nominee for the Democratic Party, and he fist-bumped Michelle after she introduced him at a rally that day. Fox News anchor

E. D. Hill flippantly dubbed this act of congratulations and encouragement as "a terrorist fist jab" during a June 6, 2008, broadcast. Ms. Hill
apologized during the next show, but it was not enough to keep her job,
as her program was replaced the following week.

Michelle appears facing Barack on the left side of the drawing. Her
outfit is strangely mismatched, as she has donned a stylish, long-sleeve
black V-neck top and camouflage-print military pants and boots. She
carries a large automatic rifle on her back, suspended by a diagonal
front strap that doubles as an ammunition belt. Ms. Obama's head is
tilted downward as she looks up at her partner with a determined, yet
approving expression, similar to her expression in the much circulated
media photo of the initial fist bump. Michelle's hair acts as a poignant
signifier in the cartoon, as she wears it in an Afro rather than her usual
straightened perm.

Ms. Obama's outfit is designed to conjure recollections of the Black
Panther Party and the more militant black nationalists and black sepa-
ratist elements of the civil rights movement. The Black Panther Party's
supposed penchant for brandishing guns is tied to its original mission,
which placed explicit emphasis on self-defense from physical attacks by
the American government or ordinary citizens. Black nationalist ideologies are fundamentally concerned with political self-determination
and economic sustainability, but the rapid dissemination of images of
armed Black Panther protestors transformed the public image of black
nationalism into a violent threat to civil society. Characterizations of the
Panthers as violent and threatening is part and parcel of a larger effort
by conservatives to paint all civil rights groups as agitators and criminals
with no respect for the rule of law. The "tough on crime" discourse of
the late twentieth century was racially encoded within the DNA of the
civil rights movement, as protestors' willingness to ignore unjust Jim
Crow laws was recast as further evidence of an unchanging culture of
black criminality.[31] Of course, Michelle was not an active participant in
the civil rights protests of the 1950s and 1960s, as she was born in 1964,
and the cartoonist, Blitt, intends to mock the notion that Ms. Obama is
a militant black nationalist (or a criminal) at heart.

The *New Yorker* cartoon contains layered meaning that can only be unpacked using intersectional analysis. As I've argued, racial meaning intersects with discourses of nationhood, and the link between whiteness and American identity is undeniable. Though the caricatures here of Michelle and Barack are ethnically distinct, as Barack is Arab and Michelle is African American, their exaggerated nonwhiteness complements the burning American flag in the fireplace. Class signifiers contribute to the visual friction of the cartoon, as both Mr. and Ms. Obama eschew the business or formal attire we might expect to be worn in such an opulent room: Barack wears sandals and Michelle wears combat boots. And of course, gender is writ large in the illustration, especially in Michelle's case, as her outfit, accessories, posture, and facial expression connote a form of aggression far afield from acceptable markers of femininity. These discourses are woven together as the Obamas are cast as intruders in the American temple, disturbing the gods and violating social norms.

Though he may have failed in the eyes of many, Blitt intended to deface the Obamas' critics rather than aid in the defamation of Michelle and Barack's public image. However, a gaggle of other commentators who disapproved of the Obamas' candidacy seemed to honestly believe that Michelle was bitter and angry, and attempted to convince the public that she was an acerbic, unpleasant character and a serious threat to the country. Many of these accusations were printed in the pages of the *National Review*, a long-standing conservative magazine founded in 1955 by William F. Buckley. In a three-week period between April 21 and May 7, 2008, the *National Review* ran an assortment of articles in print and online elaborating on the criticism born from Michelle's thesis and "proud of America" comment.[32] The exemplar of this sequence of stories is Mark Steyn's article, entitled "Mrs. Obama's America," which serves as the cover story for the April 21, 2008, print issue. The cover itself features a photograph of Ms. Obama, brow lowered, mouth opened in midsentence, a finger pointed at the reader, and a look of steely admonishment befitting a Harvard-trained lawyer. It is a decidedly threatening image, shrewdly chosen by the editors, and the caption below reads, "Mrs. Grievance: Michelle Obama and Her Discontent."[33] Steyn applies a critical eye to Michelle's thesis, and his argument about her discontent requires close reading:

The thesis is dopey, illiterate, and bizarrely punctuated, but so are the maunderings of many American students. What makes Miss Robinson's youthful opus relevant is that the contradictions it agonizes over have dominated her life. Indeed, her apparent bitterness at a society that has given her blessings she could not have enjoyed anywhere else on earth seems explicitly to derive from her inability to live either as an "integrationist who is ignorant to [the] plight" of "the Black lower class" or a "separationist" embracing its hopelessness and "desperation." Instead, she rode her privileged education to wealth and success and then felt bad about it. That's why she talks about money—her money—more than any other contender for first lady ever has: It's like an ongoing interior monologue about whether she sold out for too cheap a price.

Steyn's claim is not simply that Ms. Obama has an uncontrollable temper or that she has unbridled, unfocused contempt for the world she lives in. Nor is her problem the same as the diagnosis applied to Barack Obama by pedantic shock jock Glenn Beck, who believes that the president has "a deep seated hatred for white people or the white culture."[34] After plainly dismissing Michelle as a thinker and writer, Steyn condemns not only Michelle's anger but also her reason for it. Steyn and his compatriots at the *National Review* are aghast because, in their view, Michelle Obama has nothing to complain about. She has led a life of relative privilege, directly facilitated by the opportunities provided to her in the openly democratic and highly meritocratic society that is the United States. Steyn is dismayed because Michelle has the audacity to criticize America during and after college, even though, to use Barack Obama's words, "in no other country on earth is [her] story even possible."[35]

When Michelle Obama was booed at a NASCAR event in November 2011, Rush Limbaugh picked up where Steyn left off, explaining that the crowd was simply reacting to Michelle's "uppity" tendencies: "They [the crowd] understand it is a little bit of uppity-ism. First ladies have not been known to hop their own 757s four hours ahead of their husband when they're going to the same place."[36] Notice the intersectionality of this attack. The notion of presumptuousness, or "uppity, ism," as sin is based on racist, retrograde beliefs about blacks' acceptance of their subservient social status and the proper deference they were supposed to show to white people. Here, Limbaugh rides the racial undertow of this idea as he asserts that Michelle has forgotten not only her racial station but her proper behavior as a woman, who should know better than to upstage her husband by arriving on a separate flight. This new black womanly threat is in fact a descendant of a phenomenon identified three decades before: the black superwoman.

The New Black Superwoman

As the name suggests, the black superwoman is a figure of exorbitant strength. In her initial formulation of the black superwoman (who was not yet uppity), Michelle Wallace characterizes this mythical strength as one forged in the fire of black women's labor in arduous and undignified jobs. She is fearless and unbreakable because she has been through the worst in life. Her labor makes her physically stronger than most women, and therefore less feminine. However, the black superwoman's femininity is preserved thanks to her infinite emotional reservoir. She somehow perseveres through the mess and muck of her miserable job, while simultaneously serving as the caretaker, the leader, and the mother of the black community.[37] Wallace theorizes the black superwoman from her own experience, and she understands its connection to the long-held racist beliefs about black women as emasculating matriarchs.[38] The brilliance of her explication of black superwomanhood, however, is that Wallace describes its intuitive and seductive quality, not only for those who wish to deny or obscure black women's oppression but even for herself and others who experience and loath racism and controlling representations of black womanhood. She writes:

This woman does not have the same fears, weaknesses, and insecurities as other women, but believes herself to be and is, in fact, stronger emotionally than most men. Less of a woman in that she is less "feminine" and helpless, she is really *more* of a woman in that she is the embodiment of Mother Earth, the quintessential mother with infinite sexual, life-giving, and nurturing reserves.

In other words, she is a superwoman. . . . Even now I can hear my reader thinking, *Of course she is stronger. Look what she's been through. She would have to be. Of course she's not like other women.* Even for me, it continues to be difficult to let the myth go. Naturally black women want very much to believe it; in a way, it is all we have.[39]

↦ Rooted in muleness

The superwoman is not a representation that justifies black women's debasement. It is constructed with noble intentions, and it begins from the recognition of black women's oppression. People of goodwill, with the earnest desire to see black women treated with the respect they deserve, may exalt the superwoman as a tribute to black women's accomplishments. In spite of herself, Wallace clings to the myth out of desperation. When she surveys the range of popular representations of self that she may choose from, the superwoman is by far the most honorable. But the more she is celebrated, the more silent the superwoman grows with respect to the fallacies of the myth.

Wallace published her book in 1978, but the discourse of black superwomanhood remains relevant in the twenty-first century due to developments over the last thirty years that Wallace could not have predicted. Steyn's and Limbaugh's criticism of Michelle Obama as an uppity modern professional who speaks and acts beyond her proper station in life is a new form of racist portrayals of black womanhood. Tropes of the angry, emasculating "black bitch" combine with Wallace's superwoman and Thompson's black lady. *The black woman's super strength is no longer derived solely from her infinite emotional reserves, her mythic power to hold black communities together, or her impeccable self-denial as a sexual being. Black women's present-day, publicly displayed super strength is augmented by perceptions of her economic power: this is how she has become uppity.* The temptation to herald black women's accomplishments is bolstered when the socioeconomic situation of black women as a group is compared to that of women from other racial and ethnic groups, as well as black men. Thompson explains that one of the key reasons the black lady is perversely imagined as a social problem on par with the other damaging stereotypes of black womanhood is that her class status "appears to usurp what is considered the appropriate leadership position of the black male. The white majority considers the black lady a problem because it assumes that her successes are gained at the expense of others (whites, males) supposedly more deserving."[40] Hip-hop feminist Joan Morgan makes this dichotomy quite clear, as she explains that though she is strong, black, and female, her rejection of the "STRONGBLACKWOMAN" label is simultaneously a rejection of the idea of the "ENDANGEREDBLACKMAN." Too often, Morgan writes, strong black women accept the limitations of endangered black manhood, with dire personal and political consequences.[41]

As Cecilia Conrad notes, in 2008 black women were the primary breadwinners in 44 percent of black families with children, while across families of all races and ethnicities, women were primary breadwinners in only 24 percent of cases. Additionally, the income accumulated by black women breadwinners accounts for over 32 percent of all black family income, a proportion that far eclipses the aggregate percentage of women's contributions across all groups—roughly 14 percent.[42] These data fall in line with black women's labor history, and relative to other female wage earners in America, black women's heroics as wage earners are no myth.

Not only are black women celebrated for their indispensability to black families' economic solvency; they are celebrated for their matriculation into more elite socioeconomic strata. As her critics at the *National Review* point out, Ms. Obama is a member of the bourgeoisie. She does not scrub floors or care for white people's children. Instead, she holds degrees from Princeton and Harvard, and has worked as a corporate lawyer and well-paid public relations director for a major hospital. Michelle's education and work experience are not representative of the majority of black women, but they do hint at larger trends in black women's educational attainment during the thirty years after Wallace's book. Economist Mark J. Perry draws on estimates compiled by the Department of Education in 2009, highlighting that black women drastically outpace black men and that the gap in degree attainment between the sexes has severely worsened since 1977.[43] Table 5.1 shows the rates at which black women are awarded degrees for every one hundred black men who reach a corresponding education level.

TABLE 5.1. Rates at which black women are
awarded degrees (per 100 black men)

	1976–1977	2008–2009
Associate's	116.3	217.5
Bachelor's	133.2	193.3
Master's	170.4	254.6
Doctor's	63.6	198.5
Professional	44.1	163.1

Source: Mark J. Perry, 2012. Data from U.S. Department of
Education, Institute of Education Sciences.

Black men have a 32 percent chance of being incarcerated at some
point in their lives, and there is no doubt that the disproportionate
explosion in black male incarceration derails their prospects of educational attainment and steady employment from adolescence onward.
As of 2007, black women were incarcerated at a rate of 380 per 100,000
United States residents, a rate six times that of white women. But relative to black men, who were incarcerated at a rate of 4,618 per 100,000
residents in 2007, the rate for black women is considerably less severe.[44]
The idea of modern-day black superwomanhood is derived from comparing black women's situation to both black men and to women of different races and ethnicities. At surface level, black women's sociological
situation appears worthy of celebration and admiration, especially when
professional success is complemented with the sexual ethos demanded
by the politics of respectability.

But just as Wallace deconstructed the insidious ideology of the
superwoman myth in 1978, we must call attention to the misleading,
data-driven aura of uppity black superwomanhood in the twenty-first
century. A closer look at the quantitative evidence reveals disturbing
and durable inequality. Again, Conrad's work is especially helpful, as
she points out that black women's unemployment rate is roughly two
times the rates of both white men and white women. Black women's
poverty rates more than double those of white women, and they nearly

double those of black men. In the last quarter of the twentieth century, white women's median earnings grew by 32 percent, but black women's earnings lagged behind, showing only 22 percent growth. Perhaps most damning, as of 2005, when working the same hours, black women earned 87 cents for every dollar earned by a black man, 85 cents for every dollar earned by a white woman, and 63 cents for every dollar earned by a white man.[45]

A sharper focus on these statistics reveals even more dire circumstances for black women. Becky Pettit and Stephanie Ewert warn that studying the racial wage gap between black and white women is misleading, because the wage gap underestimates the depth of racial inequality by ignoring women who are unemployed.[46] Yvonne Newsome and Nii-Amoo Dodoo demonstrate that the 1960s and 1970s saw reduced occupational segregation and significant wage gains for both black men and black women, and that black women achieved virtual wage parity with white women by 1975. Unfortunately, the 1980s brought wage stagnation and exacerbated racial inequality among female workers.[47] Both black and white women benefited from employment gains during the dusk of the twentieth century, but black women are at far greater risk of joblessness, especially during an economic recession. The wage gap between white women and black women is partially driven by widening gaps in education, marriage, and region (residence in places without easy access to cities). Clearly, these three arenas are impacted by historically generated inequality resulting from the intersection of race- and class-based oppression. But even when the gaps in education, marriage, and region are considered cultural and nonmalicious inequities, or residue from an unfortunate but unchangeable past, much of the contemporary variance remains unexplained, which means that classic race/gender discrimination remains a factor in the current era.[48] All of these results are contextualized by well-documented declines in government jobs and a reactionary political climate that is hostile to the maintenance and expansion of equal opportunity and affirmative action programs.[49]

Michelle Obama came of age during the last quarter of the twentieth century, and she is one of many black American women from her generation who achieved upward economic mobility. Her story is cause for celebration, and her professional accomplishments should be admired. The danger arises when Ms. Obama's hypervisibility and her job as a symbol of American womanhood are mistaken for typical black women's experience. When black women are cast as invulnerable superwomen who have already "made it" in America, it detracts attention from the fragility of recent economic gains and the need for continued vigilance in the fight against intersectional oppression.

In addition, the superwoman's ladylike performance of highly reserved sexuality has particular implications for notions of marriage and family.

The Obamas and the Politics of Marriage and Family

The labor market analysis points to structural dimensions of contemporary oppression, but cultural forces exert their influence as well. The racist narrative suggests that failure to secure marriage partners leads to a cultural adaptation that makes black women more angry and therefore less feminine and desirable as partners, to men. Even when the most sexually desirable controlling image, the jezebel, is ascribed to black women, their sexuality is cast as threatening, and their prospects for long-term partnership are equally dim. The modern-day uppity superwoman has it just as bad. She is too focused on her job, too successful, and therefore too threatening to men who are only comfortable with traditional (sexist) patriarchal gender arrangements where men control the economic fate of the family and women's authority is confined to the domestic sphere.

In this context, it is tempting to identify marriage as the magical elixir. It is the key not only to escape for uppity black superwomen imprisoned by their own success but to black socioeconomic advancement. The chorus of calls for marriage rises from points across the political spectrum, from right-wing pro-family advocacy groups to minister Louis Farrakhan and the Nation of Islam. This is a romantic solution to the complex social problems born from the intersections of race, class, and gender politics; yet, prioritizing marriage at the expense of other strategies, or worse, insisting that marriage is the only active ingredient necessary for changing supposed black cultural pathology, is a mistake. Sociologist Kris Marsh and her colleagues highlight two critical flaws in the marriage-as-silver-bullet approach.[50] First, researchers who equate married-couple status with middle-class status often fixate on income, without taking expenditure into account. The most glaring analytic defect that runs parallel to this oversight is that family size (number of children) is an often-ignored component of studies on marriage and the black middle class. The second issue Marsh highlights gets at the core of the problem: causality. Marriage does not cause people to become middle class. Frequently, middle-class people seek to preserve their status through marriage, and poor people are unable to transcend their disadvantaged position through marriage. This point, about the lack of rational economic incentive for impoverished people to marry, is at the core of Wilson's research in *The Truly Disadvantaged* (1987). When Wilson's work was swept up into popular discourse, however, conservative critics adopted and adapted the argument into one about deviant and racialized cultural pathology in ghetto communities, a cultural pathology resistant to structural interventions, such as reversing labor market trends.

The error of overemphasizing marriage is plain to see when we affirm the intersectionality of gender, class, and race as the ties that bind cultural nonconformity and structural inequality. Marriage does not eliminate poverty, guarantee happiness, or eradicate racist and sexist stereotypes of black womanhood. Moreover, these explanations for black superwomen's partnering predicament and black familial cultural deviance almost uniformly assume heterosexuality as the norm. Queer people are almost completely erased from the discourse of racial inequality and from stereotypes of black masculinity and femininity. The inability to account for other versions of romantic partnership and familial life is a sure sign of the limits of the half-century-old black family debate as a useful frame for understanding and addressing inequality.

With these caveats in mind, studying the Obamas' relationship and family life is vital to understanding their appeal. Despite the fact that the Obamas are several financial echelons above middle-class standing, both Barack and Michelle Obama recognize their hypervisibility as pillars of a middle-class black family ideal that explodes stereotypes, and each public figure intervenes on the black family debate. Michelle explains, "When I was growing up in the '80s, 'The Cosby Show' meant so much to African-American families. A lot of people looked at the Huxtables and thought, 'There's no way that family exists.' But many African-Americans knew differently. If we don't see those images then the people don't believe they exist."[51]

President Obama writes about his partnership with Michelle in *The Audacity of Hope*, where he describes his courtship with his wife and the family life they have built together. He readily admits that he has failed at times to enact an equitable division of familial labor, and that Michelle has unfairly born the brunt of his choice to enter into public life, as she has assumed the lion's share of childcare and put her career on hold. Despite this failure, his reverence for family life is palpable. The first time Barack encounters Michelle's family, the Robinsons, he is struck by a sense of stability and place that characterizes their household.[52] Obama is forthright about the difference between Michelle's family upbringing and his own: his father was largely absent; his childhood was divided between two continents; and ultimately, his grandparents performed the vast majority of the parenting.

Barack's reflections on his romantic courtship with Michelle and the meaning he draws from her family speak to the broader sociological issues discussed here. Immediately after describing his relationship with the Robinsons in *The Audacity of Hope*, he laments that among African Americans, "the nuclear family is on the verge of collapse. Since 1950, the marriage rate for black women has plummeted from 62 percent to 36 percent. . . . today 54 percent of all African American children live in single parent households, compared to about 23 percent of all white children."[53] He stops short of addressing the black community directly in the text, approaching these issues from a perspective similar to that of sociologists who highlight that income from two adults has become a necessity in the contemporary economy, and that families without dual-income streams are at a severe disadvantage. In the book, Obama displays awareness of the ways "family values" discourse is tethered to the policy goals of groups that seek to restrain women's reproductive rights and prevent gay and lesbian couples from marrying. Ultimately, he issues a firm statement against the regressive movement for "traditional" marriage, where sexuality outside of marriage is condemned and women's rights and social roles are severely restricted.[54]

While he is careful not to posit marriage as a magic solution, Obama acknowledges the economic and social problems caused by a dearth of two-parent households among African Americans as a legitimate issue. Obama spoke directly to black Americans during his 2008 presidential campaign in a speech delivered to the Apostolic Church of God, a historically black church in Chicago, on Father's Day, June 15, 2008. In this speech, Obama addresses black men specifically.

If we are honest with ourselves, we'll admit that what too many fathers also are is missing—missing from too many lives and too many homes. They have abandoned their responsibilities, acting like boys instead of men. And the foundations of our families are weaker because of it. You and I know how true this is in the African-American community. We know that more than half of all black children live in single-parent households, a number that has doubled—doubled—since we were children. We know the statistics—that children who grow up without a father are five times more likely to live in poverty and commit crime; nine times more likely to drop out of schools and twenty times more likely to end up in prison. They are more likely to have behavioral problems, or run away from home, or become teenage parents themselves. And the foundations of our community are weaker because of it.[55]

Significantly, Obama stops short of advocating specifically for marriage as the sole resolution. The remainder of the speech emphasizes fathers' responsibilities to their children: supporting them financially and emotionally, spending time with them, and teaching them empathy and the value of education. Unlike right-wing "family values" discourse, Obama's speech affirms the necessity of complementary progressive legislation, such as training programs for fathers paying child support and bolstering the Earned Income Tax Credit. He mentions the fact that when he was a young man his mission in life was navigating his own course, and that fatherhood has changed that mission into a quest to leave a better world behind for his children.

Of course, this mission is more difficult to manage for women, who continue to bear primary responsibility for domestic tasks and child-rearing in modern American families, despite their gains in the paid labor force. Even in straight married families like the Obamas, where each parent is aware of women's double burden as domestic and public laborers, the scale remains tipped in men's favor. During her time in the White House, Michelle has described herself as "Mom in Chief" and emphasized her job as a public figure as one she views through the lens of motherhood. "More than anything else," Ms. Obama has explained, "I come at this as a mom. When I think about the issues facing our nation, I think about what it means for my girls . . . and I think about what it means for the world we're leaving for them and for all our children. As I travel around this country, and look into the eyes of every single child I meet, I see what's at stake."[56] We cannot know what Michelle's intentions were when she made these comments. But again, intent is beside the point. These ideas certainly impact the disagreement over Michelle's "proper place" in the White House, and may soothe those who are whipped up in a panic about the first lady's supposed nature as an uppity black superwoman. Michelle's words also directly counteract more archaic racist controlling images of black womanhood, as she constructs herself as a loving and caring figure rather than an "angry black woman," and as a proud and responsible parent rather than the lazy "welfare queen."

Emphasis on parenthood and managing different responsibilities is not the same as emphasizing marriage. Michelle explained the toll this has taken on her during her speech to a largely black audience at Howard University.

This issue is something that I have dealt with my whole life, trying to figure out how to juggle work-family balance in the process of getting an education. There isn't a day that goes by, particularly after having kids, that I don't wonder or worry about whether I'm doing the right thing for myself, for my family, for my girls. So I think this issue is particularly important for us to tackle, not just as women but men, as well. . . . The one message that I have is for all of you struggling with this issue, is just remember there is no right answer. It took me a long time to figure that out. There is no one right way to do any of this. And the choices and the decisions will change, given your circumstances.[57]

The humility and flexibility embedded in this answer are crucial, again, because Michelle Obama seems to be the modern black woman who has it all—and perhaps she does. But her seemingly effortless embodiment of the American family/marriage ideal, valuable as it might be as a symbol of respectable blackness that counteracts racism, is not in fact her day-to-day reality as a working mother and wife. Michelle Obama is not merely a superwoman icon; she is human, and she struggles. Ms. Obama does not simply instruct her audience to be strong and follow her lead, or strive to embody the mythic, heterosexual middle-class white nuclear family model; she wants young people to improvise and adjust. One of the most important adjustments young adults can make in the pursuit of a happy and healthy family life is to rely on informal networks for support. As Michelle tells Katie Couric,

I know the struggles of trying to balance work/life/family. And I know that it's something that every woman that I know is struggling with. . . . The only way that I manage every day is because of all these informal support structures in my life, whether it's my mom or a set of girlfriends or the flexibility on a job because I'm a vice president and I can set my hours when I need to. I've managed because of that. But how on earth are single-parent mothers doing it, nurses and teachers and folks who are on shifts?[58]

This is not a staunch commitment to the imagined heteronormative white bourgeois nuclear family ideal, nor is it a condemnation of single mothers. Instead, Michelle actually identifies with single mothers, pointing out that her struggles as a happily married mother of two are similar to those of women who cannot rely on a partner to shoulder the burdens of raising and providing for children. Ms. Obama deconstructs the imagined ideal of the superstrong and self-sufficient wife-mother-professional, and points to informal networks as extended family, indispensable elements for child-rearing[59] as well as her own mental health. But this is not the only way Ms. Obama breaks free from traditional and updated stereotypes of black womanhood. Michelle's response to her constrained position betwixt and between various stereotypes of black womanhood is to attack the core of the problem: the regulation of black women's bodies and their sexuality.

Body Language and Love's Revolution

When Michelle Obama revealed the "secret" to her workout for perfectly toned arms, it became national news.[60] This revelation, however, did not quell the debate and fascination over the gender politics surrounding this particular body part,[61] as CNN and *Fitness* magazine are two of the many outlets that use Michelle's arms as the ideal goal of suggested workout plans.[62] Michelle has gracefully weathered the storm of public attention about her workout regimen by turning health and fitness into one of her defining public issues, with the "Let's Move!" campaign. But the story about Michelle's arms is not an innocent case of celebrity flattery or fitness gossip; it is part and parcel of the American public's obsessive concern with the public presentation of Ms. Obama's body.

Ms. Obama's body is under absurd scrutiny, and in many cases the connections to intersectional race/gender stereotypes are painfully clear. While noting that the media is responsible for her status as a symbol representing all black women, she simultaneously validates the notion that black women do look to her as a reflection of themselves. "When Black women see me," Michelle says, "they recognize themselves in me. Whether it's my shape, my dress, the way I walk."[63] If there is one body image issue about Michelle that trumps the ongoing arms story, it is her choice of clothing. Jackie O's ghost appears once again, as commentators frequently invoke Onassis with reference to Michelle's fashion sense; "Mrs.-O," a highly trafficked blog "dedicated to following the fashion of Mrs. Obama," has been featured by seemingly every major newspaper and publication in the country, including the *Wall Street Journal*, the *New York Times*, and the *Washington Post*.[64] For a glamorous celebrity, Ms. Obama has crafted a decidedly down-to-earth public image that is a weapon against the uppity black superwoman stereotype. This image is reflected in Ms. Obama's frequently "off the rack" clothing choices, as her fashion sense is heralded for being just as refined as Jackie's but more sensible—proof that she is not the bourgeois elite that her education, occupation, and income would suggest. In *Everyday Icon: Michelle Obama and the Power of Style* (2011), Kate Betts makes the case that Michelle's embrace of her role as a fashion trailblazer breaks down the dichotomy between style and substance, and challenges the notion that for women, playing it safe with one's wardrobe is a prerequisite for being taken seriously as an intellectual. As bell hooks points out, "Rigid feminist dismissal of female longings for beauty has undermined feminist politics."[65] Celebrating a woman's effort to actively construct herself as beautiful and, for that matter, sexual is not capitulation to patriarchy and sexism. When beauty and sexuality are rooted in infantilization and objectification, and physical appearance chokes out women's intellectual expression, we have a problem.

Betts points out that when Barack Obama clinched the Democratic Party's nomination in June 2008, Michelle's approval rating stalled at 43 percent. From that point on, Michelle ditched the "corporate armor of sleek jackets and pantsuits" in favor of a more comfortable, colorful, and traditionally feminine aesthetic. After crossing the 50 percent approval threshold, she has never dipped below the halfway mark again. A cynic might argue that Michelle Obama has shrewdly accommodated the norms of respectable middle-class womanhood and that she does not deserve to be called a trailblazer simply because she follows the fashion advice of the Obamas' public relations team. But even if we dismiss the political import of her clothing choices, we are confronted with another set of bodily acts that imbue the first lady with revolutionary political significance: the way Michelle and Barack express their love for each other in public displays of affection.

As noted above, the key to creating oppressive black female stereotypes that live in the American imagination is to demonize, regulate, and desecrate black women's sexuality. Moreover, in the contemporary culture industry, black bodies have long been circulated as voiceless icons designed to bestow consumables of all kinds with the stamp of mythic physicality, danger, and sexual power. In some cases, such as Michael Jordan's trademark silhouette, which appears as the stamp of athletic virtuosity on Nike's Jordan Brand basketball clothing line, these bodies circulate as derivatives of themselves. In other cases, live bodies become the stamps of power; hoards of scantily clad black and brown women decorate the videos of hip-hop's most recognizable stars.

Michelle and Barack's use of their bodies in public displays of love and affection is revolutionary for at least three reasons. First, as historian Stephanie Coontz observes, "We've seen love in the White House before, but in many cases it was the adoring wife, along the lines of Nancy Reagan. What the Obamas have is a jocular, playful love, a mutual respect, and on Michelle's part, a lack of awe and of adoration."[66] Even without an intersectional lens, this poses a clear challenge to the idea of the first lady. Second, the Obamas carry out acts of intimacy that are leagues away from the vulgar sexualization of love and romance that permeates so much of American popular culture. Photographs of Michelle and Barack dancing, touching each other gently and laughing, looking at each other amorously, and holding hands portray romance and underlying sexual attraction as fundamentally cooperative and subjective phenomena rather than explosions triggered by the visual stimuli of objectified bodies or body parts.[67]

Finally, Barack and Michelle are *black sexual beings with voices rather than icons or symbols silenced by the metalanguage of race.* As mentioned earlier, Barack Obama writes extensively about his love for Michelle in *The Audacity of Hope,* demonstrating awareness that the meaning of their love resonates beyond their two-person partnership. Michelle reinforces this truth as she describes her physical intimacy with her husband.

My oldest daughter, now that she's ten, she's very precocious, and now can really articulate how she feels about this stuff. And she says, "you know, it makes me feel good to see you and dad hold hands." We forget about that, or we think that they don't care about that. But they like the fact that they know that we love each other. . . . They want to know that my mother and father love each other, and if they love each other that much, they're going to love me.[68]

This statement illustrates a connection between the bodily language of love (holding hands) and the stability of the family unit. Michelle reframes displays of affection between her and Barack as public statements received and interpreted by onlookers, including her children. It is important to maintain intersectional discipline and acknowledge the privileges enjoyed by the Obamas. This is not just "black love." This is black love glamorized and legitimized because the couple is straight, married, wealthy, and monoracial (assuming Barack is considered solely black). But even as Michelle Obama benefits from those elements of her social identity that bestow her with privilege, her bodily enactment, self-awareness, and public statements about intimacy shatter stereotypes and expand the range of publicly available representations of black womanhood.

Superwoman's Fight

Despite Michelle Obama's negotiation of the racist stereotypes and scripts she is subject to, three major concerns remain. America celebrates Michelle Obama in no small part because she comes as close as a black woman can to the normative, sexist, racist, and bourgeois ideal of honorable femininity. The danger is that Ms. Obama stands as proof that this ideal is a morally legitimate goal for black women (indeed, all women) to aspire to, when crippling structural disadvantages and discrimination restrict social mobility for black women at all class levels and, more broadly, all working-class Americans. Though Michelle repeatedly troubles these expectations, continuing the fight against stereotypes of black womanhood requires action on multiple fronts. It is not enough to demand that women with symbolic cachet continue to use their voices to add layers to the flat representations most commonly available. Serious changes to the structural economy are necessary. Not only do data demonstrate that old-fashioned race- and sex-based discrimination continue to pollute the labor market; the socioecological conditions in which impoverished black people live isolate black Americans from functioning schools and the legitimate economy. Cultural concerns about social disorganization, including familial instability and an absence of healthy role models, spring from this inadequate structural and ecological foundation.

Second, despite Ms. Obama's visibility and the increased attention paid to representations of black womanhood, we are still missing the link that connects conversations about black women's oppression to greater patterns of social injustice. Clearly, black women deal with different sets of intersecting challenges from those of other oppressed groups, but the systems of oppression are connected. Rather than simply debunking racist and sexist depictions of the first lady as they make their way into the public sphere, commentators and critics should explain how representations of black women are injurious to all marginalized groups, because they depend upon entrenched class privilege, straight privilege, male privilege, and white privilege.

Third, black women in the public eye, including Michelle Obama, remain under pressure to suppress their anger and frustration due to the risk of being labeled "angry black women." The silence and public secrecy explained in the opening chapter of this book weigh especially heavily on women of color due to the intersectional demands of "honorable," sexist, femininity. In "The Uses of Anger" (1981), Audre Lorde explains that fear of anger prevents all of us, especially women, from understanding racism (which is hostile by definition) and adequately addressing it. Expressing anger, rather than burying it, is fundamental to resisting racism and, for Lorde, an important step in her own personal growth.[69] Lorde emphasizes that anger is loaded with information and energy that must be translated into action while its power is ripe for use. Michelle Obama has handled public scrutiny and racist criticism with uncommon grace; her actions have deflected and deflated the stereotypes of black womanhood at every opportunity. But the stereotypes were never legitimate to begin with, and they do not depend on black women's behavior for their vitality, so Michelle remains a target no matter which tactics of resistance she uses. It would be devastatingly powerful to see someone with the symbolic weight accorded by the office of the first lady broaden her repertoire of resistance by standing up and saying, "I am furious about the way black women are portrayed and discussed, and about racism and sexism in all their forms."

Perhaps such an emancipatory proclamation lies in Michelle Obama's future; we do not yet know the arc of her career as a public figure. Hillary Clinton provides a less radical model for the transition from the office of the first lady to electoral politics, and at this stage of their respective careers Michelle's political prospects compare favorably to Hillary's. Regardless of the path she chooses, Michelle will remain an icon of black womanhood with an unreasonable burden to represent those who identify with her. She will not please all of her constituents all of the time, and she cannot be "every woman," as funk/soul music legend Chaka Khan might suggest. But as long as she continues to speak out about her own social position and the public and private issues she negotiates, Michelle provides material for teachers and culture workers to produce feminist criticism and construct black women "in a broader sense" than has been previously imagined.

CHAPTER 6

A PLACE CALLED "OBAMA"

We live our lives in literal terms, not metaphorical ones. . . .
Barack Obama is simply a man and a president. His election is best
understood as a passing respite, a brief moment of rest before it
falls to us to once again turn our shoulder to the wheel of history.
—*William Jelani Cobb*[1]

In looking at one of the most famous celebrities in the world, my purpose is not to expose or gossip about Barack Obama's private life, nor is to provide a pseudo-psychological account of what makes him tick. Instead, my goal is to explain how racial meaning is generated and how race does its work. When we speak of the political power and cultural influence of celebrities like Obama, we are not just speaking about the purposeful interventions of such figures. To talk about the political power of celebrities is to affirm the ways their mass-mediated actions, and our reactions to them, echo throughout and shape our lives. Centering sociological or otherwise scholarly texts on prominent historical figures should not be misread as hero worship, biography, or "great man" social history, where the journey from then to now is described as the results of brilliant decisions and callous mistakes made by the guardians of society. Rather, such work harnesses the power of popular culture and the cult of celebrity in the service of exposing collective, institutional phenomena and complex processes of social change. Just as celebrities use their fame to draw attention to various charitable and political causes, this book uses "Obama-mania" to map the meaning and politics of race.

Such mapping, however, is hard work. The chief problem identified in the opening chapter is that even when we wish to grapple with race and racism, we find it difficult to do so because race can be public, secret, formless, firm, and volatile all at once. At the outset, I posited "intersectionality" and "race as metalanguage" as the guiding lights for racial exploration and the keys to triumphing over the intimidating messiness and shame of race. The arguments and findings of each chapter, constructed through a commitment to intersectionality and metalanguage, are significant. Chapter 2 demonstrates that our ideas about race and nation are mutually constitutive and tragically dependent on the politics of inheritance, an epistemology that is obsessed with bodies as symbols and lineage as destiny in the pursuit of political righteousness. The racist and altogether suffocating implications of this form of knowledge are clear from the research cited. There is simply no denying the contemporary linkage between white supremacy and many of the most prevalent forms of and appeals to American nationalism and patriotism. A close reading of Obama's memoir is offered as means to deconstruct the politics of inheritance, and new possibilities for racial and national identity are presented. Specifically, I argue for a new American nationalism that eschews bodily inheritance in favor of collective action and social critique as its defining principles.

Of course, redemption and newness have been recurring themes in public discourse about what Barack Obama means, and Chapters 3 and 4 interrogate "the new" in two ways. Chapter 3 features the voices of a young cohort of multiracial Americans, as multiracial people are often viewed as futuristic, postracial political subjects. The interviewees explain how the intersections of race, gender, and nation influence public perceptions of President Obama, lament the racism that he is subjected to, and maintain space for Obama within the bounds of multiracial identity despite the fact that the president regularly identifies as black and does not carry the flag for any sort of multiracial movement. The malleability of multiracialism speaks to the metalinguistic character of race, as categories of mixedness regularly shift their shape and meaning. Despite this instability, white supremacy, rather than a general sense of racial discord, is identified by respondents as the essence of racism. These findings are important because they allow multiracial people to speak for themselves, counteracting the narratives and representations that reduce multiracial people to futuristic, postracial symbols. The findings are also important because they suggest that the development of multiracial identity is an ongoing project, even among those who already claim it. The category "multiracial" is not protected with rigid boundaries that separate the lives, experiences, and politics of multiracial people from other ethnoracial groups. Multiracial subjectivity is not postracial or antiracist by definition. But the respondents I spoke with disdain racism, and the interpretations they offer suggest that multiracial identity can be galvanized to combat racist oppression, even if such organization and mobilization have not yet come to pass on a grand scale.

Chapter 4 digs deeper into postracialism, a concept that has been repeatedly scrutinized and battered by critics who recognize the continued importance of race and racism in America. Beyond dismissing postracialism, the analysis focuses on the current state of the real and virtual spaces where black political talk occurs: the black counterpublic. This is a new era in counterpublic politics, because much of the safety that is so crucial to black political institutions has eroded, and class cleavages and technological changes have changed the rules of political communication. Contemporary black politics and the counterpublic reflect these intersectional changes rather than Obama's personal transcendence of race. When we obsess over questions of individual leadership and charisma, the institutional processes that shape leadership are often ignored. If we are dissatisfied with current black American leadership, we would be wise to dedicate time and energy to reconfiguring the institutions that shape leaders and bestow political influence rather than demonizing (or deifying) the individuals themselves.

The intersection of race and class is critical to the analysis in Chapter 5 as well, as these identity markers combine with gender to cast first lady Michelle Obama in ways that both recast and transform traditional representations of black womanhood. Before turning to Ms. Obama, the text foregrounds the canon of intersectionality theory, focusing on the work of Kimberle Crenshaw, Patricia Hill Collins, and the other black feminist scholars who initially developed intersectionality as an analytic tool. After cataloguing the historically dominant representations of black womanhood, I describe how a current representation, the uppity black superwoman, has been grafted onto the old and deployed as a weapon of racist criticism against Michelle. It is crucial that the racist objectification of Michelle Obama is understood in the historical context of controlling images of black womanhood, because these insults are not isolated attacks on an individual public figure; they are tied to long-standing processes of inequality, stereotyping, and marginalization that impact all black women. Refuting these offenses requires the voices and actions of black women themselves, and Ms. Obama publicly discusses the multiple roles she plays as a professional black woman who manages domestic and civic responsibilities while reclaiming her body and her capacity for romantic intimacy.

Beyond the specific implications of each chapter, what else does intersectionality do for us and demand of us? Jennifer Nash argues that intersectionality has established itself among race and gender scholars and made at least three critical interventions on social theory and the way we think about politics: intersectionality disrupts race/gender binaries and forces a reconsideration of identity; it provides vocabulary for moving between different and multiple forms of identity; and it highlights the ways multiply marginalized subjects are excluded from various liberation movements, including feminism.[2] However, Nash insists that there is much to be done with respect to the actual aims and untapped potential of contemporary intersectional scholarship. One area she identifies as a space ripe for development is intersectional research that reveals how both disadvantage *and* privilege can be inscribed simultaneously on the very same subject, in some cases, paradoxically reinforcing each other.[3] With respect to Obama, this theme crops up in my pointing out the ways the president is privileged by his gender, sexual orientation, and class. These characteristics both accent the stain of race for his bigoted critics and provide protection from other forms of racist attacks that less privileged people of color are subject to. The chapter on Michelle Obama is also directly applicable, as the key ingredient in the particular formula of racist stereotyping she is subject to is her exceptional class standing, which paradoxically enables the circulation of old and new controlling images of black womanhood. In addition, the multiracial respondents in Chapter 3 carry the privilege of enrollment in elite colleges or universities, which provides time, social space, and vocabulary for experimenting with and building complex racial subjectivity, despite the oversimplified stereotypes of mixedness that continue to impact their lives.

The implications of refocusing intersectionality on privilege reach far beyond figures like the Obamas. Applying an intersectional lens to privilege means expanding the purview of intersectional research to multiply privileged spaces and personalities: to people and institutions that benefit from white supremacy, patriarchy, class exploitation, and homophobia all at once. Doing so will provide much needed insight into specific processes and patterns of exclusion and inequality from the inside of privileged spaces out to the margins. We need intersectional studies of elite schools, banks, law firms, and the lives of wealthy straight white men, just as we need intersectional treatments of women of color and feminist theory.

Intersectionality scholars should also aim to increase the impact of their work in the realm of policy. A great deal of intersectional work focuses on experience, subjectivity, and cultural production, and if the causes of suffering and inequality are linked to each other, choosing a specific intervention can seem daunting. However, Kimberle Crenshaw's initial formulation of intersectionality is specifically designed to correct institutionalized practice: the way the courts understand race and gender as wholly separate entities in discrimination cases renders intersectional forms of discrimination invisible. A reconsideration of antidiscrimination *policy* is the aim of Crenshaw's work; all subsequent developments in intersectionality are rooted in this initial purpose.

One contemporary study that beautifully upholds this tradition and combines an intersectional approach to individual subjectivity, culture, and policy is Nikki Jones's *Between Good and Ghetto* (2009). Jones documents the experiences of young black women in a poor urban setting, with special attention to violence, safety, and the acquisition of respect. In discussing the relationship between domestic abuse policy and the actual lived experiences of the young women in her study, Jones reveals a complicated relationship between the courts, law enforcement, and her respondents. The current policy response to the intersectional problem of domestic abuse and other forms of violence directed against these women is to arrest, incarcerate, and forcibly remove the attackers from these women's lives. But this policy carries all sorts of unintended and unwanted consequences for the women in the study, including familial disruption, economic risk, social isolation, and cultural stigmatization from their peers. Jones's work reveals that respondents use the authorities as means of negotiation with the offending parties rather than uniform penalization.[4] Policy-makers have no choice but to take such findings seriously if they aim to interrupt cycles of violence and improve the conditions of citizens' lives. A criminal justice complex that disproportionately penalizes black and brown people and fails to understand its intersection with health and wellness policy, education, and the labor and housing markets cannot possibly serve the greater good.

These first two suggestions deal specifically with *scholarship* that takes intersectionality and race as metalanguage seriously. But obviously, these tools for thinking and talking about race hold tremendous promise for people who work outside of classrooms and legislative halls. Perhaps the most ordinary, and daunting, alteration we can make to harmful racial meanings and patterns of thought is a commitment to speak about race as carefully and correctly as possible. Too often, we allow and expect a racial term to communicate and mean more than it possibly can without proper context or intersections. The problems of race as metalanguage and the truths of intersectionality demand an individual commitment to racial *mindfulness* from each of us. Much to the dismay of those who fashion themselves unfiltered "straight shooters," this necessitates a reconsideration of political correctness and an appreciation for precision when discussing race and ethnicity.

Those who disparage political correctness offer two basic objections. First, political correctness is framed as dishonesty and inauthenticity.

It becomes a character flaw for those who practice it, because someone who watches what she says and tries not to offend everyone she meets is incapable of genuine social interaction. The second objection to political correctness describes how the individual failings of those who live by the politically correct code produce greater social problems. The claim is that those who spend too much time crying and complaining about poor word choice are missing the big picture and distracting themselves from more important issues. It is certainly possible to improve the lives of oppressed ethnoracial minorities without perfect clarity about the meaning of every single racial term in our lexicon. But as the policy-driven implications of intersectionality demonstrate, optimal improvement can only come through awareness of intersectionality.

The operative word in the phrase "politically correct" is "correct." It is the opposite of "wrong." It is not politically correct to say "Asians are bad drivers" or "women are crazy," not just because that sort of "authentic" folk wisdom rubs nerdy academics the wrong way, but because the stereotypes are wrong and they impact the way we treat each other. It is not politically correct to say "Jews are cheap" or "the Irish are drunks," not merely because these statements are "political" in that they draw lines of separation between groups, but because they are insulting and untrue. It is not politically correct to say "Latinas are spicy" or to make jokes about the size of black men's penises, because these statements are inaccurate and they epitomize bigotry though intersectional exoticism of black and brown bodies. The common threads tying politically incorrect pearls of wisdom together are that (1) they are grounded in racist and sexist mythology designed to protect white privilege and cement the "normalcy" of straight, Anglo, Christian masculinity, and (2) they ignore the diversity of groups marked by race, ethnicity, gender, nationality, and other axes of distinction. We cannot allow defending the right to speak freely and the pleasures of reveling in anecdote to morph into foolhardy generalizations about group differences. When this happens, shorthand racial and cultural "truths" (falsehoods) become metalinguistic smokescreens for processes of separation and social control. Additionally, politically incorrect "common knowledge" calcifies into scripts that regulate ideas about authenticity and belonging within groups, marginalizing those who do not conform to the erroneously assumed norm. Mindful awareness of metalanguage and intersectionality during racial conversation gets us far closer to the true meanings of race than does "shooting from the hip."

One of the most severe plagues unleashed by centuries of racial terror and oppression is a kind of dementia. We are unsure of what we see and hear, and the right words evade us when we try to describe ourselves and our world. Trepidation and shame lead to silence in the face of our own illness, and symptoms worsen and spread to our neighbors. Obama is no miracle cure, and his life and triumph are no metaphor for the black struggle or the political history of the United States. But if instead of a predetermined path he can be a gathering place, where we take the measure of our stock and distinguish between sickness and health, then we might lead each other down the road to recovery.

Appendix I
A Discussion of Racial Inequality

The first chapter describes two different understandings of white privilege. In the cultural realm, the realm where meaning is generated and beliefs and values are held, white privilege is the idea that whiteness is normal and unremarkable. Racism marks people of color not only as distinct but as deviant from the norm, and the character of their racial deviance is determined by the intersection of race with other social forces. When white experiences are accepted as universal norms, the myth that racism is no longer relevant gains traction.

Of course, interpersonal and institutional racism continue to exert their influence on our lives, not only in the realm of individual experience and identity but at the level of the collective social order. When faced with the facts of inequality in American society, we can conceive of white privilege in a more basic and naked sense: white privilege refers to the empirical reality that whites hold social, political, and economic advantages over nonwhites. These empirical advantages, born from the historical legacy of legalized discrimination as well as contemporary prejudice and institutional racism, are evident across a range of fields.

Health
Nonwhites receive substandard health care and health education relative to their white counterparts. In addition, the overlay of race- and class-based residential segregation ensures that many nonwhites grow up in neighborhoods

without suitable health clinics, dwellings, recreational space for exercise, and markets that stock food for a healthy diet.

- Blacks' life expectancy in the United States is 6–10 years shorter than that of whites.

- The age-adjusted cancer death rate is roughly 25 percent higher for blacks than it is for whites.

- The black-white gap in infant mortality widened between 1980 and 2000, despite the fact that overall infant mortality declined.

- Black women comprised two-thirds of new HIV infections in 2005, and are infected at a rate 23 times that of white women. AIDS is the leading cause of death for black women aged 25–34 years. Black women and Latinas comprise 82 percent of reported AIDS cases among women, despite accounting for only 24 percent of the female population in the United States.[1]

- 30.7 percent of Hispanics and 19.1 percent of blacks lack health insurance, compared with 10.8 percent of whites.[2]

Employment and Wealth

Nonwhites continue to face discrimination in hiring, promotion, and firing practices across a range of professions and are more heavily dependent on public funding for employment than are whites. Social networks are indispensable for learning about and seizing employment opportunities, and whites have more social capital, meaning their networks are flusher with people who have knowledge about job openings and the power to actually hire employees. Finally, economic wealth is transmitted from one generation to the next, which allows whites to continue to reap the benefits of centuries of legal racial discrimination.

- In July 2011, the white unemployment rate was 7.9 percent; Hispanic unemployment was 11.2 percent; and black unemployment was 16.2 percent.[3]

- In 2004, the median net worth of white households was $134,280, compared with $13,450 for black households, according to an analysis of Federal Reserve data by the Economic Policy Institute. By 2009, the median net worth for white households had fallen 24 percent to $97,860; the median black net worth had fallen 83 percent to $2,170. In other words, the average black household had two cents for every one dollar of wealth held by the average white household.[4]

- As of 2010, 75 percent of white families owned a home, compared with 47.4 percent of black families and 49.1 percent of Hispanic families.[5]

- Blacks and Hispanics are more than three times as likely as whites to live below the poverty line.[6]

Education

The public education system maintains its commitment to neighborhood schooling rather than economic and ethnoracial integration. As wealth is concentrated in primarily white neighborhoods and those communities are spatially and socially segregated from nonwhites, white students in public schools benefit from superior economic and human resources from elementary through high school.

- The high school dropout rate is 10.8 percent for whites, 13 percent for blacks, and 26 percent for Hispanics.[7]
- Only 47 percent of black males nationwide graduate high school with their cohort, compared with 78 percent of white males. In New York state, only 25 percent of black males graduate with their cohort.[8]
- In New York state school districts with a white voter base and a large number of nonwhite students, increases to public school budgets are voted down at a far higher rate than in districts with white voters and white students.[9]
- The average white student attends a school where more than 78 percent of the students are white and less than 20 percent of students fall below the poverty line. In contrast, roughly 90 percent of predominantly black and Latino schools are characterized by concentrated poverty (with 40 percent of the student population below the poverty line).

Incarceration

The late twentieth century has seen the unprecedented expansion of the carceral state, as the American prison population rose from 350,000 in the 1970s to 2.3 million by 2008. Search and seizure laws have been amended, expanding the power of the police to make arrests based on reasonable suspicion rather than probable cause. The "War on Drugs" waged by the Ronald Reagan administration prioritized and incentivized the treatment of low-level, nonviolent drug offenders as criminals who belong in jail. Prosecutorial power increased as judicial discretion waned, and public defenders are increasingly overworked and underpaid, unable to devote adequate attention to each case. The advent of mandatory minimum sentencing combined with a rise in plea bargains keep our nation's prisons and jails full; once prisoners are released, there is little infrastructure for reintegration into society, which leads to high rates of recidivism. Poor black and Hispanic neighborhoods are disproportionately affected by these developments.[10]

- In 2007, 1 out of every 10 black men aged 25–29 years was incarcerated. For Hispanics the proportion was 1 out of every 28 males, and for whites it was 1 out of every 59 males.
- Black men have a 32 percent chance of being incarcerated at some point in their lives. Hispanic men have a 17 percent chance, and white men have a 6 percent chance.

• Blacks comprise roughly 12 percent of the United States population, and approximately 40 percent of persons in prison or jail are black. Hispanics comprise roughly 15 percent of the population, and approximately 20 percent of prisoners are Hispanic.[11]

American Indians and Asian Americans

Tremendous class and status diversity exists within each of the racial and ethnic groups mentioned above—not all black and Hispanic people teeter on the brink of abject poverty and poor health (the majority do not). However, these figures provide a bird's-eye view of the racial and ethnic order. American Indians and Alaska natives are excluded from these data, and though they only comprise roughly 2 percent of the United States population, on balance members of these groups are politically marginalized and mired in poverty and other quantifiable disadvantages that closely resemble those of African Americans. One of the great weaknesses of contemporary racial and ethnic studies is an inability to integrate the experiences and political predicament of American Indians into larger narratives about race and ethnicity. European colonists' and early Americans' attempted extermination of the indigenous population gave way to geographic and cultural isolation on government reservations, and this alienation from the most powerful institutions of American social and political life has balkanized the field of study and marginalized American Indians from political discourse.

Asian Americans' and Pacific Islanders' positions in the United States racial hierarchy are more directly linked to the most formative structures and discourses of the American social order, but they are also difficult to generalize. As a group, Asians' median household income level actually eclipses that of whites, though the poverty rate for Asians is 3 percent higher than for whites.[12] However, as is the case with other racial groups, there is substantial ethnic, class, and generational variation among Americans lumped into the Asian category. For example, Asians of Japanese ancestry have markedly higher levels of educational attainment and income than Asians of Filipino or Cambodian descent. In addition to differences *between* ethnic groups, there is even further variation in status attainment *within* each ethnic group, often depending on the era in which the families arrive in the United States. The outcomes above are not solely the product of present-day racial discrimination, and the effects of multigenerational disadvantage need not be augmented by contemporary racism to produce inequality.

Regardless of Asians' class position, the bodily stain of nonwhiteness connotes deviance, just as it does for all people of color who live in a racist society. Frank Wu identifies two key stereotypes that dominate perceptions and representations of Asians in America: the perpetual foreigner and the model minority.[13] The stigma of foreignness is drawn from United States military history in the Far East in combination with language differences and archaic mythologies about Asian mysticism. Gender intersects with race, producing representations of Asian women as sexually exotic and submissive, and assigning violence, impotence, and untrustworthiness (occasionally amplified by stoicism) to Asian men.

The "model minority" stereotype is derived from aggregate data pointing to educational and status achievement among Asians that far outpaces other nonwhite groups. The insidiousness of the model-minority stereotype is threefold. First, it erases variation among Asians and ignores experiences of millions of Asian Americans who reside in the socioeconomic margins of society and never achieve the educational success at the core of the stereotype. As Jennifer Gonzalez points out, "Nearly half of all Asian-American and Pacific Islander students . . . attend community colleges, and many of their ethnic groups have some of the lowest high-school-graduation and college-degree-attainment rates in the United States."[14] Second, the model-minority myth attributes status attainment among high-achieving Asian Americans to "natural" intellectual aptitude rather than immigration trends and cultural and behavioral choices that have nothing to do with biology. Finally, the model-minority myth implicitly compares Asians to blacks and Hispanics, as if all nonwhites' socioeconomic starting points and battles against racism are essentially the same. The function of the myth is to cover up continued racism and discrimination against Asians, disregard the social justice issues that plague economically underprivileged Asian American communities, and invalidate the complaints of blacks and Hispanics by pointing to Asians and saying, "They made it, why can't you?"

Studying Racial Inequality

No singular axis of distinction holds the secret that explains racial meaning or inequality. The most useful approaches for studying race developed over the last thirty years are devoted to specifying the relationship between structure (economic realities) and culture. Stuart Hall's central contribution is the notion of "articulation," which is the idea that there is a complex unity "between the structure of modes of production and the specific forms of political domination and ideological legitimation."[15] Class ("modes of production") matters, but it does not overdetermine the nature of social order and social change, such that hard-and-fast rules of oppression and resistance can be applied to any historical and political context. Modes of production combine with cultural phenomena to organize societies in historically particular, and sometimes counterintuitive, ways. As I write these words, we are living in strange times, as a black/multiracial working-class community organizer turned constitutional scholar presides over the steady disappearance of the middle class and one of the most extreme exacerbations of racial inequality in this country's history.

Michael Omi and Howard Winant make use of Hall's work, as their racial formation theory states that racial meanings and racial orders are constructed on multiple levels. At the macro level, hegemonic institutions such as the capitalist economy, the state, and the family constrain our political lives through coercion and brute force, regulating racial hierarchy and constricting the range of concepts available for social identity. At the micro level, we use the words, signs, and symbols at our disposal to give meaning to individual experiences. Our expressions of experience simultaneously rely on and influence institution-ally enforced political conventions.[16]

Even if we never fully sketch the precise process by which racial inequality is sustained and reinvented, the statistics above confirm that we are truly liv-ing through a disaster. Lani Guinier uses the metaphor of the "miner's canary" to describe the predicament of the most marginalized and underrepresented groups in the American economy and polity. Miners would carry these small birds in cages as they plunged beneath the earth, using the animals as living, breathing warning signals. Canaries' lungs are more delicate than humans', so when a bird began to choke and struggle for oxygen, the laborers knew the air was unsafe. Impoverished people of color were struggling prior to the economic collapse of 2008, but most Americans refused to hear their cries as warning signs about the defects in the economy. When the crisis struck, those deep in the mine were least able to defend themselves from the fallout, and what little eco-nomic stability has since been achieved has not yet trickled down to the most vulnerable. The institutional racism that produces such deeply rooted inequality will not be vanquished by public opinion data that suggest decreased feelings of animus towards people of color. The policies and practices of banks, schools, health care providers, courts, and corporations must be changed if we are to do away with unjust racial hierarchy, and serious government intervention is needed if these populations are to survive and ward off disaffection and unrest.

Appendix II
Interviewing Multiracial Students

Existing research focuses on how young adults of multiracial descent arrive at and understand their own racial identities, relative to existing racial categories and social structures. This study makes contributions to the literature by probing the following research topics:

1. Multiracial people's personal conceptions of multiracial identity
2. The influence of race on Obama's identity management and political career
3. The relationship between Obama's multiracialism and multiracial identity more broadly
4. Obama's impact on America's racial history and the future of racism

Respondents, who are given pseudonyms in the text, were recruited via solicitation letters sent to student organizations comprising multiracial students. In most cases, letters were forwarded by the leaders of these organizations to other group members, as well as other students whom they knew to be multiracial but may not have been part of the group. Snowball sampling was also used, as respondents who did not occupy leadership positions were free to refer other participants who qualified for the study. Though all respondents identified as multiracial in some form and were recruited through the network of multiracial student groups, not every respondent was an active member of such groups. The vast majority of interviews were conducted on the students' college campuses, though on occasion cafés or bookstores off campus proved to be more convenient sites. All interviews were conducted between summer 2010 and spring 2011, and each respondent was paid twenty dollars for his or her participation.

Two of the forty-nine respondents were months removed from receiving their Bachelor of Arts degree, and the rest were enrolled as undergraduates at the time of the interview. Respondents in the sample hailed from twelve different colleges and universities, described here in three groups:

- 4 respondents attended two large public universities with applicant acceptance rates between 60 percent and 70 percent.
- 11 respondents attended two private colleges and universities with applicant acceptance rates between 40 percent and 50 percent.
- 34 respondents attended eight private colleges and universities with applicant acceptance rates no greater than 26 percent.[1]

Thirty-four of the respondents were women; fifteen were men. The racial and ethnic characteristics of the forty-nine respondents' biological parents are as follows:

- 45 respondents had at least one parent of European descent.
- 21 respondents had at least one parent of African descent.
- 20 respondents (15 women and 5 men) reported one white parent and one East Asian parent. The first letter in every abbreviation indicates the mother's race, and the second letter indicates the father's race, so this combination of parents is denoted as "AW" when the respondent had an Asian mother and white father, and "WA" when the respondent had a white mother and Asian father.
- 17 respondents (11 women and 6 men) reported one white parent and one black parent. Again, the first letter corresponds to the mother's race, so these parents are denoted as a combination of the letters "B" and "W."
- 4 respondents (3 women and 1 man) reported one white parent and one Latino parent. This is denoted with the letters "L" and "W."
- 1 man reported one white parent and one Native American parent ("WNA").
- 1 woman reported one white parent and one Middle Eastern parent ("WME").
- 1 man reported one black parent and one East Asian parent ("AB").
- 1 woman reported one white parent and one black/Latino parent ("BLW").
- 1 woman reported one East Asian parent and one Latino parent ("LA").
- 1 woman reported one black parent and one Latino parent ("LB").
- 1 man reported one black parent and one South Asian parent ("SAB").
- 1 woman reported one white parent and one South Asian parent ("WSA").

Sorting respondents by socioeconomic class is more difficult, because a young person's class is a function of income, family wealth, neighborhood, and parents' education. Though I collected data about each of these characteristics,

the groups below are organized primarily according to parents'/guardians' esti-
mated reported income. According to the 2010 Census, the median household
income in the United States was $50,221.[2] The Tax Policy Center, a joint project
of the Urban Institute and the Brookings Institution, calculated $85,811 as the
75th percentile for household income in 2011.[3] Considering that most of the respondents attended highly competitive private colleges and universities, it is no
surprise that so many of the young adults I spoke with hailed from a relatively
privileged class.

- 6 respondents reported family incomes under $50k (beneath the median).
- 11 respondents reported family incomes between $51,000 and $85,811 (between the median and the 75th percentile).
- 5 respondents did not report family income, and of those two reported that
  their families were "well off" and "upper middle class," and two had other
  family characteristics, including parents' education and home neighborhood, suggesting that family income was above the 75th percentile.

As a conservative estimate, thirty-one of the forty-nine respondents came
from households that reside in the 75th income percentile or above. This is consistent with what the literature tells us about which households are most likely
to produce children that identify as multiracial or are labeled as such by their
parents or guardians. None of the respondents reported living below the poverty line, though the poverty line is not always an accurate measure of whether
a family is living in need. A handful of respondents reported going through
periods when they knew their families' finances were tight, or lived in places
that they described as lower- or working-class neighborhoods.

Respondents described their home lives in seventeen different states and
several countries other than the United States. States from the Northeast,
South, Midwest, Southwest, and west coast of the country were represented.
Many of the respondents moved around quite a bit during their upbringing,
but interviews focused on experiences during their middle and high school
years, and they were geographically sorted according to those spaces. The states
with greatest representation in the sample are New York (nine respondents),
Massachusetts (eight), California (seven), and New Jersey (five). Thirty-two
respondents were raised in suburban communities, and the other seventeen
were raised in urban neighborhoods. Two respondents described their suburban spaces as rural/suburban hybrids, but nobody reported being raised in a
definitively rural community. The geographic and spatial diversity disrupts the
notion of class homogeneity derived from the household income data; an $85k
family income carries far less purchasing power in New York City than it does
in suburban Phoenix, especially if the household contains multiple children.

In recruiting students to participate in this research, a form letter was sent
to the leaders of multiracial student groups at various colleges on the east coast,

and the sample was built through replies to the letter and referrals. Here is the full text of the form letter:

> Greetings:
>
> I am a professor at Wellesley College, in the midst of an interview-based research project about young people's ideas regarding mixed race identity. Each interview unfolds as a conversation about a number of topics, including experiences at home and at college, and impressions of Barack Obama. The purpose of the study is to add to what is a growing field of research that focuses on the experiences of people who identify as having a biracial or multiracial heritage. Eventually, the data will be analyzed and published as part of an academic article or book on the topic.
>
> Each interview is conducted in person, and takes about 1 hour. Each respondent is paid $20 for his/her participation. Yours is one of many student organizations that have been contacted for data collection, and I hope to speak with as many students as possible before the end of the semester. If you would like to participate, I am happy to meet each respondent at a time and place that is convenient for him/her to complete the interview. I am more than willing to meet on campus, or anywhere else in the [city or town] area, if that is what works best. I am completely willing to work around your schedule.
>
> If you are not interested in the study, but you know of someone between the ages of 18–25 years old who you think might like to participate, I hope you will forward this letter to him/her on my behalf. If you have any questions about the study, please email me at mjeffrie@wellesley.edu or call me at [number].
>
> Your participation is very important to the field, and deeply appreciated. I hope to hear from you soon.
>
> Best regards,
> Michael P. Jeffries, Ph.D.
> Assistant Professor
> Department of American Studies
> Wellesley College
> mjeffrie@wellesley.edu

My home institution was excluded from the list of recruitment sites, as I had already interacted with a number of students in the designated campus group. In some cases, the students were previously enrolled in my "Race, Ethnicity, and Politics" course, which includes a unit on multiracialism. I did not want our previous discussions to influence data collection.

The interview schedule contains a number of topics, as the subject matter gradually evolves from descriptions of personal experiences, to more general ideas about race, to impressions and analysis of Obama and his political career. Here is the list of questions:

How old are you? What year of school are you in (if applicable)?

Can you describe the neighborhood you grew up in for me? (probe class, race and ethnicity, religion, sexuality)

Can you describe your school for me? (probe class, race and ethnicity, religion, sexuality)

Can you say a bit about your parents? (race and ethnicity, religion, education, occupation)

How would you describe your race and/or ethnicity?

When asked to indicate your race/ethnicity on forms, such as the census, how do you/would you identify yourself?

Have you always described it in this way?

Is there a set of rules you think all people should follow when faced with such questions? Are the rules different depending on who is filling out the form?

Can you explain how you arrived at this description? (probe school/peers, parents, specific events)

How would you describe the race of most of your friends or people you hang out with, including significant others?

Are there times when you find yourself to be especially aware of your racial identity?

Do you believe people usually assume things about your racial identity?

Have there been times when you felt you were mistreated because of your race? How did you respond?

. . .

How has your experience at college impacted the way you think about your race, or race more generally? How would you describe the student organization you are a part of?

How would you define race?

How would you define racism? (probe solution to racism)

Where did this definition of racism come from? Has it evolved over time?

How, if at all, does racism affect people who have a mixed-race background?

What do you think of Barack Obama?

Were you involved in his campaign, in any way? If you were of voting age, did you cast your vote for him?

How would you evaluate his term as president thus far?

Has Obama's race played a role in the way he is treated or understood? (probe by media, by private citizens; has Obama been a victim of racism?)

What is your understanding of Obama's racial identity? Where does this understanding come from?

What do you think Obama thinks about his own racial identity? Does it impact the way he presents himself, either to the country as a whole, or in a given context?

Has Obama's mixed-race background played a role in any of these understandings? (probe advantage or disadvantage in getting elected or politics more generally)

What do you think Obama thinks about racism? (probe definition, how to counteract it)

How has Obama dealt with race during his campaign and/or during his first term? Would you like to see him address or deal with specific racial issues differently than he has, either with respect to his own biography or politics more generally?

What impact, if any, do you think Obama has had on the way Americans think about race, racism, or about people of mixed-race background? Why?

What impact, if any, do you think he has had on the way mixed-race Americans think about race or their own identity?

Whether or not there has been an impact thus far, do you think his rise to the presidency will affect the way we all think about race in the future? Will it have a future impact on racism?

Are there any questions that you wished I would have asked, or is there anything that you are thinking of now that you didn't get a chance to say?

Thank you.

My discussions with respondents were immensely rewarding. The young men and women I spoke with were thoughtful and honest in their replies and took great care to give specific examples and anecdotes from their personal lives when appropriate. Ethnographers must consider insider/outsider dynamics when interacting with respondents. Every qualitative interview I have ever conducted was part of a larger project about race, but this is the first project wherein suppositions about my own multiracial identity may have labeled me a clear "insider" and added to respondents' comfort level during the interview. Extant research confirms the miscommunication and anxiety that can occur between multiracials and monoracials in situations where the boundaries of authenticity are rigidly policed, and a number of respondents describe uncomfortable interactions with people of color who view multiracial affiliation as a slight to the more traditional racial group. Though I primarily identify as African American, my skin tone marks me as a subject outside the expected bounds of traditional blackness. While it is certainly possible that I reaped some "insider" benefits, it would be absurd to assume that I was immediately and instantly marked as a sympathetic ear during the interviews, considering the ambiguity, contingency, and fluidity of multiracial identification and affiliation, as explained in Chapter 3. After the interview, a number of respondents asked me to clarify my racial background, enumerate the publication goals for the project, and disclose my feelings about some of the issues we discussed. While I was always forthcoming about my background and my aspirations for the research, I often dodged questions about interview topics on the chance that this feedback might somehow make its way into subsequent interviews with referred respondents.

Kristin Esterberg's description of "open" and "focused" coding guides my data analysis. I analyzed the interviews using "open coding" to home in on recurrent themes and data points that speak to the research questions.[4] My field notes from the interviews were especially helpful, as I was able to jot down key words that served as the basis for codes and data clusters. In many cases, manually reviewing and coding each of the forty-nine answers to a given question on the interview schedule proved to be the most effective means of data analysis. In others, I used the Atlas.ti program to cull responses based on key words and themes, such as "Tea Party" and "coolness." Grouping all the mentions of a term is a first step, followed by further, more-focused coding to sketch the symbolic boundaries and mental maps offered up by respondents.[5] The prevalence of shared meanings, permeability of group boundaries, capacity for contradiction, and the nuanced differences between emotions like sadness, anger, and disappointment all require focused reading of the qualitative data after they have been sorted.

Symbolic boundaries are "conceptual distinctions made by social actors to categorize objects, people, practices, and even time and space. They are tools by which individuals and groups struggle over and come to agree upon definitions of reality. Examining them allows us to capture the dynamic dimensions of social relations, as groups compete in the production, diffusion, and institutionalization of alternative systems and principles of classifications."[6] Collective identities are invoked through performance and conversation; my conversations with respondents delve into the boundaries between multiracial people and other groups, and how multiracial identity is built.

Lamont and Molnar are quick to point out that we should not confuse symbolic boundaries with social boundaries, which are "objectified forms of social differences rooted in unequal access to and unequal distribution of resources (material and non-material) and social opportunities."[7] Not all symbolic boundaries and mental maps correspond to empirically verifiable social divisions or political behavior. However, William Gamson and Melissa Harris-Perry each demonstrate the importance of everyday talk to political ideologies and action, and the "symbolic work" we perform gives our lives meaning.[8]

Notes

CHAPTER ONE: THROUGH THE FOG

1. Barbara J. Fields, "Ideology and Race in American History," in *Region, Race, and Reconstruction: Essays in Honor of C. Vann Woodward*, ed. J. Morgan Kousser and James M. McPherson (New York: Oxford University Press, 1982), 153.

2. "Will American Voters Elect a Black President?" NPR, December 18, 2006, http://www.npr.org/templates/story/story.php?storyId=6642868.

3. In *The White Racial Frame: Centuries of Racial Framing and Counter-Framing* (New York: Routledge, 2009), Joe Feagan provides a detailed theoretical map of white privilege, or "white racial framing," explaining how virtuous and normative whiteness combines with violence and is institutionalized as the frame through people interpret moral reality.

4. Howard Winant, "Just Do It: Notes on Politics and Race at the Dawn of the Obama Presidency," *Du Bois Review* 6, no. 1 (2009): 53.

5. For a thorough treatment of how Obama has navigated such racial controversies, please see Randall Kennedy, *The Persistence of the Color Line: Racial Politics and the Obama Presidency* (New York: Random House, 2011).

6. This phrase is the title of Bonilla-Silva's 2003 text, *Racism Without Racists: Color-Blind Racism and the Persistence of Racial Inequality in the United States* (New York: Rowman & Littlefield, 2003).

7. Ibid.

8. For a snapshot of this crisis as measured in health, income/employment, education, and incarceration outcomes, please refer to Appendix I.

9. Michael Taussig, *Defacement: Public Secrecy and the Labor of the Negative* (Stanford: Stanford University Press, 1999), 5–7. Emphasis in original.

10. Eviatar Zerubavel, *The Elephant in the Room: Silence and Denial in Everyday Life* (New York: Oxford University Press, 2006), 9.

11. Jake Tapper, "Gingrich Says Obama Must Have 'Cognitive Dissonance' About Plight of African-American Community," ABC News, December 2, 2011, http://abcnews.go.com/blogs/politics/2011/12/gingrich-says-obama-must-have-cognitive-dissonance-about-plight-of-african-american-community/.

12. Charles M. Blow, "Newt Gingrich and the Art of Racial Politics," *New York Times*, January 17, 2012, http://campaignstops.blogs.nytimes.com/2012/01/17/newt-gingrich-and-the-art-of-racial-politics/.

13. Alex Seitz-Wald, "Romney: Obama's Bringing Welfare Back," Salon, last modified August 7, 2012, http://www.salon.com/2012/08/07/romney_obamas_bringing_welfare_back/.

14. Tali Mendelberg (*The Race Card: Campaign Strategy, Implicit Messages and the Norm of Equality* [Princeton: Princeton University Press, 2001]) and Valentino et al. ("The Sword's Other Edge," *Public Opinion Quarterly* 75, no. 2 [2002]: 201–26) find that this awareness may not actually change voters' behaviors, and suggest that observed effects may be limited to those with low levels of educational attainment and weak attachments to the norm of equality. But even if voting behavior does not change, Bruce Western (*Punishment and Inequality in America* [New York: Russell Sage, 2007]) notes that respondents are awakened to their own dissonance, as racist stereotypes persist in the context of professed antiracist beliefs—certainly, a positive development.

15. Audre Lorde, *Sister Outsider: Essays and Speeches by Audre Lorde* (Berkeley: Crossing Press, 2007 [1984]), 123. The full quotation is, "For we have, built into all of us, old blueprints of expectation and response, old structures of oppression, and these must be altered at the same time as we alter the living conditions which are a result of those structures. For the master's tools will never dismantle the master's house."

16. Toni Morrison, "Introduction: Friday on the Potomac," in *Race-ing Justice, En-Gendering Power: Essays on Anita Hill, Clarence Thomas, and the Construction of Social Reality* (New York: Pantheon, 1992), xxviii–xxix.

17. See the lecture film entitled "Race: The Floating Signifier" (1997), directed by Sut Jhally, Media Education Foundation (1997). The transcript is available at http://www.mediaed.org/cgi-bin/commerce.cgi?preadd=action&key=407. Stuart Hall explains that race is a "floating signifier" that has different meanings dependent on both discursive and historical context. In this way, race operates more like a language than a static means of categorization, or a historical or biological fact.

18. See Evelyn Higginbotham, "African-American Women's History and the Metalangauge of Race," *Signs* 17, no. 2 (1992): 255. Understanding race as

metalanguage moves beyond the notion that racial code words and images are invoked in order to prime fear and antipathy. Coding and implicit priming are encompassed within metalanguage, but metalanguage operates without intentionality as prerequisite.

19. Hall, "Race: The Floating Signifier."

20. Bob Raissman, "Packer Listens to Jesse 'No Way A Racist,'" *New York Daily News*, March 6, 1996, http://articles.nydailynews.com/1996-03-06/sports/17997298_1_billy-packer-tough-monkey-racist.

21. For a thorough explanation of why the old litmus tests of intent and determinism are no longer sufficient for understanding and combating racism, please see Imani Perry, *More Beautiful and More Terrible: The Embrace and Transcendence of Racial Inequality in the United States* (New York: New York University Press), 13–22.

22. Blacks are not the only racial minority to be depicted as apes in American popular culture. John Dower catalogues racist depictions of Japanese and Japanese American people during World War II in *War Without Mercy: Race and Power in the Pacific War* (New York: Pantheon, 1987), and apes are a recurring source of material for caricaturized racist depictions of the United States' Asian enemy.

23. Tom Callahan, "Sport: A Banner Year for Meanness," *Time*, March 14, 1983, http://www.time.com/time/magazine/article/0,9171,951986-1,00.html.

24. Laurie Whitwell, "Russian Racism Shame as Robert Carlos Demands Action for Banana Throwing Incident," *Daily Mail*, March 24, 2011, http://www.dailymail.co.uk/sport/football/article-1369378/Russian-racism-shame-. Taunting black players with bananas is a recurring theme in professional European football. Fans will even taunt black players on their own teams, as is in the case of Carlos Kameni and Marc Zoro, highlighted by Jeremy Schapp, "European Soccer Combats Racial Abuse," ABC News, June 11, 2006, http://abcnews.go.com/WNT/ESPNSports/story?id=2064033&page=1.

25. "Flyers Game Marred by Banana Throwing Incident," CBS News, September 23, 2003, http://philadelphia.cbslocal.com/2011/09/23/flyers-game-marred-by-banana-throwing-incident/.

26. Scott Conroy, "Man at Palin Rally Displays Monkey Doll Donning Obama Sticker," CBS News, October 11, 2008, http://www.cbsnews.com/8301-502443_162-4515246-502443.html.

27. Dan Amira, "Makers of Racist Obama Monkey Would Like to Transcend Racism," *New York Magazine*, June 13, 2008, http://nymag.com/daily/intel/2008/06/the_makers_of_a_racist_obama_t.html.

28. The full text of this blog post has been removed, though its content was widely reported on the Internet, including by Claudio E. Cabrera, "French Magazine Calls the Obamas' Style 'Black-geiosie,'" The Root, January 25, 2012, http://www.theroot.com/french-elle-magazine-obamas-black-fashion.

29. Intersectionality is the central theoretical and analytic contribution of black feminist scholarship, and I want to emphasize my debt to this tradition here. Higginbotham's work is formative, and a deeper discussion of the roots of intersectionality appears in Chapter 4, where due credit is given to Kimberle Crenshaw, bell hooks, Patricia Hill Collins, and others. It needs to be emphasized that intersectionality is not a matter of simple multiplication, whereby race and gender combine to create a double burden, multiplying the intensity of the oppression of women of color. Intersectionality is not the same as "double (or triple) jeopardy," another catch phrase that emerged at the pinnacle of black feminist theoretical development to signify the double or triple intensity of black women's suffering. The multiple jeopardy framework may be useful in some cases, but it does not fully capture the utility of intersectionality.

30. Processes of discipline and categorization may in fact take place along a single axis of differentiation, such as race, gender, or class. That is, in some cases, people are divided and penalized strictly based on race or gender, and in others, the intersection of race and gender does the work of stratification and categorization. My argument here concerns *the meaning of the racial term itself*, which is always intersectional, even when those intersections are not explicit.

31. Antonia Darder and Rodolfo Torres, *After Race: Racism After Multiculturalism* (New York: New York University Press, 2004), 17.

32. Ellen M. Wood, *Democracy Against Capitalism: Renewing Historical Materialism* (New York: Cambridge University Press, 1995), 258.

33. Orlando Patterson's *Rituals of Blood: Consequences of Slavery in Two American Centuries* (New York: Basic Civitas Books, 1999) and Adolph Reed's *Stirrings in the Jug: Black Politics in the Post-Segregation Era* (Minneapolis: University of Minnesota Press, 1999) advance similar arguments about the commerce and commoditization of black culture.

34. Michelle Wallace, *Black Macho and the Myth of the Superwoman* (New York: Dial Press, 1978).

CHAPTER TWO: MY (FOUNDING) FATHER'S SON

1. As quoted in John Heilemann and Mark Halperin, *Game Change: Obama and the Clintons, McCain and Palin, and the Race of a Lifetime* (New York: Harper, 2010), 331.

2. A brief caveat: Chapter 3 emphasizes Obama's multiracial identity rather than solely his blackness, but in this chapter, I collapse multiracialism into blackness as a reflection of the way Obama self-identifies and is most commonly viewed.

3. The ideas in this paragraph are commonly shared by historians, sociologists, and political scientists, but for further reference, see succinct explanations by Anthony Marx, *Making Race and Nation: A Comparison of South Africa, the United States, and Brazil* (New York: Cambridge University Press, 1998), 4;

and Lauren L. Basson, *White Enough to Be American: Race Mixing, Indigenous People, and the Boundaries of State and Nation* (Chapel Hill: University of North Carolina Press, 2008), 13.

4. Rogers Brubaker, "In the Name of the Nation: Reflections on Nationalism and Patriotism," *Citizenship Studies* 8, no. 2 (June 2004): 116. In "Narrating the Nation" (in *Nationalism*, ed. John Hutchinson and Anthony D. Smith [Oxford: Oxford University Press, 1994]), Homi Bhabha observes that "nation" always carries a certain ambivalence, because it emerges out of signification rather than definitive historical roots. It is always a transitional social reality.

5. Alfred Cobban ("The Rise of the Nation-State System," in Hutchinson and Smith, *Nationalism*, 245–51) notes, "Although nation states had existed for centuries, before the nineteenth century no specific relationship had been posited between culture or language and the political state" (247). In "Nationalism and Ethnicity" (*Annual Review of Sociology* 19 [1993]: 211–39), Craig Calhoun provides a comprehensive literature review tracing the history of ethnicity and nation. While the definition I give approximates what Calhoun describes as an "ideal type" of nationalism, he observes the tension in all invocations of nationalism, which seem to imply that there is something fundamentally modern about the idea (reflected in the Cobban quotation), while relying on ancient ethnic history. He writes, "most variants of nationalist rhetoric claim the nation as an always-already existing basis for action, whether as the continuation of ancient ethnicity or as the result of historically specific acts of foundation" (214).

6. Benedict Anderson, *Imagined Communities: Reflections on the Origin and Spread of Nationalism* (London: Verso, 1991), 7.

7. Brubaker, "In the Name of the Nation," 121.

8. Barack Obama, "Keynote Speech at the 2004 Democratic National Convention," *Washington Post*, transcript published July 27, 2004, http://www.washington post.com/wp-dyn/articles/A19751-2004Jul27.html.

9. Jim Sidanius, Seymour Feshbach, Shana Levin, and Felicia Pratto, "The Interface Between Ethnic and National Attachment: Ethnic Pluralism or Ethnic Dominance?" *Public Opinion Quarterly* 61 (1997): 103–33.

10. See ibid., and Jim Sidanius and Felicia Pratto, *Social Dominance: An Intergroup Theory of Social Hierarchy and Oppression* (New York: Cambridge University Press, 1999).

11. By "classical racism," I mean documented beliefs about the inherent, unchanging inferiority of ethnoracial out-groups.

12. Sidanius et al., "Interface Between Ethnic and National Attachment," 118–23.

13. See Yesilernis Pena and Jim Sidanius, "American Patriotism and Ideologies of Group Dominance: A Tale of Asymmetry," *Journal of Social Psychology* 142 (2002): 782–90. The quotation appears in the article's abstract.

14. Christopher S. Parker, Mark Q. Sawyer, and Christopher Towler, "A *Black* Man in the *White* House?: The Role of Racism and Patriotism in the 2008 Presidential Election," *Du Bois Review* 6, no. 1 (2009): 207. Symbolic racism, discussed later in this chapter, is a theory driven by the idea that nonwhite bodies symbolize deviance, threat, and anti-American values. Laissez-faire racism is grounded in the notion that cultural (rather than biological) deficiencies among subjugated groups explain racial hierarchy rather than prejudice, discrimination, and institutional inequality. Laissez-faire racism is also characterized by the belief that the government should take a "hands off" approach in addressing racial inequality and that there is no reason to alter the way our institutions function.

15. Eric Hehman, Samuel L. Gaertner, and John F. Dovidio, "Evaluations of Presidential Performance: Race, Prejudice, and Perceptions of Americanism," *Journal of Experimental Psychology* 47, no. 2 (2011): 430–35.

16. The connections between whiteness and Americanness as normative categories present themselves beyond social psychology and political science. See Ruth Frankenberg, "Whiteness and Americanness: Examining Constructions of Race, Culture, and Nation in White Women's Life Narratives," in *Race*, ed. Steven Gregory and Roger Sanjek (New Brunswick: Rutgers University Press, 1994), 62–77. In her qualitative study of white women's self-narratives about white and American identity, Ruth Frankenberg finds that both whiteness and Americanness operate as "unmarked marker[s] . . . often viewed as substantively empty and yet taken as normative," and at times these terms become interchangeable for respondents (65–66). In "Differences from Somewhere: The Normativity of Whiteness in Bioethics in the United States," *American Journal of Bioethics* 3 (2003): 1-11, Catherine Myser extends the argument into the realm of bioethics, pointing out that although the notion of sociocultural diversity was introduced as a corrective to the notion of white normalcy, the "dominant white center of mainstream U.S. bioethics" has never been problematized, and the resulting research paradigm simply reifies white American normativity and the white/other racial binary.

17. Barack Obama, "Remarks by the President at the Memorial Service for Richard Holbrooke," *The White House*, published January 14, 2011, http://www.whitehouse.gov/the-press-office/2011/01/14/remarks-president-memorial-service-richard-holbrooke.

18. Ronald Takaki, *A Different Mirror: A History of Multicultural America* (Boston: Little, Brown, 1993), makes this argument explicitly, and the examples that follow in this paragraph show how the principle is applied to a range of nonwhite racial and ethnic groups in the United States. This particular ideology of citizenship is somewhat unique in that it combines two archetypes from Rogers Brubaker's *Nationhood Reframed: Nationhood and the National Question in the New Europe* (Cambridge: Cambridge University Press, 1996): citizen-

ship grounded in the place of residence at birth, and one grounded in blood. The importance of the place of residence component is evident in the fact that United States citizenship is born out of explicit comparison to citizenship in another place: Great Britain. The importance of blood is evident in the racial restrictions on United States citizenship.

19. See Edmund Morgan, *American Slavery, American Freedom* (New York: Norton, 1993), 369–70; and Matthew F. Jacobson, *Whiteness of a Different Color: European Immigrants and the Alchemy of Race* (Cambridge: Harvard University Press, 1999), 29–30.

20. Jacobson, *Whiteness of a Different Color*, 49–50, 87.

21. See Mae Ngai, "The Architecture of Race in American Immigration Law: A Reexamination of the Immigration Act of 1924," *Journal of American History* 86, no. 1 (June 1999): 67–92. President Theodore Roosevelt was especially fond of eugenics, and endeavored to build an America with the best possible mix of all the white races, as noted by Gary Gerstile, *American Crucible: Race and Nation in the Twentieth Century* (Princeton: Princeton University Press, 2001), 14–43.

22. For the most thorough treatment of the history of American immigration law, the legal inscription of whiteness as prerequisite for citizenship, and the construction of the "illegal alien" as a political subject, please see Mai Ngai, *Impossible Subjects: Illegal Aliens and the Making of Modern America* (Princeton: Princeton University Press, 2004).

23. Alondra Nelson, *Body and Soul: The Black Panther Party and the Fight Against Medical Discrimination* (Minneapolis: University of Minnesota Press, 2011), 10.

24. This formulation of the difference between public state identities and private ethnic identities comes from Anthony D. Smith, *The Ethnic Origins of Nations* (Cambridge: Blackwell, 1987), 151, though he does not discuss the feminist critique, which emphasizes the contradictions and power relations inherent to public/private dichotomies. These difficulties are common to a range of nation-states, but from the earliest days of America's nationhood they are exemplified by the experiences and critiques of African Americans. As W.E.B. Du Bois laments, "One ever feels his twoness—an American, a Negro; two souls, two thoughts, two unreconciled strivings; two warring ideals in one dark body, whose dogged strength alone keeps it from being torn asunder" (see *The Souls of Black Folk*, in *Three Negro Classics* [New York: Avon Books, 1903 (1965)], 207–390, 215).

25. Jon Swaine, "Mitt Romney Would Restore 'Anglo-Saxon' Relations Between Britain and America," *Daily Telegraph*, last modified July 24, 2102, http://www.telegraph.co.uk/news/worldnews/mitt-romney/9424524/Mitt-Romney-would-restore-Anglo-Saxon-relations-between-Britain-and-America.html.

26. Donald R. Kinder and David O. Sears, "Prejudice and Politics: Symbolic Racism Versus Racial Threats to the Good Life," *Journal of Personality and*

Social Psychology 40, no. 1 (1981): 414–31; Donald R. Kinder and Lynn M Sanders, *Divided by Color: Racial Politics and Democratic Ideals* (Chicago: University of Chicago Press, 1996). The reader should note that while symbolic racism is engrained during childhood, racist associations can be changed over the course of one's life.

27. See Thierry Devos and Mahzarin R. Banaji, "American = White?" *Journal of Personality and Social Psychology* 88, no. 3 (March 2005): 447–66; Sapna Cheryan and Benoit Monin, "'Where Are You Really From?': Asian-Americans and Identity Denial," *Journal of Personality and Social Psychology* 89, no. 5 (November 2005): 717–30. I am not the first to compare these theories to each other, as Lawrence D. Bobo uses symbolic racism as foil to develop his theory of group position prejudice ("Whites' Opposition to Busing: Symbolic Racism or Realistic Group Conflict?" *Journal of Personality and Social Psychology* 45 [1983]: 1196–1210) and laissez-faire racism ("The Color Line, the Dilemma, and the Dream: Race Relations in America at the Close of the Twentieth Century," in *Civil Rights and Social Wrongs: Black-White Relations Since World War II*, ed. John Higham [University Park: Pennsylvania State University Press, 1997], 31–58); and Eduardo Bonilla-Silva offers a similar comparison prior to explaining color-blind racism as his alternative in *Racism Without Racists: Color-Blind Racism and the Persistence of Racial Inequality in the United States* (New York: Rowman & Littlefield, 2003), 5–7. However, Bonilla-Silva also includes racial optimism, the notion that we are steadily progressing towards a more racially just and equitable society, an idea rendered suspect by the evidence presented in this chapter.

Bobo is critical of symbolic racism because it is a distinctly psychological approach that overemphasizes implicit attitudes and predispositions learned early in childhood; it wrongly denies the influence of self-interest on these beliefs and overlooks "realistic group conflict" between racial groups struggling to obtain and keep material resources. Prejudice is not simply about individuals learning that nonwhite bodies symbolize deviance or dishonor; it is about building a conception of one's own racial group as part of a socioeconomic hierarchy. Group position prejudice occurs when someone believes her racial group is more deserving of a privileged spot in the hierarchy than another. For further reference, see Lawrence Bobo and Mia Tuan, *Prejudice and Politics: Group Position, Public Opinion, and the Wisconsin Treaty Rights Dispute* (Cambridge: Harvard University Press, 2006).

This group-based notion of prejudice is built into Bobo's theory of *laissez-faire racism*, a term that emphasizes the government's hands-off approach and failure to intervene in the face of historical and contemporary prejudice and discrimination against nonwhite groups. Bobo emphasizes that classic racial prejudice and beliefs about blacks' inherent biological inferiority decreased throughout the twentieth century, but the public's shift in racial principles is unaccompanied by a shift in policy. By and large, the American public does not hold the government responsible for correcting racial inequality—it is not part of the national mission. More discouragingly, though beliefs about inherent *biological* inferiority have waned, many Americans affirm damaging stereotypes about black *cultural* pathology (Bobo, "Color Line, the Dilemma, and the Dream," 41).

Bonilla-Silva acknowledges the usefulness of both symbolic racism and laissez-faire racism but takes slight issue with each as he argues for a third conception, *color-blind racism*. The crucial difference between color-blind racism and other approaches is that prejudice and stereotyping is largely irrelevant to the theory. Antipathy and suspicion of racial others may exist, but these sentiments need not be articulated or empirically documented to verify the existence of racism. In fact, focusing too much attention on these psychological phenomena individualizes what is a profoundly structural problem. All that is needed is a racially inequitable social hierarchy and groups of actors at various levels who allow the hierarchy to sustain itself. For further reference, see Eduardo Bonilla-Silva, "Rethinking Racism: Toward a Structural Interpretation," *American Sociological Review* 62, no. 3 (1997): 465–80.

In sum, racism is a combination of (1) implicit bias and the tendency to associate nonwhites with deviance or threat, (2) belief that one's group deserves a specific place in the racial hierarchy, which may be accompanied by antipathy towards, or belief in the inferiority of, racial others, and (3) an ethic of denial and personal and governmental nonintervention when it comes to racial oppression and injustice.

28. Anthony D. Smith, *The Ethnic Origins of Nations* (Cambridge: Blackwell, 1987), 149.

29. I owe this distinction between history and memory to David Blight. In "Historians and 'Memory,'" *Common-Place* 2, no. 3 (2002), http://www.common-place.org/vol-02/no-03/author/, Blight explains,

History is what trained historians do, a reasoned reconstruction of the past rooted in research; it tends to be critical and skeptical of human motive and action, and therefore more secular than what people commonly call memory. History can be read by or belong to everyone; it is more relative, and contingent on place, chronology, and scale.

If history is shared and secular, memory is often treated as a sacred set of absolute meanings and stories, possessed as the heritage or identity of a community. Memory is often owned, history interpreted. Memory is passed down through generations; history is revised. Memory often coalesces in objects, sites, and monuments; history seeks to understand contexts in all their complexity.

30. Lawrence D. Bobo, "Somewhere Between Jim Crow & Post-Racialism: Reflections on the Racial Divide in America Today," *Daedalus* 140, no. 2 (Spring 2011).

31. Kyle Trygstad, "Poll: Majority of Republicans Doubt Obama's Birthplace," Roll Call, February 15, 2011, http://www.rollcall.com/news/Poll-Majority-GOP-Birthers-203418-1.html.

32. "CNN Debunks False Report About Obama," CNN, January 22, 2007, http://articles.cnn.com/2007-01-22/politics/obama.madrassa_1_islamic -school-madrassa-muslim-school?_s=PM:POLITICS.

33. "Hillary Clinton Drops Madrassa Bomb on Obama," Fox News, January 22, 2007, http://www.foxnews.com/story/0,2933,245582,00.html.

34. As quoted in Alex Koppelman, "Why the Stories About Obama's Birth Certificate Will Never Die," Salon, December 5, 2008, http://www.salon.com/ news/feature/2008/12/05/birth_certificate.

35. See "Limbaugh: 'Barack Obama Has Yet to Have to Prove He's a Citizen. All He Has to Do Is Show a Birth Certificate," Media Matters, July 20, 2009, http://mediamatters.org/mmtv/200907200028; and Ben Smith, "Palin: Obama Birth Certificate 'A Fair Question,'" Politico, December 3, 2009, http://www .politico.com/blogs/bensmith/1209/Palin_Obama_birth_certificate_a_fair_ques tion.html?showall.

36. Andrew Zajac, "John Boehner: 'Not My job' to Convince Skeptics on Obama Birth, Religion," *Chicago Tribune*, last modified February 13, 2011, http://www.chicagotribune.com/news/nationworld/sc-dc-boehner-obama -birth-20110213,0,861253.story. Emphasis in original. Catalina Camia, "Romney Surrogate Sununu Sorry for Slamming Obama," *USA Today*, last modified July 17, 2012, http://content.usatoday.com/communities/onpolitics/post/2012/07/ john-sununu-obama-american-mitt-romney-/1.

37. "About the Tea Party," Tea Party Patriots, February 9, 2012, http://www .teapartypatriots.org/about.

38. Christopher S. Parker is the principal investigator of the "Multi-State Survey of Race and Politics," published on the Internet by the University of Washington Institute for the Study of Ethnicity, Race and Sexuality, at http:// depts.washington.edu/uwiser/racepolitics.html (accessed August 10, 2011).

39. Huffington Post compiled a photo journal of the ten most offensive Tea Party signs captured on film. It is available at http://www.huffingtonpost .com/2009/04/16/10-most-offensive-tea-par_n_187554.html. See also Zachary Roth, "Conservative Activist Forwards Racist Pic Showing Obama as Witch Doctor," Talking Points Memo, last modified July 23, 2009, http://tpmmuck raker.talkingpointsmemo.com/2009/07/conservative_activist_forwards_ racist_pic_showing.php; Associated Press, "Iowa Tea Party Billboard Compares Obama to Hitler," Fox News, last modified July 13, 2010, http://www.foxnews .com/politics/2010/07/13/iowa-tea-party-billboard-compares-obama-hitler/.

40. See Kenneth P. Vogel, "Tea Party 'Expulsion' Reveals New Rifts," Politico, last modified July 20, 2010, http://www.politico.com/news/stories/ 0710/39940.html; and Eugene Washington, "The Tea Party Must Purge Racism from Its Ranks," *Washington Post*, July 20, 2010, http://www.washingtonpost. com/wpdyn/content/article/2010/07/19/AR2010071903686.html.

41. For two of the more measured treatments of this topic, please see Joan

Walsh, "Too Much Tea Party Racism," Salon, March 20, 2010, http://www.salon
.com/news/opinion/joan_walsh/politics/2010/03/20/tea_party_racism; and Eugene Washington, "Racism and the Tea Party Movement," Real Clear Politics,
November 2, 2010, http://www.realclearpolitics.com/articles/2010/11/02/race_
and_the_tea_partys_ire_107805.html.

42. See James B. Peterson, "Tea Party Tar Babies," Huffington Post, August 15, 2011, http://www.huffingtonpost.com/james-peterson/tea-party-tar
-babies_b_922353.html.

43. In "Tea Time with the Posse: Inside an Idaho Tea Party Patriots Conference," Institute for Research on Education and Human Rights, April 18, 2011,
http://www.irehr.org/issue-areas/tea-parties/19-news/79-tea-time-with-the
-posse-inside-an-idaho-tea-party-patriots-conference, Devin Burghart details
the anti-Jewish propaganda on display at the Tea Party Patriots conference in
April 2011, though this is hardly the first instance of documented Tea Party
anti-Semitism. Michael McAuliff reports on hostile encounters with Tea Party
sympathizers in the halls of Congress during March 2010 in "Make That the
Nas-Tea Party," New York Daily News, March 20, 2010, http://www.nydaily
news.com/blogs/dc/2010/03/make-that-the-nas-tea-party.html.

44. Matt Taibbi provides two poignant examples in his lengthy Rolling
Stone piece describing his time at Tea Party rallies, entitled "The Truth About
the Tea Party," September 28, 2010, http://www.rollingstone.com/politics/news/
matt-taibbi-on-the-tea-party-20100928. Koch Industries (owned by billionaire
and Wisconsin labor union antagonist David Koch) funds Americans for Prosperity, and Steve Forbes is a major funding provider for FreedomWorks.

45. Kenneth Jackson (Crabgrass Frontier: The Suburbanization of the United
States [Oxford: Oxford University Press, 1987]) and Ira Katznelson (When Affirmative Action Was White: An Untold History of Racial Inequality in Twentieth
Century America [New York: Norton, 2005]) provide thorough historical accounts of these initiatives that demonstrate how they maintained and exacerbated racial inequality.

46. Jill Lepore, The Whites of Their Eyes: The Tea Party Revolution and the
Battle over American History (Princeton: Princeton University Press, 2010), 7–8.

47. Nilanjana Dasgupta and Kumar Yogeeswaran, "Obama-Nation? Implicit Beliefs About American Nationality and the Possibility of Redefining
Who Counts as 'Truly' American," in The Obamas and (Post) Racial America,
ed. Gregory S. Parks and Matthew Hughey (Oxford: Oxford University Press,
2011), 72–90.

48. Barack Obama, Dreams from My Father: A Story of Race and Inheritance
(New York: Three Rivers Press, 1995), xvi.

49. Ibid., 10.

50. Ibid., 11.

51. Ibid., 16.

52. Ibid., 25.

53. Ibid., 25–26.

54. Ibid., 45.

55. Ibid., 47.

56. Ibid., 51.

57. Ibid., 52.

58. Ibid., 220.

59. Ibid., 220–21.

60. Ibid., 328.

61. Ibid., 329.

62. Ibid., 331.

63. Ibid., 435.

64. Ibid., 433.

65. Ibid., 294.

66. Craig Calhoun, "Is It Time to Be Postnational?" in *Ethnicity, Nationalism, and Minority Rights*, ed. Stephen May, Tariq Modood, and Judith Squires (Cambridge: Cambridge University Press, 2004), 238.

67. Joseph Stiglitz, "Of the 1 Percent, By the 1 Percent, For the 1 Percent," *Vanity Fair*, May 2011, http://www.vanityfair.com/society/features/2011/05/top-one-percent-201105?currentPage=1.

68. Sabrina Tavernise, "Soaring Poverty Casts Spotlight on 'Lost Decade,'" *New York Times*, September 13, 2011, http://www.nytimes.com/2011/09/14/us/14census.html?_r=2&hp.

69. Christopher Hayes, *Twilight of the Elites: America After Meritocracy* (New York: Crown, 2012), 61.

70. Stiglitz, "Of the 1 Percent, By the 1 Percent, For the 1 Percent"; and Bob Herbert, "When Democracy Weakens," *New York Times*, February 11, 2011, http://www.nytimes.com/2011/02/12/opinion/12herbert.html.

71. These basic stipulations are outlined in the introduction of John L. Campbell's useful work on the recent crisis in neoliberalism, "Neoliberalism in Crisis: Regulatory Roots of the U.S. Financial Meltdown," in *Markets on Trial: The Economic Sociology of the U.S. Financial Crisis: Part B Research in the Sociology of Organizations, Volume 30*, ed. Michael Lounsbury and Paul M. Hirsch (Bingley, U.K.: Emerald Group), 66.

CHAPTER THREE: "MUTTS LIKE ME"

1. "Obama Prefers 'Mutt Like Me,'" CNN, November 7, 2008, http://www.cnn.com/video/#/video/politics/2008/11/07/sot.obama.dog.cnn (accessed August 10, 2011).

2. Shelby Steele, "The Loneliness of the Black Conservative," *Hoover Digest* 1, January 30, 1999, http://www.hoover.org/publications/hoover-digest/article/7691.

3. Shelby Steele, *The Content of Our Character: A New Vision of Race in America* (New York: HarperCollins, 1990), 2–3.

4. See Steele, "Loneliness of the Black Conservative," as well as *A Dream Deferred: A Second Betrayal of Black Freedom in America* (New York: Harper-Collins, 1998), and *White Guilt: How Blacks and Whites Together Destroyed the Promise of the Civil Rights Era* (New York: HarperCollins, 2006).

5. Shelby Steele, *A Bound Man: Why We Are Excited About Obama and Why He Can't Win* (New York: Free Press, 2008), 38.

6. Ibid., 71.

7. See Benoit Monin and Dale T. Miller, "Moral Credentials and the Expression of Prejudice," *Journal of Personality and Social Psychology* 8, no. 1 (2001): 33–43.

8. Kimberly McClain DaCosta, "All in the Family: The Familial Roots of Racial Divisions," in *The Politics of Multiracialism: Challenging Racial Thinking*, ed. Heather Dalmage (Albany: SUNY Press 2004), 20. Emphasis in original.

9. Ibid., 29.

10. Werner Sollors, "Introduction," in *Interracialism: Black-White Intermarriage in American History, Literature, and Law*, ed. Werner Sollors (Oxford: Oxford University Press, 2000), 4–5.

11. For a comprehensive treatment of antimiscegenation law history and enforcement, please see Randall Kennedy, *Interracial Intimacies: Sex, Marriage, Identity, and Adoption* (New York: Pantheon, 2003), 214–43. Kennedy explicitly notes that since the early eighteenth century, all antimiscegenation laws prohibited black-white partnership (220).

12. Maria P.P. Root, *Love's Revolution: Interracial Marriage* (Philadelphia: Temple University Press, 2001), 34–35.

13. For further reference, see Naomi Zack, "American Mixed Race: The United States 2000 Census and Related Issues," in *Mixing It Up: Multiracial Subjects*, ed. Sansan Kwan, Kenneth Speirs, and Naomi Zack (Austin: University of Texas Press, 2004), 14–15.

14. Hazel Carby, *Reconstructing Womanhood: The Emergence of the Afro-American Woman Novelist* (New York: Oxford University Press, 1987), 89.

15. "Judge Defends Denied Interracial Marriage," CBS News, October 19, 2009,
http://www.cbsnews.com/stories/2009/10/19/earlyshow/main5396242
.shtml.

16. Erica Chito Childs, "Black and White: Family Opposition to Becoming Multiracial," in *Mixed Messages: Multiracial Identity in the "Color-Blind" Era*, ed. David Brunsma (Boulder: Lynne Rienner, 2006), 243.

17. Root, *Love's Revolution*, 38. In *Challenging Multiracialism* (Boulder: Lynne Rienner, 2006), 68–69, Rainier Spencer points out that the research on multiracialism does not establish a *causal* relationship between the *Loving* deci-

sion and the rise in interracial unions, so I want to be clear that I am not making such a claim by presenting these data.

18. "Interracial Marriage Rising, but Not as Fast," CBS News, May 26, 2010, http://www.cbsnews.com/stories/2010/05/26/national/main6520098.shtml.

19. It is an impossible task to list all the works in "the canon" of assimilation research; good places to start include Richard Alba and Victor Nee, *Remaking the American Mainstream: Assimilation and Contemporary Immigration* (Cambridge: Harvard University Press, 2003); Herbert Gans, "Symbolic Ethnicity: The Future of Ethnic Groups and Cultures in America," *Ethnic and Racial Studies* 2, no. 1 (1979): 1–20; Noel Ignatiev, *How the Irish Became White* (New York: Routledge, 1995); Alejandro Portes and Min Zhou, "The New Second Generation: Segmented Assimilation and Its Variants," *Annals of the American Academy of Political and Social Science* 530, no. 1 (November 1993): 74–96; and Mary Waters, *Ethnic Options: Choosing Identities in America* (Berkeley: University of California Press, 1990), and *Black Identities: West Indian Immigrant Dreams and American Realities* (Cambridge: Harvard University Press, 1999). There are many different theories of assimilation and integration, and Alba and Nee provide a thorough summary of the range of theories and the historical development of the field.

20. United States Census, "Married Couple Family Groups, by Presence of Own Children/1 In Specific Age Groups, and Age, Earnings, Education, and Race and Hispanic Origin/2 of Both Spouses," published 2010, http://www.census.gov/population/socdemo/hh-fam/cps2010/tabFG4-all.xls (accessed August 10, 2011).

21. David Parker and Miri Song, "Introduction: 'Rethinking Mixed Race,'" in *Rethinking Mixed Race*, ed. David Parker and Miri Song (London: Pluto Press, 2001), 1–22.

22. This paragraph summarizes Kim Williams, *Mark One or More: Civil Rights in Multiracial America* (Ann Arbor: University of Michigan Press, 2006), which is the most highly specified academic work on multiracialism as it pertains to the 2000 Census.

23. Kimberly McClain DaCosta, *Making Multiracials: State, Family, and Market in the Remaking of the Color Line* (Stanford: Stanford University Press, 2007), 29–30, identifies a paradox here, in that these are claims based on the rights of a given *individual*, but activists were simultaneously arguing for the creation and protection of a *group*.

24. Williams, *Mark One or More*, 2.

25. Molefi Kete Asante, "Racing to Leave the Race: Black Postmodernists Off-Track," *Black Scholar* 23, nos. 3–4 (Spring/Fall 1993): 50–51.

26. Herbert J. Gans, "The Possibility of a New Racial Hierarchy in the Twenty First Century in the United States," in *The Cultural Territories of Race*, ed. Michele Lamont (Chicago: University of Chicago Press, 1999), 371–390.

27. Charles Gallagher, "Racial Redistricting: Expanding the Boundaries of Whiteness," in *The Politics of Multiracialism: Challenging Racial Thinking*, ed. Heather Dalmage (Albany: SUNY Press, 2004), 74.

28. DaCosta, *Making Multiracials*, 6.

29. See James P. Smith and Barry Edmonston, *The New Americans: Economic, Demographic, and Fiscal Effects of Immigration* (Washington: National Academies Press, 1997).

30. Each bullet point is a direct excerpt from Susan Saulny, "Census Shows Rise in Multiracial Population of Youths," *New York Times*, modified March 24, 2011, http://www.nytimes.com/2011/03/25/us/25race.html.

31. Though, as Michele Elam notes in "Why Obama Is Black Again," *Stanford Report*, January 29, 2009, http://humanexperience.stanford.edu/race-elam, two years before the 2010 Census, the OMB reported that the number of people self-identifying as mixed had actually been declining since 2006.

32. Kimberly McClain DaCosta, "Selling Mixedness: Marketing with Multiracial Identities," in Brunsma, *Mixed Messages*, 185–93.

33. Michele Elam, *The Souls of Mixed Folk: Race, Politics, and Aesthetics in the New Millennium* (Stanford: Stanford University Press, 2011).

34. Ibid., 39.

35. See Kerri Ann Rockquemore and David L. Brunsma, *Beyond Black: Biracial Identity in America* (Thousand Oaks: Sage, 2001); Natalie Masuoka, "The 'Multiracial' Option: Social Group Identity and Changing Patterns of Racial Categorization," *American Politics Research* 39, no. 1 (2011): 176–204.

36. See Stephanie Dunning, "'Brown Like Me': Explorations of a Shifting Self," in Kwan, Speirs, and Zack, *Mixing It Up*, 123–140; David R. Harris and Jeremiah Joseph, "Who Is Multiracial? Assessing the Complexity of Lived Race," *American Sociological Review* 67, no. 4 (August 2002): 614–27; Wendy Roth, "The End of the One-Drop Rule? Labeling of Multiracial Children in Black Intermarriages," *Sociological Forum* 20, no. 1 (March 2005): 35–67; Natalie Masuoka, "Political Attitudes and Ideologies of Multiracial Americans," *Political Research Quarterly* 61, no. 2 (2008): 253–67.

37. Masuoka uses the same data set in both her 2008 and 2011 articles.

38. See Masuoka, "Political Attitudes and Ideologies of Multiracial Americans" and "'Multiracial' Option." In the earlier work, she notes two exceptions: "multiracial blacks have similar perspectives on race-based policy solutions as monoracial blacks, and multiracial Asians have similar perspectives on racial discrimination as monoracial whites" (261).

39. Melissa R. Herman, "'Do You See What I Am?': How Observers' Backgrounds Affect Their Perceptions of Multiracial Faces," *Social Psychology Quarterly* 73, no. 1 (2010): 58–78.

40. Richard Jenkins, *Social Identity* (London: Routledge, 1996).

41. Arnold K. Ho, Jim Sidanius, Daniel T. Levin, and Mahzarin R. Banaji,

"Evidence for Hypodescent and Racial Hierarchy in the Categorization and Perception of Biracial Individuals," *Journal of Personality and Social Psychology* 94 (2011): 1–15.

42. Nicholas A. Valentino and Ted Brader, "The Sword's Other Edge: Perceptions of Discrimination and Racial Policy Opinion After Obama," *Public Opinion Quarterly* 75, no. 2 (2011): 201–6; Michael I. Norton and Samuel R. Sommers, "Whites See Racism as a Zero-Sum Game That They Are Now Losing," *Perspectives on Psychological Science* 6, no. 3 (2011): 215–18.

43. Felicia R. Lee, "Pushing Boundaries, Mixed-Race Artists Gain Notice," *New York Times*, July 5, 2011, http://www.nytimes.com/2011/07/06/arts/mixed-race-writers-and-artists-raise-their-profiles.html?pagewanted=1&_r=2.

44. David A. Hollinger, *Postethnic America: Beyond Multiculturalism* (New York: Basic Books, 2005), 181.

CHAPTER FOUR: POSTRACIALISM RECONSIDERED

1. As quoted in Jann S. Wenner, "Ready for the Fight: *Rolling Stone* Interview with Barack Obama," *Rolling Stone*, April 25, 2012, http://www.rollingstone.com/politics/news/ready-for-the-fight-rolling-stone-interview-with-barack-obama-20120425.

2. "MSNBC's Matthews on Obama: 'I Forgot He Was Black Tonight,'" RealClearPolitics, January 27, 2010, http://www.realclearpolitics.com/video/2010/01/27/msnbcs_matthews_on_obama_i_forgot_he_was_black_tonight.html.

3. Sumi Cho, "Post-Racialism," *Iowa Law Review* 94, no. 2 (2009): 1598.

4. Roland Martin, "Washington Watch with Roland Martin: In Conversation with Michelle Obama," TVOne, August 24, 2008, http://tvoneblogs.com/roland/news/tv-ones-michelle-obama-interview-wins-image-award-977.htm/comment-page-20, and http://www.youtube.com/watch?v=UIrd4MOatko.

5. William Julius Wilson, *The Declining Significance of Race* (Chicago: University of Chicago Press, 1978), 1–3.

6. Matt Bai, "Post-Race—Is Obama the End of Black Politics?" *New York Times Magazine*, August 6, 2008, http://www.nytimes.com/2008/08/10/magazine/10politics-t.html?em.

7. In "The Conceptualization of Deracialization" (in *Dilemmas of Black Politics*, ed. Georgia Persons [New York: HarperCollins, 1993]) Joseph McCormick and Charles Jones define "deracialization" as a campaign strategy that avoids explicit discussion of racial issues in favor of issues deemed racially transcendent. Black candidates employ these tactics to gain the support of and mobilize a large swath of the electorate, rather than building outward from a small base of black voters. Even when candidates hold court with a black audience, staunch commitment to deracialization requires avoiding direct racial appeals for support and discussion of race-specific political issues.

8. Here I am indebted to Andra Gillespie, who establishes this historical content and builds a useful, three-category historical typology of black political leadership in "Meet the New Class: Theorizing Young Black Leadership in a 'Postracial' Era" (in *Whose Black Politics?: Cases in Post-Racial Black Leadership*, ed. Andra Gillespie [New York: Routledge, 2009], 13–14).

9. Ron Walters, "Barack Obama and the Politics of Blackness," *Journal of Black Studies* 18, no. 1 (September 2007): 16. Walters notes that these points summarize his arguments in his 2005 book, *Freedom Is Not Enough* (Lanham: Rowman & Littlefield), but they are presented in the 2007 article in a more succinct and straightforward manner.

10. Gwen Ifill, *The Breakthrough: Politics and Race in the Age of Obama* (New York: Doubleday, 2009), 24–25.

11. Ibid., 38.

12. Ibid., 44.

13. Sekou Franklin makes a strong case for situational, rather than absolute, deracialization in "Situational Deracialization, Harold Ford, and the 2006 Senate Race in Tennessee" in Gillespie's previously cited *Whose Black Politics?*, 220.

14. Manning Marable, "Introduction: Racializing Obama: The Enigma of Postblack Politics and Leadership," in *Barack Obama and African American Empowerment: The Rise of Black America's New Leadership*, ed. Manning Marable and Kristen Clarke (New York: Palgrave MacMillan, 2009), 11.

15. Mary Pattillo-McCoy, "Middle Class, yet Black: A Review Essay," *African American Research Perspectives* 5, no. 1 (1999).

16. United States Census Bureau, "Poverty in the United States: 2000," last modified 2001, www.census.gov/prod/2001pubs/p60-214.pdf.

17. Erick Eckholm, "Recession Raises Poverty Rate to 15-Year High" *New York Times*, September 16, 2010, http://www.nytimes.com/2010/09/17/us/17poverty.html?_r=1&pagewanted=all.

18. The classic texts on this issue are Dalton Conley's *Race, Wealth, and Social Policy in America* (Berkeley: University of California Press, 1999); and Melvin Oliver and Thomas Shapiro's *Black Wealth/White Wealth: A New Perspective on Racial Inequality* (New York: Routledge, 1995).

19. See Mary Pattillo-McCoy, *Black Picket Fences: Privilege and Peril Among the Black Middle Class* (Chicago: University of Chicago Press, 1999).

20. George Wilson, "Racialized Life-Chance Opportunities Across the Class Structure: The Case of African Americans," *Annals of the American Academy of Political and Social Science* 609 (January 2007): 222–23.

21. Patrick Sharkey, "The Intergenerational Transmission of Context," *American Journal of Sociology* 113, no. 4 (January 2008): 931.

22. Wilson, "Racialized Life-Chance Opportunities Across the Class Structure," 220–21.

23. In *Black Visions: The Roots of Contemporary African-American Political Ideologies* (Chicago: University of Chicago Press, 2001), Michael Dawson is careful to note that these patterns of political behavior do not indicate a lack of ideological variation among blacks, who disagree vehemently about a host of political issues and political strategies. The common strand, however, that links many of these ideologies is an insistence on racial dynamics as vital determinants of one's social and political experiences.

24. Frederick C. Harris, Valeria Sinclair-Chapman, and Brian D. McKenzie, "Macrodynamics of Black Political Participation," *Journal of Politics* 67, no. 4 (November 2005).

25. Jason E. Shelton and George Wilson, "Race, Class, and the Basis of Group Alignment: An Analysis of Support for Redistributive Policies Among Privilege Blacks," *Sociological Perspectives* 52, no. 3 (Fall 2009).

26. This paragraph summarizes Michael Dawson's arguments in two key works: Michael C. Dawson, "A Black Counter Public?: Economic Earthquakes, Racial Agendas, and Black Politics," in *The Black Public Sphere: A Public Culture Book*, ed. Black Public Sphere Collective (Chicago: University of Chicago Press, 1995), 199–227; and the aforementioned *Black Visions*.

27. Jürgen Habermas, *The Structural Transformation of the Public Sphere: An Inquiry into a Category of Bourgeois Society* (Cambridge: MIT Press, 1991).

28. Michael Hanchard, "Black Cinderella?: Race and the Public Sphere in Brazil," in Black Public Sphere Collective, *Black Public Sphere*, 173.

29. Nancy Fraser, "Rethinking the Public Sphere: A Contribution to the Critique of Actually Existing Democracy," *Social Text* 25/26 (1990): 67.

30. Dawson emphasizes this point about black counterpublics in *Black Visions*, though Felski makes it earlier, pointing out that counterpublics must direct their energy outward and engage greater society.

31. Dawson, *Black Visions*, 35.

32. Ibid., 41.

33. Melissa V. Harris-Perry (Harris-Lacewell), *Barbershops, Bibles, and BET: Everyday Talk and Black Political Thought* (Princeton: Princeton University Press, 2004), xxiii.

34. See Fredrick C. Harris, *Something Within: Religion in African-American Political Activism* (Oxford: Oxford University Press, 1999); Michael L. Owens, *God and Government in the Ghetto: The Politics of Church-State Collaboration in Black America* (Chicago: University of Chicago Press, 2007); and Eric L. McDaniel, *Politics in the Pews: The Political Mobilization of Black Churches* (Ann Arbor: University of Michigan Press, 2008).

35. Harris-Perry, *Barbershops, Bibles, and BET*, 202.

36. Houston Baker, "Critical Memory and the Black Public Sphere," in Black Public Sphere Collective, *Black Public Sphere*, 23.

37. Harris-Perry, *Barbershops, Bibles, and BET*, 6.

38. Marshall McLuhan, *Understanding Media: The Extensions of Man* (Cambridge: MIT Press, 1994 [1964]), 7.

39. Marshall McLuhan, *The Gutenberg Galaxy: The Making of Typographic Man* (Toronto: University of Toronto Press, 1962).

40. McLuhan, *Understanding Media*, 5.

41. As quoted in Robert J. Downey, "'Barbershop' Attacked by Revered Jesse Jackson," MTV News, September 25, 2002, http://www.mtv.com/news/articles/1457788/20020925/ice_cube.jhtml.

42. See Dawson, *Black Visions*; and Gwendolyn Pough, *Check It While I Wreck It: Black Womanhood, Hip-Hop Culture, and the Public Sphere* (Boston: Northeastern University Press, 2004).

43. Jennifer C. Lena, "Social Context and Musical Content of Rap Music, 1979–1995," *Social Forces* 85, no. 1 (2006): 479–95.

44. See http://www.cnn.com/SPECIALS/2009/black.in.america/ (accessed August 30, 2011).

45. See Ann Coulter, "Throw Grandma Under the Bus," AnnCoulter.com, March 19, 2008, http://www.anncoulter.com/cgi-local/article.cgi?article=241; Rush Limbaugh, "Obama's Double Life Exposed: His Racist, Hatemonger Pastor," RushLimbaugh.com, March 13, 2008, http://www.rushlimbaugh.com/home/daily/site_031308/content/01125106.guest.html; and Bill O'Reilly, "Talking Points: Obama Pastor Controversy Continues," Fox News, March 17, 2008, http://www.foxnews.com/story/0,2933,338488,00.html.

46. Here is the full excerpt from Wright's 2003 sermon, "Confusing Government and God," ABC News, April 24, 2008, http://abcnews.go.com/Blotter/story?id=4719157&page=2, known for its "God damn America" quotation, for further reference:
The British government failed, the Russian government failed, the Japanese government failed, the German government failed, and the United States of America government, when it came to treating her citizens of Indian descent fairly, she failed. She put them on reservations. When it came to treating her citizens of Japanese decent fairly, she failed. She put them in internment prison camps. When it came to treating her citizens of African descent fairly, America failed. The government put them in chains. She put them on slave quarters, put them on auction blocks, put them in cotton fields, put them in inferior schools, put them in sub-standard housing, put them in scientific experiments, put them in the lowest paying jobs, put them outside the equal protection of the law, kept them out of their racist bastions of higher education, and locked them into positions of hopelessness and helplessness. The government gives them the drugs, builds bigger prisons, passes a three strike law, and then wants us to sing God Bless America . . . no, no, no.
Not God bless America, God damn America! That's in the Bible, for killing innocent people. God damn America for treating her citizens as less than human! God damn America for as long as she acts like she is God and she is supreme!

47. Barack Obama, "A More Perfect Union," delivered March 18, 2008, in Philadelphia, http://www.americanrhetoric.com/speeches/barackobamaperfect union.htm.

48. Ibid.

49. Obama, *Dreams from My Father*, 200–201.

50. Ibid., 273–74.

51. Ibid., 286.

52. Eugene Robinson, "Obama's Road Map on Race," *Washington Post*, March 18, 2008, http://www.washingtonpost.com/wp-dyn/content/article /2008/03/18/AR2008031802649.html.

53. Jonathan Kaufman and Gary Fields, "Election of Obama Recasts National Conversation on Race," *Wall Street Journal*, November 10, 2008, http:// online.wsj.com/article/SB122627584403012071.html.

54. Sarah Kershaw, "Talk About Race? Relax It's Okay," *New York Times*, January 15, 2009, http://www.nytimes.com/2009/01/15/world/americas/15iht-15 race.19375220.html.

55. "How Does Your Country Talk About Race?" National Public Radio, February 26, 2009, http://www.npr.org/templates/story/story.php?storyId =101195212.

56. Sheryl Stolberg and Marjorie Connelly, "Obama Is Nudging Views on Race, a Survey Finds," *New York Times*, April 27, 2009, http://www.nytimes.com /2009/04/28/us/politics/28poll.html?_r=1&hp.

57. Susan Saulny, "Voices Reflect Rising Sense of Racial Optimism," *New York Times*, May 3, 2009, http://www.nytimes.com/2009/05/03/us/ politics/03race.html?_r=1&hp.

58. Mendelberg, *Race Card*.

59. For reference, please view the video at "Anti-Harold Ford Ad Draws Racism Charges," Truthdig, October 24, 2006, http://www.truthdig.com/ avbooth/item/20060124_harold_ford_ad/.

60. The phrase "the real Barack Obama" became a catchphrase of the McCain campaign during its final months, as noted by Michael Cooper, "Who Is the Real Barack Obama?" *New York Times*, October 6, 2008, http://thecaucus .blogs.nytimes.com/2008/10/06/mccain-who-is-the-real-barack-obama/.

61. Republican Party of Pennsylvania, "The Real Barack Obama: Judgment," available at YouTube.com, http://www.youtube.com/ watch?v=yoGcYKu_zFo (accessed January 10, 2010).

62. While not identical, the language of these bullet points is extremely close to that used in the summary report of the "Pew Internet and American Life Project." The original document can be found at http://www.pewinternet .org/Reports/2009/6—The-Internets-Role-in-Campaign-2008.aspx?r=1, and the citation for the complete report is Aaron Smith, "The Internet's Role in Campaign 2008," April 2009, available on the Pew Internet and American Life

Project website at http://www.pewinternet.org/Reports/2009/6—The-Internets
-Role-in-Campaign-2008.aspx?r=1 (accessed January 10, 2010).

63. These potential benefits are outlined by Bruce Bimber, "The Internet
and Political Transformation: Populism, Community, and Accelerated Pluralism," *Polity* 31, no. 1 (1998): 133–60.

64. See Lawrence K. Grossman, *The Electronic Republic: Reshaping Democracy in America* (New York: Viking, 1995); and Anthony Corrado and Charles
M. Firestone (eds.), *Elections in Cyberspace: Toward a New Era in American Politics* (Washington: Aspen Institute, 1996).

65. Bimber, "Internet and Political Transformation," 136.

66. Bimber, "Internet and Political Transformation," 152. See also Michael
Cornfield, "The Internet and Democratic Participation," *National Civic Review*
89 (2000): 235–40.

67. Omar Wasow, "The First Internet President," The Root, November 5,
2008, http://www.theroot.com/views/first-internet-president.

68. Michel Marriott, "Digital Divide Closing as Blacks Turn to the Internet," *New York Times*, March 31, 2006, http://www.nytimes.com/2006/03/31/
us/31divide.html.

69. See Wasow, "First Internet President"; and Traci Burch, "Can the New
Commander in Chief Sustain His All-Volunteer Standing Army?" *Du Bois
Review* 6, no. 1 (2009): 159.

70. Emphasis added, as quoted in Roger Simon, "Obama: 'I Have the Potential of Bringing People Together," Politico, February 7, 2007, http://www
.politico.com/news/stories/0207/2689.html.

71. Alex Beam, "Is Your President This Cool?" *Boston Globe*, November 14,
2008, http://www.boston.com/lifestyle/articles/2008/11/13/is_your_president
_this_cool/; also see Damien Cave, "Generation O Gets Its Hopes Up,"
New York Times, November 7, 2008, http://www.nytimes.com/2008/11/09/
fashion/09boomers.html?pagewanted=all.

72. This testimony can be found at http://my.barackobama.com/page/
community/blog/stateupdates/2008/06 (accessed January 10, 2010).

73. Pippa Norris, *Digital Divide: Civic Engagement, Information Poverty,
and the Internet Worldwide* (Cambridge: Cambridge University Press, 2001),
230–31.

74. Matthew S. Hindman, *The Myth of Digital Democracy* (Princeton:
Princeton University Press, 2009), 131–33.

75. Ibid., 138.

76. See Raul H. Ojeda, Albert Jacquez, and Paula C. Takash, "The End of
the American Dream for Blacks and Latinos: How the Home Mortgage Crisis
Is Destroying Black and Latino Wealth, Jeopardizing America's Prosperity and
How to Fix It," William C. Velasquez Institute, June 2009, http://www.wcvi.org/
data/pub/wcvi_whitepaper_housing_june2009.pdf (accessed August 10, 2011).

77. This is not speculation; Nicolas D. Kristof's "A Banker Speaks, with Regrets," *New York Times*, November 30, 2011, includes statements from former Chase Bank vice president James Theckston confirming these tactics. See also, Jacob Rugh and Douglas Massey, "Racial Segregation and the American Foreclosure Crisis," *American Sociological Review* 75, no. 5 (2010): 629–51.

78. Kenneth J. Cooper, "Lending to Blacks, Hispanics Plummets During Housing Crisis," *Chicago Sun-Times*, March 15, 2011, http://www.suntimes .com/business/3803378-420/lending-to-blacks-hispanics-plummets-during -housing-crisis.html.

CHAPTER FIVE: THE PERILS OF BEING SUPERWOMAN

1. As quoted during her 2008 TV One interview with Roland Martin, "Washington Watch with Roland Martin: In Conversation with Michelle Obama," clip retrieved May 19, 2011, at http://tvoneblogs.com/roland/news/tv -ones-michelle-obama-interview-wins-image-award-977.htm/comment-page-20.

2. Frank Newport, David W. Moore, and Lydia Saad, "Most Admired Men and Women 1948–1998," Gallup, December 13, 1999, http://www.gallup.com/ poll/3415/most-admired-men-women-19481998.aspx (accessed August 10, 2011).

3. Robert P. Watson, "'Source Material': Toward the Study of the First Lady: The State of Scholarship," *Presidential Studies Quarterly* 22, no. 2 (June 2003): 425.

4. Ibid., 431–32. Robert P. Watson also provides the most comprehensive book-length historical account of American first ladies in *The Presidents' Wives: Reassessing the Office of the First Lady* (Boulder: Lynne Rienner, 2000), though Myra G. Gutin predates him with *The President's Partner: The First Lady in the Twentieth Century* (New York: Greenwood Press) and offers a comparable typology.

5. Anthony J. Eksterowicz and Kristen Paynter, "The Evolution of the Role and Office of the First Lady: The Movement Toward Integration with the White House Office," *Social Science Journal* 37, no. 4 (2000): 549.

6. Ibid., 549.

7. Shawn J. Parry-Giles and Diane M. Blair, "The Rise of the Rhetorical First Lady: Politics, Gender, and Women's Voice, 1789–2002," *Rhetoric and Public Affairs* 5, no. 4 (Winter 2002): 581.

8. Ibid., 581.

9. Ibid., 575, 586.

10. Mona Harrington, *Care and Equality: Inventing a New Family Politics* (New York: Routledge, 2000), 103–4.

11. Krissah Thompson and Vanessa Williams, "African American Women See Their Own Challenges Mirrored in Michelle Obama's," *Washington Post*, January 23, 2102, http://www.washingtonpost.com/politics/african-american -women-see-their-own-struggles-mirrored-in-michelle-obamas/2012/01/19/ gIQA5k4DMQ_story.html.

12. The canon of black feminism, which includes both single-authored texts and influential anthologies, includes the following: Hazel Carby, *Reconstructing Womanhood: The Emergence of the Afro-American Woman Novelist* (New York: Oxford University Press, 1987); Barbara Christian, "The Race for Theory," *Feminist Studies* 14, no. 1 (1988): 67–79; Patricia Hill Collins, *Black Feminist Thought: Knowledge, Consciousness, and the Politics of Empowerment* (New York: Routledge, 1991); Kimberle Crenshaw, "Demarginalizing the Intersection of Race and Sex: A Black Feminist Critique of Antidiscrimination Doctrine, Feminist Theory and Antiracist Politics," *University of Chicago Legal Forum* (1989): 139–67; Angela Davis, *Women, Race, and Class* (New York: Random House, 1981); Paula Giddings, *When and Where I Enter: The Impact of Black Women on Race and Sex in America* (New York: William Morrow, 1984); Darlene Clark Hine, "Rape and the Inner Lives of Black Women in the Middle West: Preliminary Thoughts on the Culture of Dissemblance," *Signs* 14, no. 4 (Summer 1989): 912–20; Beverly Guy-Sheftall (ed.), *Words of Fire: An Anthology of African-American Feminist Thought* (New York: New Press, 1995); bell hooks, *Ain't I a Woman: Black Women and Feminism* (Boston: South End Press, 1981); *From Margin to Center* (Boston: South End Press, 1984); *Talking Back: Thinking Feminist, Thinking Black* (Boston: South End Press, 1989); Gloria T. Hull, Patricia Bell Scott, and Barbara Smith (eds.), *But Some of Us Are Brave* (Old Westbury: Feminist Press, 1982); Cherrie Moraga and Gloria Anzaldua (eds.), *This Bridge Called My Back: Writing by Radical Women of Color* (Watertown: Persephone Press, 1981); Barbara Smith, "Introduction," in *Home Girls: A Black Feminist Anthology*, ed. Barbara Smith (New York: Kitchen Table Press, 1983), xix–lvi; Alice Walker, *In Search of Our Mothers' Gardens* (New York: Harcourt Brace, 1983).

13. In *Gender Trouble: Feminism and the Subversion of Identity* (New York: Routledge, 1990), Judith Butler expertly explains how the maintenance of dichotomous male/female sex/gender categories engenders oppression and cripples feminism.

14. Crenshaw, "Demarginalizing the Intersection of Race and Sex," 140.

15. Ibid., 151.

16. Ibid., 149.

17. The ideological/symbolic realm, where controlling images of black womanhood are produced, is one of three dimensions identified by Collins. The other two dimensions are labor and politics, as Collins documents the implications of black women's severe exploitation from the moment they arrived in the West, and emphasizes the overlay of economic oppression with political disenfranchisement that cripples black women within their own communities and in mainstream politics (Collins, *Black Feminist Thought*, 6). My summary of the four controlling images is drawn from Collins, *Black Feminist Thought*, 71–77.

18. The list of scholars who have written about this document is endless, but William Julius Wilson provides current and sensible synopsis, complete

with a fair assessment of the report's virtues and blemishes, in *More Than Just Race: Being Black and Poor in the Inner City* (New York: Norton, 2009).

19. Collins, *Black Feminist Thought*, 76.

20. Of course, Collins is not the only researcher to highlight this truth. For further reference, Dorothy Roberts provides an equally incisive account in her award-winning text, *Killing the Black Body* (New York: Pantheon, 1997).

21. Lisa B. Thompson, *Beyond the Black Lady: Sexuality and the New African American Middle Class* (Urbana: University of Illinois Press, 2009), 3.

22. Alex Koppelman, "Fox News Calls Michelle Obama 'Obama's Baby Mama,'" Salon, June 11, 2008, http://www.salon.com/news/politics/war_room/2008/06/11/fox_obama/index.html.

23. MacKenzie Weinger, "Jim Sensenbrenner Sorry for 'Big Butt' Quip," Politico, December 22, 2011, http://www.politico.com/news/stories/1211/70788.html.

24. Nicole Marie Melton, "Lawmaker Apologizes for Email Calling First Lady 'Mrs. YoMama,'" January 7, 2012, http://www.essence.com/2012/01/07/lawmaker-apologizes-for-email-calling-first-lady-mrs-yomama/.

25. The transcript and footage of this interview can be found at "Michelle Obama: No Tension with Husband's Aides," CBSNews, January 11, 2012, http://www.cbsnews.com/8301-505270_162-57356770/michelle-obama-no-tension-with-husbands-aides/.

26. Both quotations appear as reported in Michael Cooper, "Cindy McCain's Pride," *New York Times*, February 19, http://thecaucus.blogs.nytimes.com/2008/02/19/cindy-mccains-pride.

27. "Michelle Obama Retools 'I'm Proud' Remark," CBS News, June 28, 2009, http://www.cbsnews.com/stories/2008/02/20/politics/main3855129.shtml.

28. The entire thesis paper can be downloaded through the link in the following article: Jeffrey Ressner, "Michelle Obama Thesis Was on Racial Divide," Politico, February 22, 2008, http://www.politico.com/news/stories/0208/8642.html.

29. The transcript and footage of this incident are available at "Hannity Repeatedly Distorts Passage in Michelle Obama's Senior Thesis to Suggest Alumni Views on Race Are Her Own," Media Matters, February 29, 2008, http://mediamatters.org/research/200802290007.

30. Nico Pitney, "Barry Blitt Defends His New Yorker Cover Art of Obama," Huffington Post, July 13, 2008, http://www.huffingtonpost.com/2008/07/13/barry-blitt-addresses-his_n_112432.html.

31. See Katherine Beckett, *Making Crime Pay: Law and Order in Contemporary American Politics* (Oxford: Oxford University Press, 1997); and Bruce Western, *Punishment and Inequality in America* (New York: Russell Sage Foundation, 2006).

32. I am referring here to the triad of articles published by Yuval Levin ("America's Unhappiest Millionaire: Michelle Obama's Gospel of Misery," *Na-*

tional Review, May 5, 2008, http://www.nationalreview.com/articles/224394/
americas-unhappiest-millionaire/yuval-Levin), Michelle Malkin ("His Bitter
Half: Michelle Obama, Queen of the Grievance Mongers," *National Review*,
May 7, 2008, http://www.nationalreview.com/articles/224411/his- bitter-half/
michelle-malkin), and Mark Steyn ("Ms. Obama's America," *National Review*
60, no. 7, April 21, 2008, http://nrd.nationalreview.com/article/?q=MWUoYz
QwZTZjODZhZTNkODc5ODlhMGUiMDkzZjRjODc=), which are exem-
plary, though not exhaustive, examples of the sort of content produced by the
National Review on the topic of Ms. Obama's anger.

33. Steyn, "Ms. Obama's America."

34. "Glenn Beck: 'Obama Is a Racist,'" CBS News, July 29, 2009, http://
www.cbsnews.com/stories/2009/07/29/politics/main5195604.shtml.

35. Barack Obama, "Keynote Speech at the 2004 Democratic National
Convention," *Washington Post*, transcript published July 27, 2004, http://www
.washingtonpost.com/wp-dyn/articles/A19751-2004Jul27.html.

36. Evan McMorris-Santoro, "Rush Limbaugh: Michelle Obama Booed at
NASCAR Event Over 'Uppity-ism,'" Talking Points Memo, http://2012.talking
pointsmemo.com/2011/11/rush-limbaugh-michelle-obama-booed-at-nascar-event
-over-uppityism-audio.php.

37. Michele Wallace, *Black Macho and the Myth of the Superwoman* (New
York: Dial Press, 1978), 107.

38. Ibid., 95.

39. Ibid., 107. Emphasis in original.

40. Thompson, *Beyond the Black Lady*, 26.

41. Joan Morgan, *When Chickenheads Come Home to Roost* (New York:
HarperCollins, 1999), 86–87.

42. Cecilia A. Conrad, "Black Women: The Unfinished Agenda," American Prospect, September 22, 2008, http://www.prospect.org/cs/articles?article
=black_women_the_unfinished_agenda.

43. Table courtesy of Dr. Mark J. Perry, University of Michigan—Flint.
Data are drawn from United States Department of Education, Institute of
Education Sciences, available at http://nces.ed.gov/FastFacts/display.asp?id=72
(accessed May 24, 2012).

44. William J. Sabol and Heather Couture, "Prison Inmates at Midyear
2007," United States Department of Justice, http://bjs.ojp.usdoj.gov/content/
pub/pdf/pim07.pdf (accessed August 10, 2011).

45. Conrad, "Black Women."

46. Becky Pettit and Stephanie Ewert, "Employment and Wage Declines:
The Erosion of Black Women's Relative Wages Since 1980," *Demography* 46, no.
3 (August 2009).

47. Yvonne D. Newsome and F. Nii-Amoo Dodoo, "Explaining the Decline
in Black Women's Earnings," *Gender and Society* 16, no. 4 (August 2002): 447.

48. Ibid., 489.

49. Newsome and Dodoo, "Explaining the Decline in Black Women's Earnings."

50. Kris Marsh, William A. Darity Jr., Philip N. Cohen, Lynne M. Casper, and Danielle Salters, "The Emerging Black Middle Class: Single and Living Alone," *Social Forces* 85, no. 2 (2007): 4–5.

51. Debbie VanTassel, "With Michelle Obama, Many African American Women Feel They Have an Accurate Reflection of Themselves," *Cleveland Plain Dealer*, November 9, 2008, http://www.cleveland.com/living/index.ssf/2008/11/black_women_discuss_their_view.html.

52. Barack Obama, *The Audacity of Hope: Thoughts on Reclaiming the American Dream* (New York: Three Rivers Press, 2006), 331.

53. Ibid., 333.

54. Ibid., 334.

55. Barack Obama, "Text of Obama's Fatherhood Speech," Politico, June 15, 2008, http://www.politico.com/news/stories/0608/11094.html.

56. Z. Byron Wolf, "'Mom-in-Chief Hits the Campaign Trail,'" ABC News, October 13, 2010, http://abcnews.go.com/Politics/vote-2010-elections-mom-chief-michelle-obama-hits/story?id=11870916#.T5-Osr-sqKw.

57. Michelle Obama, "Home, Work, Community: The Roles of African American Women as Change Agents," speech delivered February 11, 2009, as transcribed in *Michelle Obama: In Her Own Words*, ed. Susan A. Jones (New York: SoHo Books, 2010), 241–42.

58. Katie Couric, "Michelle Obama on Love, Family, and Politics," CBS Evening News, February 15, 2008, http://www.cbsnews.com/stories/2008/02/15/eveningnews/main3838886_page3.shtml.

59. Carol Stack's *All Our Kin* (New York: Harper, 1974) is the classic anthropological text on this subject, especially as it pertains to economically disadvantaged African American mothers.

60. Bill Hutchinson, "Secret Behind First Lady Michelle Obama's Arms Finally Revealed," *New York Daily News*, September 8, 2009, http://articles.nydailynews.com/2009-09-08/news/17930892_1_health-and-fitness-hammer-curls-cardio-workout.

61. Jeanine Stein, "Michelle Obama's Toned Arms Are Debated," *Los Angeles Times*, March 29, 2009, http://www.latimes.com/features/image/la-ig-arms29-2009mar29,0,4782966.story.

62. See Madison Park, "How to Get Michelle Obama's Toned Arms," CNN, February 26, 2009, http://articles.cnn.com/2009-02-26/health/toning.obama.arms_1_arms-strength-training-first-lady?_s=PM:HEALTH; and Donna Raskin, "How to Get Michelle Obama's Arms: The Workout Plan," *Fit-

ness Magazine, May 13, 2011, http://www.fitnessmagazine.com/workout/arms/exercises/how-to-get-michelle-obamas-arms-the-workout-plan/.

63. As quoted in Martin, "Washington Watch with Roland Martin: In Conversation with Michelle Obama," TVOne, August 24, 2008, http://tv oneblogs.com/roland/news/tv-ones-michelle-obama-interview-wins-image-award-977.htm/comment-page-20, and http://www.youtube.com/watch?v=UIrd4MOatko (accessed August 10, 2011).

64. See http://mrs-o.org/press-coverage/.

65. hooks, *Feminism Is for Everybody*, 36.

66. As quoted in "Obama Marriage Inspires Fascination, Imitation," MSNBC, February 12, 2009, http://today.msnbc.msn.com/id/29167200/.

67. For a slideshow of the Obamas' "Greatest PDA Moments," visit Huffington Post at http://www.huffingtonpost.com/2008/11/03/the-obamas-greatest-pda-m_n_130947.html.

68. This excerpt is culled from the same 2008 Martin interview as above, though the relevant portion of the video only appears at the second Internet address: http://www.youtube.com/watch?v=UIrd4MOatko.

69. Audre Lorde, "The Uses of Anger," *Women's Studies Quarterly* 25, no. 1 (Spring–Summer 1997): 278. Lorde's essay was originally published in 1981.

CHAPTER SIX: A PLACE CALLED OBAMA

1. William Jelani Cobb, *The Substance of Hope: Barack Obama and the Paradox of Progress* (New York: Walker, 2010), 174.

2. Jennifer C. Nash, "Re-Thinking Intersectionality," *Feminist Review* 89 (2008): 2–3.

3. Ibid., 11–12.

4. Nikki Jones, *Between Good and Ghetto: African American Girls and Inner-City Violence* (New Brunswick: Rutgers University Press, 2009), 118.

APPENDIX I

1. The figures presented in the first four bullet points are drawn from pp. 9–11 of "Unequal Health Outcomes in the United States," a report submitted to the United Nations Committee on the Elimination of Racial Discrimination in 2008. The report, which includes contributions from multiple scholars and nonprofit organizations, can be found widely on the Internet, including at www.prrac.org/pdf/CERDhealthEnvironmentReport.pdf (accessed August 20, 2011).

2. "The State of Black America 2010: Responding to the Crisis," National Urban League, http://www.nul.org/content/state-black-america-executive-summary (accessed August 20, 2011).

3. Andy Kroll, "The Persistent Black-White Employment Gap," Salon, July 5, 2011, http://www.salon.com/news/politics/war_room/2011/07/05/unemployment_scandal; Lynn Sweet, "Republican National Committee Memo:

Obama Won't Hold Colorado, Nevada, and New Mexico," *Chicago Sun-Times*, July 20, 2011, http://blogs.suntimes.com/sweet/2011/07/republican_national_ committee_12.html.

4. The first sentence in this bullet point is a direct quotation from Jesse Washington's "Black Economic Gains Reversed in Great Recession," Yahoo Finance, July 9, 2011, http://finance.yahoo.com/news/Black-economic-gains -reversed-apf-625380746.html?x=0. The second sentence paraphrases a quotation from Algernon Austin's quotation in the same piece.

5. National Urban League, "State of Black America 2010."

6. Ibid.

7. Ibid.

8. "Yes We Can: The Schott 50 State Report on Public Education and Black Males," Schott Foundation for Public Education, http://www.blackboys report.org/ (accessed August 20, 2011).

9. Sam Roberts, "Racial Patterns Are Found in Recent School Budget Elections," *New York Times*, August 24, 2010, http://www.nytimes.com/2010/08/25/ nyregion/25districts.html?ref=nyregion.

10. For more on these developments, please see Michelle Alexander's *The New Jim Crow: Mass Incarceration in the Age of Colorblindness* (New York: New Press, 2010). The statistic on the rise of the prison population from 350,000 to 2.3 million is taken from p. 92 of Alexander's book.

11. These figures are drawn from Nicole D. Porter, "The State of Sentencing 2010: Developments in Policy and Practice," The Sentencing Project, http:// sentencingproject.org/doc/publications/publications/Final State of the Sentencing 2010.pdf.

12. Erik Eckholm, "Recession Raises Poverty Rate to 15-Year High," *New York Times*, last modified September 16, 2010, http://www.nytimes.com/2010 /09/17/us/17poverty.html?_r=1&pagewanted=all.

13. Frank Wu, *Yellow: Race in America Beyond Black and White* (New York: Basic Books, 2003).

14. Jennifer Gonzalez, "Asian American and Pacific Islander Students Are Not Monolithically Successful," *Chronicle of Higher Education*, last modified June 27, 2011, http://chronicle.com/article/Asian-AmericanPacific/128061/.

15. Stuart Hall, "Race, Articulation, and Societies Structured in Dominance," in *Sociological Theories: Race and Colonialism*, ed. UNESCO (Paris: UNESCO, 1980), 322.

16. See Michael Omi and Howard Winant, *Racial Formation in the United States: From the 1960s to the 1980s* (New York: Routledge, 1986). Winant refers to Hall's notion of articulation as a central component of racial formation theory in a later article entitled "Race and Race Theory," *Annual Review of Sociology* 26 (2000).

To summarize the racial formation approach: (a) It views the meaning of race and the content of racial identities as unstable and politically contested; (b) It understands racial formation as the intersection/conflict of racial "projects" that combine representational/discursive elements with structural/institutional ones; (c) It sees these intersections as iterative sequences of interpretations (articulations) of the meaning of race that are open to many types of agency, from the individual to the organizational, from the local to the global. (182)

APPENDIX II

1. See *U.S. News and World Report*, based on 2010 data, at http://colleges.us news.rankingsandreviews.com/best-colleges (accessed June 29, 2011).

2. See United States Census, at http://quickfacts.census.gov/qfd/states/00000.html (accessed June 29, 2011).

3. See Tax Policy Center, at http://taxpolicycenter.org/numbers/display atab.cfm?DocID=2970 (accessed August 2011).

4. See Kristin Esterberg, *Qualitative Methods in Social Research* (New York: McGraw-Hill, 2001).

5. For further reference on symbolic boundaries and "mental maps," please see Frederick Barth, *Ethnic Groups and Boundaries* (Boston: Little, Brown, 1969); Herbert J. Gans, *Popular Culture and High Culture* (New York: Basic Books, 1974); Michele Lamont, *Money, Morals, and Manners: The Culture of the French and American Upper-Middle Class* (Chicago: University of Chicago Press, 1992); and Michele Lamont and Virag Molnar, "The Study of Boundaries in the Social Sciences," *American Review of Sociology* 28 (2002): 167–95.

6. Lamont and Molnar, "Study of Boundaries in the Social Sciences," 168.

7. Ibid.

8. William. A. Gamson, *Talking Politics* (Cambridge: Cambridge University Press, 1992); Harris-Perry, *Barbershops, Bibles, and BET*. The phrase "symbolic work" is taken from Paul Willis, *Common Culture* (Buckingham: Open University Press, 1990).

Index

ABC News, 96

Adam and Eve, 34

African descent, people of: bodies of, 9, 143–44; and census categories, 60; class and, 89–90; economic disadvantages experienced by, 84–85, 89–90, 111–12, 123, 145, 158; education of, 159; families of, 138–39; health of, 157–58; incarceration of, 159–60; multiracialism and, 60, 66; and politics of inheritance, 40; racist imagery associated with, 5–10, 122–36, 173*n*22; safety of, 93–96; sexuality of, 103, 123–25; social disadvantages and stigma experienced by, 2, 60, 66–67, 76, 145–46. *See also* Black counterpublics; Black women

AIDS, 158

American dream, 20, 21, 35–37

American Indians, 55, 160

American values and Americanness: the body and, 28–33; and inclusiveness, 45–46; innocence and, 36; Michelle Obama and, 126, 129–30; Obama on, 36–38, 41–42, 98–99; Obama perceived as lacking in, 24–25, 30–31, 33, 103–4, 127; race and, 27, 176*n*16; Wright's criticism of, 96–99. *See also* National identity

Anderson, Benedict, 23

Anger, attributed to black women, 122–23, 125–29, 132, 146

Ape imagery, 7–10, 173*n*22

A Place for Us, 59

Articulation, 161, 198*n*16

Asante, Molefi, 60

Asian descent, people of, 55, 67, 160–61

Assimilation, 23, 57

Association of Multiethnic Americans, 59